# HOW TO USE THIS BOOK

1. COME ON IN. Have a look around. Check out the Table of Contents to see if anything catches your eye.

2. ALL OF OUR WORKSHOPS ARE DIFFERENT, SO ALL OF OUR LESSON PLANS ARE TOO. Generally, there's **an outline of the lesson** for you and sometimes a **handout for the students**. We've tried to make them as user-friendly as possible.

3. TO HELP YOU PLAN YOUR CLASS, **WE'VE HEADED EACH LESSON PLAN WITH A TIME ESTIMATE.** This is how long the class generally runs. In your classroom it might go slower or faster, but we've tried to ballpark it for you.

4. AS MUCH AS WE'VE TRIED TO MAKE THINGS FUN, **WE'VE ALSO TRIED TO KEEP THINGS SIMPLE.** A three-ring writing circus with actual trained animals and cotton candy machines would be great fun for your students, but a great big headache for you, so **we've tried to keep the supplies and prep to a minimum.** We've headed each lesson plan and activity with the list of materials it requires. Most of the time this will consist of things you already have on hand. Fancier fixings are optional.

5. **WE ENCOURAGE YOU TO ADAPT THESE LESSONS TO SUIT YOU AND YOUR STUDENTS.** These lessons were taught in an after-school environment, with students who were there by choice, so we expect they'll need some tweaking to work for you. Make them yours.

6. SOMETIMES **YOU MIGHT HAVE EXTRA TIME AND WANT TO DO SOMETHING REALLY, REALLY SPECIAL.** When you do, look for the Superteacher bonus activity icon. It looks like this:

## SUPERTEACHER BONUS ACTIVITIES

Superteacher bonus activities are optional additions to the lesson plan that require a little more effort, but are guaranteed to dazzle your students.

7. IN THE APPENDIX YOU'LL FIND SOME OTHER TOOLS WE HOPE WILL MAKE YOUR LIFE EASIER: **evaluation rubrics to guide grading, student self-assessment checklists**, and charts to **show you which Core Curriculum guidelines each lesson plan meets.**

8. WE'D LOVE TO HEAR HOW IT GOES. Any suggestions? Comments? **You can contact us at** info@826national.org. Send us your own favorite lesson plan, or samples of your students' fabulous work. We'd love to see it.

# DON'T FORGET to WRITE

WITHDRAWN

### for the SECONDARY GRADES

**50** ENTHRALLING *and* EFFECTIVE WRITING LESSONS

AGES **11** AND **UP**

826 NATIONAL | EDITED BY JENNIFER TRAIG

JOSSEY-BASS
A Wiley Imprint
www.josseybass.com

Published by Jossey-Bass
A Wiley Imprint
989 Market Street, San Francisco, CA 94103-1741—www.josseybass.com

Jossey-Bass books and products are available through most bookstores. To contact Jossey-Bass directly call our Customer Care Department within the U.S. at 800-956-7739, outside the U.S. at 317-572-3986, or fax 317-572-4002.

Wiley also publishes its books in a variety of electronic formats and by print-on-demand. Not all content that is available in standard print versions of this book may appear or be packaged in all book formats. If you have purchased a version of this book that did not include media that is referenced by or accompanies a standard print version, you may request this media by visiting http://booksupport.wiley.com. For more information about Wiley products, visit us www.wiley.com.

**Library of Congress Cataloging-in-Publication Data**

Don't forget to write for the secondary grades : 50 enthralling and effective writing lessons (ages 11 and up) / 826 National. — 1st ed.

  p. cm.

 ISBN 978-1-118-02432-4 (pbk.)

 1.  English language – Composition and exercises – Study and teaching (Secondary) – United States. I. 826 National (Organization)

 LB1631 .D59 2011

 808'.0420712 – dc23

                                                                                         2011025957

Printed in the United States of America

FIRST EDITION

*PB Printing*  10 9 8 7 6 5 4 3 2 1

# TABLE OF CONTENTS

## LESSON PLANS

*by* DAVE EGGERS

In this three-part lesson, students learn to draw details from real life to create unforgettable characters and compelling stories.

*by* KATHRYN RIDDLE

Curious what Elizabeth Bennet's, Harry Potter's, Bella Swan's, or Percy Jackson's Facebook profile would look like? In this workshop, students create a mock Facebook profile based on their favorite literary character.

*by* TOM PERROTTA

The author of *Little Children* and *Election* shares his tips for finding inspiration in your own neighborhood.

*by* WILLIAM JOHN BERT

Writing about the time you *didn't* get away with it.

# FOREWORD

THE FIRST INDICATION THAT THIS ISN'T YOUR NORMAL WRITING CENTER IS the storefront you have to pass through to get to the classroom. It might be a pirate shop, featuring a large selection of peg legs and eye patches, or it could be a robot repair lab, presided over by a burping automaton. It might be a time travel mart, offering dodo chow and 50-year calendars; or a superhero supply store with a phone-booth changing room. Past the shelves of student-authored books, zines, and newspapers, students slip through the secret door to the classroom. This doesn't look normal, either. There are plush couches inviting you to curl up and read, big mahogany tables begging you to hunker down and write, and some fixtures that make no sense at all, like portholes, or a fully functional grocer's scale. The teacher appears to be wearing a wig and a Viking helmet. Just what is going on here?

This is how we do things at the 826 National centers. From the time we opened our doors in San Francisco in 2002, our emphasis has been on fun, and there's been plenty of that. But something else happened: we helped students produce some great writing. Then we did it again. Students returned over and over and told their friends. Before long our workshops had long waiting lists.

We'd come up with a formula that worked. Soon we started hearing from people who wanted to bring our methods to their own hometowns. We expanded to eight centers across the country, each offering free after-school tutoring, in-class support for teachers and students, and workshops on topics ranging from spycraft to space exploration to screenwriting.

Word continued to spread. Teachers wrote, called, and came in, asking for ideas for their own classrooms. By 2005 we'd had so many requests we decided it was time to put all our best ideas in one place, so we published *Don't Forget to Write,* a collection of lesson plans from our best workshops and favorite authors. Six years and several hundred workshops later, it seemed high time to publish a new edition.

We ended up with so many lesson plans, in fact, that we had to publish two volumes, one for elementary grades, and one for middle and high school. In this volume, you'll find lessons on topics that appeal to more mature writers, both to those who like writing and reading (The Essay, Literary Facebooks, Writing from Experience) and those who don't (Writing for Gamers, Bad Writing, This Class Sucks). It's also a great resource for the writer of any age looking for exercises to challenge him - or herself at home. There's a particular emphasis on fun, yes, but also on honing your craft: the nuances of narrative, character development, self-expression. How do you create a detailed, rounded, real protagonist? What stories lurk on your block? What can words do? You'll learn how to mutate Shakespeare; how to lie for fun, profit, and literary acclaim; why it's okay for first drafts to be awful; and what a *blazon* is. And, of course, you'll learn how to bring 826's methods to your own classroom.

What makes 826 workshops different? Well, first of all, they are often completely nuts. We think fun and engagement are paramount, so we use lots of props, costumes, and drama. Our tutors are invited to teach courses on anything related to writing. Sometimes it's very practical, like a workshop on writing the perfect college application essay. Sometimes it's just

goofy, like Writing for Pets (though this, too, has a pedagogical rationale: reading to a non-judgmental listener, like a dog, is great way to boost students' skills and confidence).

Whatever the topic, it's taught by a specialist in the field, from journalists to sportswriters to musicians. At 826LA, the first workshop was taught by filmmaker Spike Jonze. In San Francisco, when workshop teacher Michael Chabon told his colleague Stephen King that he was using his work in our Horror and Dark Fantasy class, Stephen decided to come to teach the lesson himself.

We would love to be able to dispatch pros like these to your classroom too. Instead, we've done the next best thing: we asked them to write lesson plans for you. A working screenwriter wrote the screenwriting lesson. Professional sportswriters wrote the sportswriting lesson, and professional cartoonists wrote the comic book lesson. Other contributors include classroom teachers (the most expert experts of all), college professors, poets, journalists, and two bona fide TV stars. Our favorite authors pitched in, too. We think the end result is like having Sarah Vowell stop by to teach a class on revisions, or Audrey Niffenegger lead a workshop on playing with time lines.

The whole enterprise is the classroom equivalent of hiding the good-for-you vegetables under the potato chips in the secretly nutritious casserole. We've based our activities on proven pedagogy. The students think they're having fun, and of course they are, but they're also engaged in very academic endeavors. They are organizing their ideas, crafting arguments, revising their work, stating their point of view, peer-editing a friend's work, and generally learning an awful lot about the hard work and craft of writing. They're goofing around, but they're also getting real experience. For two hours they're a music critic, a reporter, a playwright, getting an idea of what it's really like to do this for a living.

And they leave with concrete proof. All of our workshops are project-based. Everyone likes to have something to show for their time, so we strive to produce something in every class, be it a chapbook, a play, a newspaper, a short film, or a radio segment. We know that the process of making that product is the important part, but having something to hold on to at the end is the perfect punctuation to work well done. Also, making them is incredibly satisfying and enjoyable.

We hope you'll enjoy the process, too. Supporting teachers is our first priority, and we've tried to create a book that will make your job just a little bit easier and fun. We know that teachers are pressed for time trying to ensure content and skill requirements are met. To this end, we've made sure the lessons in this book meet the Common Core Curriculum standards. We created some charts to show you (see Appendix).

If you're nearby, come pay us a visit (see Appendix for a listing of all our centers). Workshops are only a part of what we do at 826. We also offer free after-school tutoring, free writing field trips, and free in-school support. You can learn more about our programs at www.826national.org. We'd love for you to come see all the excitement for yourself.

We hope you have as much fun as we have.

JENNIFER TRAIG, GERALD RICHARDS, *and* DAVE EGGERS

 # ACKNOWLEDGMENTS

LIKE ALL 826 NATIONAL PROJECTS, THIS BOOK WAS MADE POSSIBLE BY THE contributions of an incredibly creative and generous group of people who were kind enough to share their time and talents. We're especially grateful to 826 National cofounder Nínive Calegari for all her work putting the project together in the first place. Thanks, also, to the executive directors of all the chapters, and to the many staffers who helped and contributed, especially Amy Sumerton, Julius Diaz Panoriñgan, Joan Kim, Kait Steele, Chris Molnar, Ryan Smith, Maya Shugart, Lindsey Plait Jones, Karen Sama, Lauren Hall, and Mariama Lockington. Thanks to the wonderful volunteers who let us offer inventive workshops at all our chapters. Thanks to everyone at Jossey-Bass, especially Kate Gagnon, Tracy Gallagher, and Justin Frahm. Thanks to the very talented Tony Millionaire for his artwork, especially his Superteacher icon figure. Finally, thanks to our brilliant lesson plan contributors, some of them old friends, some of them new. We were blown away by their work and can't thank them enough.

# THE AUTHORS

**826 NATIONAL** IS A NETWORK OF NONPROFIT ORGANIZATIONS DEDICATED TO HELPING students, ages 6 through 18, with expository and creative writing, and to helping teachers inspire their students to write. 826 chapters are located in San Francisco, Los Angeles, New York, Chicago, Ann Arbor, Seattle, Boston, and Washington, D.C. Our mission is based on the understanding that great leaps in learning can happen with one-on-one attention, and that strong writing skills are fundamental to future success. We offer innovative and dynamic project-based learning opportunities that build on students' classroom experience, and strengthen their ability to express ideas effectively, creatively, confidently, and in their own voices.

Each 826 chapter offers after-school tutoring, field trips, workshops, and in-school programs—all free of charge—for students, classes, and schools. We target students in public schools, particularly those with limited financial, educational, and community resources.

**Jennifer Traig** is the author of the memoirs *Devil in the Details* and *Well Enough Alone,* and the editor of *The Autobiographer's Handbook.* A longtime 826 volunteer, she has a PhD in literature and lives in Ann Arbor, where she serves on the board of directors for 826michigan.

## 826's History

826 Valencia opened its doors in 2002, growing out of a desire to partner the professional literary and arts community of San Francisco with local students in need of engaging learning opportunities. The tutoring and writing center was designed to be a vibrant setting for rigorous educational activities. Connecting students with local authors, artists, and college students while providing a space that is whimsical and fun proved to be an excellent model for achieving results, and the idea was replicated in seven additional cities.

Since 2004, 826 chapters have opened in Brooklyn, Los Angeles, Chicago, Seattle, Ann Arbor, Boston, and, most recently, Washington, D.C., each with a unique storefront as the gateway to the writing center. While the theme of each center is varied (in Los Angeles students are encouraged to dabble in time travel; in Chicago they may begin their careers as future spies), the 826 model always holds true: if you offer students rigorous and fun learning opportunities and one-on-one attention, they will make great strides in their writing skills and confidence.

As the 826 model spread, the flagship center became home to the nationwide support of the individual chapters, determining and encouraging the use of shared best practices, setting standards for program evaluations to ensure the quality of 826 programming, and framing the national dialogue about the work of teachers and the value of teaching writing. In 2004, the legal name of 826 Valencia was changed to 826 National, to reflect this bigger-picture work. Meanwhile, in San Francisco the programs continued to grow bigger and stronger. In 2008, we made the decision to

formally separate into two legal entities to reflect the different initiatives of the local San Francisco chapter and the national one. Since July 2008, 826 National has existed as its own legal entity, apart from 826 Valencia, and it supports the individual 826 chapters across the nation.

Pirette McKamey, the teacher with whom 826 Valencia worked at Mission High School last year, said this about our collaboration: "When students work with people one-on-one on their writing, the benefit is so great. It helps students begin to recognize the relationship between their writing and communication to other people—that writing actually has the power to do that. It's great to have outside people. I think the students feel less comfortable working with outside people, so they have to do some self-struggle and overcome barriers to figure out how to communicate their ideas to someone they don't assume is sympathetic. And it's good for them—very powerful, and good for them."

## Our Student Programming

Each year, 826 is able to provide 22,000 students from low-income families and low-performing school districts with one-on-one tutoring, writing instruction, classroom support, and a wide variety of publishing opportunities. We give students high-quality, engaging, and hands-on literary programming. The result: better writing, improved grades, stronger community ties between young people and professional adults, and brighter futures.

ALL EIGHT 826 CHAPTERS OFFER THE FOLLOWING:

- AFTER-SCHOOL TUTORING: Neighborhood students receive free one-on-one tutoring five days a week in all subject areas at each center. 826 National's tutoring program is designed to inspire learning, foster creativity, and help students understand and complete their homework each day. We accomplish this by providing youth—particularly low-income youth, including those who live near our locations—free access to invaluable academic assistance.

- WORKSHOPS: Our free workshops foster creativity and strengthen writing skills in a variety of areas. All offerings directly support classroom curriculum while engaging students with imaginative and often playful themes. Workshops are project-based and taught by experienced, accomplished literary professionals. Examples of topics include: Writing for Pets (just what it sounds like!); Mad Science, in which students, wearing lab coats, isolate strings of their own DNA and then write stories about their DNA mutating in strange ways; How to Persuade Your Parents, Or: Whining Effectively; Spy Training; and How to Write a Comic Book, taught by a professional cartoonist.

- PUBLISHING: 826 publishes an array of student-authored literary quarterlies, newspapers, books, chapbooks, and anthologies, which are displayed and sold in the retail shops that front our writing centers and are distributed and sold nationwide. We use professional editors and designers to allow the students' work to shine. Our most significant student collaboration each year, the Young Authors' Book Project, partners a local high school classroom with professional writers and editors. The students spend three to four months crafting essays around a particular theme, continually collaborating with adult tutors through the editing and publishing process. When the project is complete, we celebrate the release with a festive party. The final book is a stunning reflection of months of hard work, engagement, and dedication on the part of the students and tutors.

 FIELD TRIPS: Up to four times a week, 826 chapters welcome an entire public school classroom for a morning of high-energy learning. In one field trip, Storytelling & Bookmaking, students write, illustrate, and bind their own books within a two-hour period.

 IN-SCHOOL PROGRAM: We dispatch teams of volunteers into local, high-need public schools to support teachers and provide one-on-one assistance to students as they tackle various writing projects, such as school newspapers, research papers, oral histories, and college entrance essays. We serve five thousand students annually through this deeply meaningful partnership with local schools and teachers.

Our five thousand volunteers make our work possible and our programs free of charge. They are local community residents, many of whom are professional writers, artists, college students, parents, bankers, lawyers, and retirees from a wide range of professions. These passionate individuals are found at our centers throughout the day, sitting side by side with our students after school, supporting morning field trips, and helping entire classrooms of students learn the art of writing. Our volunteers actively connect with youth every day.

If you would like to get involved in programs as a tutor or as a donor, please go to the 826 National Website, www.826national.org, to find out more information or visit one of our chapter Websites (the full list can be found at the end of the book).

# THE CONTRIBUTORS

**STEVE ALMOND** is the author of a bunch of books, most recently the story collection *God Bless America.*

**JONATHAN AMES** is the author of eight books, including *Wake Up, Sir!* and *The Extra Man,* and he is the creator of the HBO show *Bored to Death.*

**JULIANNE BALMAIN** is the author of many books, including travel books, books for kids, humor books, and guides to love and romance. Writing as Nadia Gordon, she is the author of four Napa Valley culinary mysteries, most recently *Lethal Vintage,* which was nominated for a Mystery Writers of America Mary Higgins Clark Award. Her mystery novels have been called "jolly, high-calorie pleasure" by the *Chicago Tribune,* "highly enjoyable" by the *Washington Post,* and "rapturous" by the *Los Angeles Times.*

**WILLIAM JOHN BERT** lives in Washington, D.C., and he still gets a little smile on his face when he walks by the Museum of Unnatural History on his way to work each morning. He received a DC Young Artist Grant in 2011, and his work has appeared in *Colorado Review, pacificReview, Sonora Review,* and *Anomalous Press.*

**TOM BISSELL** is the author of *Chasing the Sea: Lost Among the Ghosts of Empire in Central Asia, Speak Commentary* (with Jeff Alexander), *God Lives in St. Petersburg and Other Stories, The Father of All Things: A Marine, His Son, and the Legacy of Vietnam,* and *Extra Lives: Why Video Games Matter.* He is assistant professor of English at Portland State University.

**KYLE BOOTEN** is a Helen Zell Fellow at the University of Michigan and coeditor of online project Just (www.justzine.com). His poems have appeared in *Tin House, Hotel Amerika, Court Green,* and elsewhere.

**LISA BROWN** is an illustrator, syndicated cartoonist, and picture book writer. She coauthored and illustrated *Picture the Dead,* a Civil War ghost story for young adults, with award-winning author Adele Griffin. She lives in a spooky old house in San Francisco.

**JORDAN CRANE** is a cartoonist who's published both his own and other people's comics through his press, Red Ink. He edited and designed the ambitious anthology *NON* (which won several AIGA 365 awards). His current Fantagraphics work consists of the semi-regular solo comic *Uptight.*

**MEGHAN DAUM** has been a weekly columnist at the *Los Angeles Times* since 2005. She's the author of a memoir, *Life Would Be Perfect If I Lived In That House,* the novel *The Quality of Life Report,* and the essay collection *My Misspent Youth.* She lives in Los Angeles.

**NICHOLAS DECOULOS** is a senior at Northeastern University studying English and cinema studies and plans to continue writing. He would like to thank his family, his friends, 826 Boston, and his English teachers for giving him the encouragement to write, and providing him with plenty of good writing material.

**CORY DOCTOROW** is the coeditor of Boing Boing (www.boingboing.net) and the author of books including *For the Win, Makers,* and the best-selling *Little Brother.* His work has been nominated for the Nebula, Hugo, Sunburst, and Locus awards. He is the former European director of the Electronic Frontier Foundation and cofounded the UK Open Rights Group.

**DAVE EGGERS** is the cofounder of 826 Valencia and the founder of McSweeney's Publishing, LLC. He is also an author whose writings include *A Heartbreaking Work of Staggering Genius, You Shall Know Our Velocity, How We Are Hungry, What Is the What, Zeitoun, The Wild Things,* and *Teachers Have It Easy: The Big Sacrifices and Small Salaries of America's Teachers.*

**STEPHEN ELLIOTT** is the author of books including *Happy Baby, Looking Forward to It,* and *The Adderall Diaries,* and coauthor of *Donald.* He is the founder of www .TheRumpus.net.

**PHOEBE GLOECKNER** is the author of *Diary of a Teenage Girl: An Account in Words and Pictures* and *A Child's Life and Other Stories.* She is associate professor of art and design at the University of Michigan.

**DAPHNE GOTTLIEB** is the author and editor of nine books, most recently the poetry book *15 Ways to Stay Alive,* as well as coeditor (with Lisa Kester) of *Dear Dawn: Aileen Wuornos in Her Own Words.* Her poetry books include *Kissing Dead Girls, Final Girl, Why Things Burn,* and *Pelt.* She is also the author of the graphic novel *Jokes and the Unconscious* with artist Diane DiMassa.

**ADELE GRIFFIN** has written a number of books for young adults, including *Where I Want to Be, Amandine, The Other Shepards,* the *Witch Twins* and *Vampire Island* series, *Picture the Dead* with best selling illustrator Lisa Brown, and the "Generation Facebook" novel *The Julian Game.* She lives with her family in Brooklyn, New York.

**RYAN HARTY** received an MFA from the Iowa Writers' Workshop, and held a Truman Capote Fellowship in the Wallace Stegner Program at Stanford University. His first book, *Bring Me Your Saddest Arizona,* won the John Simmons Award for Short Fiction and was named a *San Francisco Chronicle* Best Book of the Year. He has taught at the Iowa Writers' Workshop, Stanford, the University of Michigan, and Columbia.

**NOAH HAWLEY** is the author of four novels, including *A Conspiracy of Tall Men* and *The Punch.* He is the creator of the ABC series *My Generation* and *The Unusuals* and has written and produced for the series *Bones.*

**LOUANNE JOHNSON** is a former U.S. Navy journalist, Marine Corps officer, and high school teacher, and the author of the *New York Times* best seller *Dangerous Minds* (originally *My Posse Don't Do Homework*). At present she is assistant professor of teacher education at Santa Fe Community College. Her other books include *Queen of Education, Teaching Outside the Box,* and *Muchacho.*

**EMILY KATZ** is a graduate of Bard College.

**ELLIE KEMPER** is a contributor to *McSweeney's* and *The Onion*. She plays Erin Hannon on NBC's *The Office.*

**DAN KENNEDY** is a frequent contributor to *McSweeney's Internet Tendency* and the author of the books *Loser Goes First* and *Rock On.* He is a regular host of The Moth StorySLAM in New York.

**ERIKA LOPEZ** is an artist and writer whose books include *Flaming Iguanas; Hoochie Mama; THEY CALL ME MAD DOG!;* and the latest, *The Girl Must Die: A Monster Girl Memoir,* as well as a matching postcard book. She's currently trying to make it amazing to be a human being with emotions again with her new multimedia company, Monster Girl Media. They figure in four to five years they'll get some fierce women who scream without dying back on screen.

**LISA LUTZ** is the author of the *Spellman Files* series of comedic novels, the collaborative mystery novel *Heads You Lose* (with David Hayward), and several unanswered fan letters. She lives in San Francisco.

**RONA MARECH**, a freelance journalist based in Washington, D.C., has been a staff writer at the *San Francisco Chronicle* and the *Baltimore Sun.* She helped found the *Baltimore Sun's* journalism program for high school minority students and has also taught journalism and writing at Catholic University and 826DC.

**TOM MOLANPHY** received his MFA in creative writing from the University of Montana. His essays and short stories have appeared in *Colorado College Press, Pilgrimage Review, Desert Call Magazine,* and the online journal *Blood Orange Review.* He teaches undergraduate and graduate writing and literature at the Academy of Art University.

**THAO NGUYEN** performs with Thao with The Get Down Stay Down, an alternative folk rock music group.

**AUDREY NIFFENEGGER** is the author of *The Time Traveler's Wife* and *Her Fearful Symmetry.* She trained as a visual artist at the School of the Art Institute of Chicago, and received her MFA from Northwestern University's Department of Art Theory and Practice. She is now on the faculty of the Columbia College Fiction Writing Department. She serves on the advisory board for 826CHI.

**RISA NYE** is a former college counselor who still enjoys helping students write those pesky college essays. She is coeditor of *Writin' on Empty: Parents Reveal the Upside, Downside, and Everything in Between When Children Leave the Nest.*

**MARK O'DONNELL** received the 2003 Tony Award for *Hairspray.* His books include *Elementary Education, Vertigo Park and Other Tall Tales, Getting over Homer,* and *Let Nothing You Dismay.* He has received a Guggenheim Fellowship, the Lecomte Du Nuoy Prize, and the George S. Kaufman award.

**ALVIN ORLOFF** is the manager of Dog Eared Books, an independent bookstore in San Francisco's über-vivacious Mission District. He's written three novels, *I Married an Earthling, Gutter Boys,* and *Why Aren't You Smiling?* and may very well write another.

**JULIE ORRINGER** is the author of the novel *The Invisible Bridge* and the short story collection *How to Breathe Underwater.* She is a graduate of the Iowa Writers' Workshop and has taught at Stanford, the University of Michigan, and Columbia.

**JULIUS DIAZ PANORIŃGAN** is director of education at 826LA, where he helps volunteers cook up madcap writing workshops and occasionally teaches his own. (For years, he's been reteaching and retweaking one of his babies: $8 - 2 = 6$, a math story workshop.) As far as he can recall, his atypical lesson planning started as a college senior, when he tasked his computer science section with programming a fictional robot to disrupt the always-annoying ProFro (prospective freshman) Weekend.

**CHRIS PERDUE** has drawn on his experience teaching piano, guitar, and bass lessons to conduct songwriting workshops for 826 Valencia. When he's not teaching or doing Web design, he performs in San Francisco.

**TOM PERROTTA** is the author of *The Abstinence Teacher, Little Children, Joe College, Election, The Wishbones,* and *Bad Haircut.* He serves on the literary board of 826 Boston.

**MICAH PILKINGTON** has worked as a Web editor and writer since 2000, with sporadic career digressions into film and theater. She lives in San Francisco.

**NEAL POLLACK** is the author of *Stretch: The Unlikely Making of a Yoga Dude, Alternadad, Never Mind the Pollacks,* and *The Neal Pollack Anthology of American Literature,* among other works. He writes for *Wired, Men's Journal, Yoga Journal,* and many other magazines and Websites, and lives in Los Angeles with his family.

**KAZZ REGELMAN** wandered the world after graduating from Princeton: Fulbright scholar in Taiwan, Tokyo correspondent for *Variety,* scuba instructor in the Philippines, cook on Maui, French-immersion preschool founder in San Francisco, and freelance writer whose work has appeared in publications as diverse as the *Hollywood Reporter,* the *Boston Globe,* and *Boys' Life.* With 37 countries, five continents, five languages, four food-poisoning incidents, and one overseas hospital visit under her belt, she has recently moved from San Francisco with her husband and two children to Paris.

**GERALD RICHARDS** is the CEO of 826 National, with more than 16 years of management and development experience in the nonprofit sector. Prior to joining 826, Gerald was the executive director for the Bay Area office of the Network for Teaching Entrepreneurship (NFTE). Gerald is currently a member of the Council of Chief State School Officers (CCSSO) and Ed Steps Curiosity and Creativity workgroup in Washington, D.C. He is an inaugural fellow in the California Leaders of Color Fellowship Program, a member of the 2009 class of Leadership San Francisco, and a 2008 award recipient of 101 African-American Champions for Youth in the Bay Area. He currently serves on the board of the Woodland School. Gerald has an MFA in writing from the School of the Art Institute of Chicago and a BA in film studies from Wesleyan University.

**KATHRYN RIDDLE** holds a BS from Eastern Michigan University and an MA in education from the University of Michigan. She currently teaches high school in Anchorage, Alaska, where she lives with her fiancé, Joel, and their sweet puppies, Butch and Daisy.

**JASON ROBERTS** the author of *Two Shipwrecks,* a nonfiction saga of intertwined lives in nineteenth century America and Japan. His previous book, *A Sense of the World,* was a finalist for the National Book Critics Circle Award and the international *Guardian* First Book Prize.

**MATTHUE ROTH**'S newest young-adult novel is *Losers,* an epic about Russian Jewish immigrant geeks. He is a slam poet and the cocreator of www.G-dcast.com, and he keeps a secret diary at www.matthue.com.

**KRISTEN SCHAAL** is a contributor to *The Daily Show* and the voice of Louise on *Bob's Burgers*. She played Mel on *Flight of the Conchords* and cowrote *The Sexy Book of Sexy Sex* with Rich Blomquist.

**SAM SILVERSTEIN** is a managing editor at Yahoo!

**MARK SIPOWICZ** is a teacher, writer, and guide especially interested in creative and heart-centered exploration of soul and nature. He has owned a bookstore, survived an avalanche, salmon seined in Alaska, raised two boys, studied rites of passage and literature, and is currently working toward a PhD in depth psychology.

**KAIT STEELE** is the director of education at 826CHI. Prior to joining 826CHI, she studied creative writing at Northwestern University and worked at Woodstock School in India. These days, Kait spends most of her time being awed and inspired by the profound, hilarious, and powerful words of student writers, and the volunteers who support their creativity every day. In her spare time, she is ever so slowly learning the accordion.

**REBECCA STERN** taught in a "hard-to-staff" public school in Brooklyn before becoming a middle school language arts teacher in Palo Alto. Along with Brad Wolfe, she is the coeditor of a book of essays by notable authors aimed at the middle grades to be published by Roaring Brook Press/Macmillan in 2013.

**ANDREW STRICKMAN** is senior director of experiential marketing at Yahoo! and an award-winning entertainment and pop culture journalist for such magazines as *Rolling Stone, Details,* and *ReadyMade.*

**JASON TURBOW** is the coauthor of *The Baseball Codes: Beanballs, Sign Stealing, and Bench-Clearing Brawls: The Unwritten Rules of America's Pastime.*

**VENDELA VIDA** is the author of four books, most recently *Let the Northern Lights Erase Your Name* and *The Lovers.* A founding coeditor of the *Believer* magazine, Vida lives in San Francisco.

**SARAH VOWELL** is the author of *Take the Cannoli, The Partly Cloudy Patriot, Assassination Vacation, The Wordy Shipmates,* and *Unfamiliar Fishes.* She is president of the 826NYC board of directors.

**STEVEN WEISSMAN** is the author of *Chewing Gum in Church* and other comic books. He teaches cartooning to fourth- through eighth-grade students at the Art Center College of Design.

**JEREMY WILSON** is a writer, teacher, and frequent volunteer at 826CHI. In his spare time he enjoys going to Wrigley Field with his wife and eating nachos served in batting helmets.

**BRAD WOLFE** is the founder of Hopeful Media, an organization aimed at using various forms of media to cultivate inspiration, creativity, and mindfulness in education and business. He is also the president of the Sunbeam Foundation for rare pediatric cancer research and is the lead singer of Brad Wolfe and the Moon. Along with Rebecca Stern, he is the coeditor of a book of essays by notable authors aimed at the middle grades to be published by Roaring Brook Press/Macmillan in 2013.

**LARA ZIELIN** is the author of the young-adult novels *Donut Days* and *The Implosion of Aggie Winchester.* She lives in Ypsilanti, Michigan, where she writes, eats cheese, and Beadazzles, I think stuff that she probably shouldn't.

# DETAILS (GOLDEN), CHARACTER (IMMORTAL), AND SETTING (RURAL INDIA)

*by* DAVE EGGERS

1 SESSION, 2 HOURS

THIS IS THE LESSON I USUALLY GIVE ON THE FIRST MEETING OF MY EVENING high school writing class. I'm trying to do the following things:

☞ Get the students thinking about specificity in their writing

☞ Get them thinking about the value of personal observation

☞ Get them better acquainted with each other (in my class, the students are from all over the Bay Area, but this is just as useful in a setting where the students all think they know each other)

☞ Get them started on a short story that challenges them to solve fairly sophisticated problems of setting and motive.

*Note:* Any portion of this two-hour plan could be used alone. Most steps could easily take up a 50-minute class period. The time guidelines are only included if you happen to have a 2-hour, or two-class-period, block of time available.

## Step 1: The Power of Observation (12 minutes)

Start with the head of a stuffed crocodile. Or something like that. 826 Valencia is next to a store that sells taxidermied animals, so I usually go over and borrow one of their crocodile heads. Whatever you choose to use, this object should be something fairly unusual, but it should also be something that the students have seen before. Now—without showing the students the object—pass out blank pieces of paper, and ask the students to draw the object. For example, if I have the stuffed crocodile head hidden in my desk, I would tell the students, "You have 5 minutes to draw a perfectly accurate rendering of a Peruvian caiman (a type of

1

small crocodile)." The students will laugh, but you will be serious. They have to get down to business, and draw that crocodile.

After 5 minutes, most students will have a pretty sorry-looking crocodile. They will have drawn the animal from memory, trying to recall if the crocodile's eyes are on the top of the head, or the side, and if the teeth are inside its mouth or protrude out the sides. Collect the drawings and show them to the class. Guffaws will follow.

Now take the actual crocodile head out, and place it where the students can easily see it. Now ask them to draw the Peruvian caiman again, using the actual animal as a model. After 5 minutes, you'll see a tremendous difference. Where there was guessing and vagueness and error in the first drawings, there will be detail, specificity, and accuracy, now that the students can refer to the genuine article. They'll see that the eyes are actually on top of its head. They'll see that the eyes are like a cat's—eerie and many-layered. They'll see that the snout is very long, very narrow, and very brittle-seeming.

## Step 2: Apply the Lesson of the Peruvian Caiman to Any and All Writing (5 minutes)

The lesson is pretty clear: if you draw from life, from observation, your writing will be more convincing. It doesn't matter if you're writing science fiction, fantasy, or contemporary realism—whatever it is, it will benefit from real-life observation. Is there a street performer in the novel you're writing? Go watch one in action. Is there a short-hair terrier in the story you're writing? Go observe one. Is there a meat-eating Venus flytrap plant in your poem? See how they really do it. Nothing can substitute for the level of specificity you get when you actually observe.

## Step 3: Knowing the Difference in Details (25 minutes)

My students and I talk about the three types of details. With different classes, we've given these three types different names, but here we'll call them:

- ☞ Golden
- ☞ Useful
- ☞ Not-so-good

Now let's try to define them, in reverse order so we have some drama:

*Not-so-good:* This is a very nice way of referring to clichés or clunky descriptions or analogies. First, clichés: if there's one service we can give to these students, it's to wean them off the use of clichés. Clichés just destroy everything in their path, and they prevent the student's writing from being personal or original. *He was as strong as an ox. She ate like a bird. His hands were clammy. She looked like she'd seen a ghost.* There's just no point, really, in writing these words down. When students can tell a cliché when they see one, they become better critical thinkers, better readers, smarter people. When they learn to stay away from clichés in their own writing, they're on their way to becoming far stronger writers. The other type of not-so-good detail is the clunky one. *His legs looked like square-cut carrots. Her dog was like a blancmange crossed with a high-plains cowboy.* This is, in a way, preferable to a cliché, but it's so strange and hard to picture that it disrupts the flow of the story.

*Useful:* These are descriptions that are plain but needed. *His hair was orange. Her face was long and oval.* These pedestrian details are necessary, of course. Not every description can be golden. Speaking of which . . .

*Golden:* This is a detail/description/analogy that is singular, is completely original, and makes one's subject unforgettable. *She tapped her fingernail rhythmically on her large teeth as she watched her husband count the change in his man-purse.* In one sentence, we've learned so much about these two people. He has a man-purse. He's fastidious. She's tired of him. She's exasperated by him. She has large teeth. Golden details can come about even while using plain words: *Their young daughter's eyes were grey and cold, exhausted.* Those words, individually bland, are very specific and unsettling when applied to a young girl. In one key sentence, a writer can nail down a character. This is a sample from one of my students, describing a man she saw in the park near 826 Valencia: *He wore a beret, though he'd never been to Paris, and he walked like a dancer, as if hoping someone would notice that he walked like a dancer.*

**Working this out with the class:** Getting the students to understand the differences between these three kinds of description is possible with an exercise that's always good fun. Create a chart, where you have three categories: not-so-good, useful, golden. Now give them a challenge: come up with examples of each. Tell them that they need to conjure examples for, say:

*The feeling of traveling at 100 miles an hour.*

The students in one of my classes came up with these:

*Not-so-good:* like flying; like being on a rollercoaster; so fast you want to puke; like being shot out of a cannon.

*Useful:* terrifying; dizzying; nerve-racking; hurtling.

*Golden:* like being dropped down a well; as the speed grew, I heard death's whisper growing louder and louder.

The exploration of these types of description can last a full class period, for sure. If you want to keep going, consider this game I use sometimes. This takes the concept to a new level of fun.

## Optional Game (25 minutes)

Take 25 sheets of blank paper, or one for every student in the class. At the top of each—leaving plenty of room below—write something that might need description: the smell of a grandparent; the sensation of a first kiss; the atmosphere of a funeral home; the taste of a perfect apple; the look in the eyes of someone who's just seen a car accident. Now, pass these out, one page per student. The task is to come up with the best (golden) description or analogy for each prompt. It works like this: Student A might start with the "smell of a grandparent" sheet. Student A then spends a few minutes trying to come up with the best description he can think of. When Student A has written something down, he passes the paper on to Student B, and Student A receives another one that's been passed by Student C. The next paper Student A gets might be "the taste of a perfect apple." Student A then spends a few minutes on that one. If he comes up with something, then great. If he doesn't, he can pass it on. Each student writes his or her own analogy below the rest of the descriptions. The final object is to come up with the best description for each prompt. I usually give the students 25 minutes, so those 25 minutes are pretty madcap, with the papers flying, the students searching for the prompts that inspire them. At the end of the 25 minutes, each prompt might have 10–15 descriptions written below it. The teacher then reads all the descriptions aloud, and the students vote on which one is best. Whichever student wins the most prompts is feted in some appropriate way.

## Step 4: Interviewing Your Peers While Observing Them Shrewdly (15 minutes)

Start by telling the students that they're going to interview each other for 15 minutes. The students will be paired up—try to pair up students who don't usually talk to each other much—and they'll find a quiet place to talk. One will interview the other, and after 7½ minutes, they'll switch. Before getting them started, talk about what sorts of details are useful in defining a character, making that character singular and intriguing. They'll be applying what they know from the caiman exercise, and also using good interviewing techniques, to immediately get beyond the "Where do you go to school?" sorts of questions. By asking good questions and observing closely, the interviews should produce strong results very quickly, now that the students know that they're looking for golden details.

## Step 5: Immortalizing Your Subject (30 minutes)

Once all the students have notes about their assigned peer, they can do one of two things:

### The Simple but Essential Character Sketch

You can ask them to simply write one-page character sketches of their peers, which should be compelling, true, well observed, and (of course) beautifully written. This alone is a very worthwhile assignment. When these are read aloud, the interview subjects benefit from what in most cases is the first time they've ever been thus defined. It's strange but true: it's pretty rare to have someone observe you closely, write about your gestures and freckles and manner of speech. In the process, the interviewers improve their powers of observation, while the interviewees blush and can't get the words off their brain. And these two students get to know each other far better than they would almost any other way. It's a good way to break though cliques, and create new bonds of understanding.

## Find Your Subject in Rural India (for Example)

The lesson works pretty well either way, but something extraordinary happens with this second part, the curveball part. At this stage, after the first 15 minutes, hand out pictures to the students. These pictures, one per student, should depict some unusual, strange, foreign, bizarre, or historical setting. Usually I make copies from old *LIFE* books about various cultures of the world. Thus the student might end up with a picture of a Swedish farm, a royal Thai court, a Nairobi marketplace, or a scene from rural India. Then tell the class that they need to (a) use the details they've gathered about their classmate; and then (b) place that student in a foreign setting. The writers then need to concoct a reason why their character is in rural India, or in Barbados, or in Grenada, or in the drawing room of a Scottish duke. This requires the writers to imagine this new/strange world, and also solve the problem: What is their character doing there? Is their character stuck, is he or she trying to leave? How would this student react to being lost in a marketplace in Nairobi? Who or what is he or she looking for?

If you have some time, or want to expand the exercise, have the students research their location a bit. Even by using the picture alone, they are using their observational powers, but with the added benefit of some book-oriented or Internet research, they can conjure ever-more-convincing settings.

I have to admit that I came up with this exercise on the fly. I had no idea that it would work, but it did the first time I did it, and it always works. Here's why:

☞ The process of interviewing one's classmates is always appealing to the students.

☞ The close observation makes both students, interviewer and interviewee, feel valued and singular.

☞ The curveball of putting this person in a foreign setting forces the students outside their own school/home/neighborhood, and requires the solving of a fairly sophisticated problem: Who is this person, and why is he or she here? The drama and conflict are built into the setting, and get a short story off to a quick and intriguing start.

A stellar example of one such exercise is on the following page. In their interview, 17-year-old Sally Mao's subject told her about some nightmares he'd been having, and mentioned having recently been to the hospital to visit his mother. Then Sally was given a picture of Bombay, circa 1970. From this, Sally created this story in about 20 minutes.

# DUST-SILK POUCH

Up ahead, the road widens to reveal a slipshod blockade of cars, carts, and cargo. A yellow-curry smoke stews the engine of Mr. Kendall's van as he bites at the tail of jagged traffic. James, neck pressed against the seat, awakens from a sweaty dream to the grind of sound.

He has just suffered the same nightmare again. It gallops with him wherever he goes. He sees its lean legs and mane, its relentless tawny hooves swerving outside car windows, airplane windows, bedroom doors, its acrid breath clogging his nostrils, a familiar stench. The ride up the mountain has rattled his dreamscape like some monstrous cataclysm, magnifying his terror. This time the rodents had done it. They were wearing green uniforms, the whole lot of them. They swarmed, they crawled, they carried nooses, planks, kerosene, and razor-tipped whips. They were out for blood.

James asks, "Dad, what's a Nazi?"

"Eh? Are we having this discussion again?"

"What's a Nazi, what's a Gestapo, what are they?"

"A Nazi is a kind of monster," Mr. Kendall declares. "The kind that enslaves people, that performs cruel experiments. A Gestapo is their secret police."

"What kind of monsters are they? Are they some kind of furry creature? Rodents, maybe?"

"I wouldn't say that. But Nazis are less prevalent than they used to be."

"I just had a dream. It was the chipmunks, it was the rodents who made up the Gestapo, they wanted blood, Dad, they wanted blood, and they're right here in India—I'm not sure where but I think they're further up ahead. I'm scared."

Mr. Kendall laughs. "Well, son, who could really blame the rodents? The very term 'guinea pig' implies some sort of cruel and unusual experimentation. Yes, if rodents took over the world, they'd be out for blood."

His father's hands sweat on the wheel. "This may take longer than expected," he says. "The hospital is beyond this village. If I get this right, it'd probably be within the next two towns. I hope that's the one she's staying in. Otherwise, we're out of luck."

What they are waiting for James doesn't grasp. He fidgets, chews on imaginary gum, plugs his ears. Before this trip, India was a haze of cast-bronze Hindu idols, boiled-blood sunrises, young girls in jeweled saris and deep crimson makeup, and all that kind of exotic drone that keeps a dish of samosas spicy. But like any vision, this one has been extinguished. India isn't carved out of ivory. India bakes and suffocates. India is dirty, damp, and cauldron-colored. India sticks to the inside of his skin.

—Sally Mao, 17

# LITERARY FACEBOOKS

*by* KATHRYN RIDDLE

1 SESSION, 2 HOURS
MATERIALS: *Magazines to cut up, scissors,
glue sticks (optional)*

CURIOUS WHAT ELIZABETH BENNET'S, Harry Potter's, Bella Swan's, or Percy Jackson's Facebook profile would look like? Wonder no more! In this lesson plan, students create a mock Facebook profile based on their very favorite literary character. There's lots of room for creativity. Use it as a fun wrap-up activity, or to assess student understanding of character traits.

When using the paper template, it works well to expand it onto a large piece of paper, leaving lots of room for writing and instant classroom decoration when the product is finished!

Start by having the class discuss what they have in their own Facebook profile and how it represents them. Students should then pick a book character to use for their Facebook and brainstorm what they want to include in it.

Pass out the templates and get ready to write! Students often like to have the text they are using at hand to check details. Encouragement to get creative is also important, as not all Facebook details will be found in the book. In this case, encourage students to make up details based on other character traits. Have magazines,

scissors, and glue sticks on hand so students can paste in profile pictures and other images.

Now brace yourself and be ready to be amazed by your incredibly creative and talented students. Have your students share their creations with the class. This offers an opportunity to both show their skills and prove what they know about the text (and it's a great review for those students who may have missed a chapter or two!). Because sharing the entire profile would be very time-consuming, encourage your students to pick five parts that they want to share, or ask them what they put in various areas of the page.

This lesson does not have to stop with literature lessons. Students can create pages for acclaimed scientists, famous historical figures, or celebrated mathematicians.

*Note:* Neither Jossey-Bass Publishers nor the authors of this book encourage the creation of fictitious profiles on Facebook.com; the site is a hub for individuals' authentic identities and as such fictitious profiles violate the core values of Facebook.

Wall | **Info** | Photos | SuperPoke! | Flair | Video

**Basic Information** ______________________________

Sex: ______________________________

Current City: ______________________________

Birthday: ______________________________

Hometown: ______________________________

Parents: ______________________________

Looking for: ______________________________

Political Views: ______________________________

Religious Views: ______________________________

**Likes and Interests** ______________________________

Activities: ______________________________

______________________________

Interests: ______________________________

______________________________

Favorite Music: ______________________________

Favorite Movie: ______________________________

Favorite Quotation: ______________________________

______________________________

**Friends**

_____

_____ said:

_____

_____ said:

_____ said:

# SUBURBAN EPICS

*by* TOM PERROTTA

1 SESSION, 2 HOURS

PEOPLE THINK THEIR OWN NEIGHBORHOODS ARE BORING, BUT IN MOST CASES that's not true at all. I've written any number of stories about people who live next door to me. Inevitably, they end up being stranger and more interesting than I'd thought. I don't think I'm lucky to live next to weird people; I think weird people are living next to all of us. Just this year I wrote a story about a woman who lives on my street who spends the entire fall picking up every leaf. She was a part of the landscape, and we'd started to wonder about her, what would it mean to have your life reduced to this plot of grass. She became a neighborhood anecdote, and then a short story. In this lesson plan students practice finding the stories in their own neighborhood.

## The Exercise

### 1. Make a Map

Draw a map of your street, then write a brief anecdote for each house: this lady drives like a maniac; this guy gets the newspaper in a woman's robe.

### 2. Pick the Most Interesting Anecdote

Sometimes this is easy. I lived in one house from the time I was 7 until college, and a pretty amazing thing happened next door, which became the basis for a story in my first book. The widow next door was having an affair with a married man. His wife caught them. The first time I saw this man he was standing on my porch, choking his wife. Later, my neighbor married the man—the choker—and he became my next-door neighbor for the rest of his life.

Less sensationally, I recently lived next to four classical horn players. Every hour of the day, someone was practicing the horn, so I know I'm going to write about that one day.

10

### 3. Turn the Anecdote into a Story

If that's what you want to do, that is. For the purposes of this exercise, it can be enough just to produce an anecdote and to start to *think* about expanding it. The point is just to realize that we all have a wealth of stories right around us, right in our neighborhoods.

If you do want to transform your anecdote into a story, you'll need a plot. Usually this is a matter of finding another character whose life is rubbing against the protagonist's life. When I wrote the leaf story, the narrator was a high school kid who can't play football because of too many concussions. For the first time he has nothing to do, and he gets irritated by this woman and her leaves. In the end, the story's really about him, confronting having nothing to do.

All that said, when you're first getting started, try not too get to hung up on the nuts and bolts of structuring. If you're feeling bogged down, or don't know where to begin, it can be a good idea to play around with the point of view. Try telling the story from the perspective of the neighbor, especially if it's an irritating neighbor. Think of the person who bugs you the most and imagine how he or she sees you.

### 4. As You Go, Don't Be Afraid to Make Stuff Up

You're writing fiction, so you can take as much license as you want. When do you do that? When the truth is either boring or unknown. That's most of the time. In my own work not more than 10% comes from real life. The anecdote or the kernel is really a minimal jumping-off point. I almost don't want to know too much. I'd rather just have an image in my head, or a sentence that I read in a newspaper story. It's good to have a lot of questions and a lot of empty space to fill.

### 5. Wind Down

Because your neighbors are still (presumably) alive, and their real-life story is still going on, it can be hard to figure out where to end your story. Every story is different, and you'll find it by feel. In my leaf story, I could see where it was going to end up: after having this terrible night, the narrator goes and breaks open the lady's leaf bags all over her lawn. As the story ends, we see he has nothing better to do than pick up those leaves himself, an act of acceptance that kind of rounded out the story for me. Your own story can span years or just be a brief episode, and the ending will complete an arc for the character at the center of the story.

## Alternately

Besides neighbors, another great subject is teachers. Understandably, this assignment can lead to big trouble in a classroom setting, but writers working on their own might want to try it. Take five or six teachers that you've had and come up with stories about them. Relatives can also make great subjects. The idea is that you don't have to look very far, go across the world, or go over to the dark side to find interesting people. Just running into coaches, teachers, and your friends' parents, you have all these people who've made an impression on you. You want to open up their lives and imagine more.

# BUSTED

*by* WILLIAM JOHN BERT

**3 SESSIONS, 2 HOURS EACH**

WE ALL DO THINGS WE AREN'T SUPPOSED to do, and sometimes we get caught doing them. Usually we learn something about ourselves (but not always!). This is the stuff of story: desire, conflict, climax, and resolution (or lack thereof). This workshop uses students' experiences of getting caught to set a scene, narrate character actions and motivation, build suspense, and convey what—if anything—the experience taught them.

## Session 1

To start, we go around the room and share stories about times that we got caught. The more embarrassing, the better. We pay attention to how we tell our tales: what details do we give, and in what order? How do we describe ourselves, or other people? Write down some of the elements of these tales on the board. Use them to define and explain the essential elements of a story: characters, setting, plot, and theme.

The worksheet handout helps distill the elements of our tales. We use it to draft a list of characters, a setting, a plot, and a lesson/message/moral, or lack thereof. But a worksheet is not a story. What does a story look like? It's complete sentences and paragraphs of narration. It introduces characters,

describes settings, and relates the events of the plot in a flow of language, sometimes withholding key details until late in the story to create suspense. So now we write out our getting caught stories. It's okay if they're not perfect—we're going to keep working on them—but try to draft out the whole thing, all the way to the end.

To wrap up, we put away the drafts and do an exercise: describe the story's setting using each of the five senses at least twice. After reading this, our readers should know what the settings look like, sound like, smell like, and so forth. This helps convince them that the story really happened by forming images in their minds, and it will come in handy when we revise the stories over the next two workshops.

## Session 2

A *character* is a person, but *character* is a quality that answers the question, Why do people do what they do? So, why did we do the thing we weren't supposed to do? We ask the students to write a monologue justifying why this illegal thing was worth breaking the rules for. We tell them not to dwell on being sorry for it. If it was an item you took, why did you want it? If it was an action, then how did you think taking the action would change your life? Use concrete details to show what the character (you) was thinking, hoping, envisioning.

Next, we do a point of view (POV) exercise. POV has to do with who is telling the story—the narrator. What does the narrator see or think? When does he or she learn new pieces of information? How does this change the story? This exercise helps us answer those questions.

1. We take a few minutes to write about the room or building we're in right now as it looks to someone walking by outside who has never been inside. What does that person see and think? What questions does he or she have? By the end, the passerby should decide whether to enter or walk away.

2. Now we write about this place as it looks to a homeless person who walks by it every single day but has never been inside. By the end, the person should decide whether or not to go inside. How is this POV different from the person in part 1?

3. Finally, we write about the building from the POV *of the building itself.* What would it be like to be a place? How would a place talk and think? Put your imagination to use.

Next we rewrite our Session 1 getting caught story from the POV of the person(s) who caught us. We use our imaginations to get in their head, see what they see, and feel what they felt, from before they caught us up until afterward. How did their opinion of us change?

If there's time, we share these POV stories with each other. Identify the characters, setting, plot, and concrete details. Discuss the differences in writing from this POV. Do we understand what the characters know and when they know it? Do we understand our characters' motivations?

# Session 3

For a quick 15-minute warm-up exercise, we tell the students:

1. Write down a list of everything that happened to you today, from when you woke up until now.

2. Pick the thing from that list that you disliked the most. Write about it as if you really loved it, as if it were the best part of your day.

3. Now pick the thing that you liked the best and describe it in incredibly concrete detail, being sure to describe the scene, including sense descriptions to convey to the reader just what you liked so much about it.

Once we've done all these exercises, it's time to revise. That means reading over our drafts and exercises and any comments or suggestions we've received. It means finding ways to make our story come alive and seize the reader's imagination and attention. It can mean adding concrete detail and texture, withholding information, explaining character motivation, or adding backstory.

We have a choice here: do we want to revise our original getting caught story, or the story from the POV of the person who caught us? Make a choice, and then incorporate everything we've done so far—concrete detail, character motivation, POV—to revise it into the best story possible. When everyone's done, we share the stories with each other.

If there's time, after each person reads, talk about choosing a title (students hardly ever title their own stories without being prompted). A title can reflect the theme of the story, or it can be a significant detail within the story, a key thing that the main character wants, thinks, or feels.

# BUSTED WORKSHEET

Copyright © 2011 by 826 National

Who are your CHARACTERS? You need at least two: YOU and THE PERSON WHO CAUGHT YOU. You can have more characters if more people were involved in the story.

1. _____
2. _____
3. _____
4. _____

WHERE did the story take place? This is your SETTING. Be sure to include concrete details such as SIGHTS, SOUNDS, SMELLS, TEXTURES, and TASTES.

1. _____
2. _____
3. _____
4. _____

What happened? This is your PLOT. List WHAT HAPPENED step-by-step from beginning to end. Continue on the back side of the paper if you need to.

1. _____
2. _____
3. _____
4. _____
5. _____
6. _____
7. _____
8. _____

What do you THINK about what happened? How do you FEEL about what happened? Did you LEARN anything? Ever get caught doing the same again? Or doing something different? Share your thoughts.

1. _____
2. _____
3. _____
4. _____

# HOW TO WRITE SCIENCE FICTION

*by* CORY DOCTOROW

3 SESSIONS, 1 HOUR EACH

WRITING A SCIENCE FICTION STORY IS like building a machine with two gears: a big one (the world you're creating) and a little one (the characters in it). The little gear turns the big one around. The big wheel doesn't have a lot of torque; what it has is a lot of stuff. The characters, meanwhile, don't have a lot of stuff, but they've got the emotions that keep things happening in the big world and keep readers interested. In this exercise students will create a big world and a small group of characters, then bring them together to create the beginnings of a science fiction story.

## Step 1: Imagine a World

Every story has to happen somewhere, but it's very common for new writers to start in a white room. That's because even *you* don't know what's there yet. But the more that's there, the more it's going to feel like the story is really happening, which is going to help your readers care about what's going on. One way to do that is to make this world somewhere you really know. It can be an imaginary place you've thought a lot about, or it can be somewhere real. We tend to think of science fiction as always happening in outer space, but lots of science fiction stories take place in actual cities.

Real or imaginary, you'll want some kind of premise—some problem or question your story's going to explore. In my book *Little Brother* the premise I started with was that I wanted to write a story in which the technology actually *works*. I've seen innumerable thrillers where the computers are treated as narrative conveniences without regard to how computers actually function, which is too bad, because real-life computers can do some really amazing stuff. So I started brainstorming scenarios in which computers do exciting things: cat-and-mouse games, kids hiding from schools, individuals hiding from authorities and from criminals.

From there the story followed naturally. Once you've got an idea of what your world will be like, you can start to populate it with things, structures, infrastructures, and so on, all of which usually emerges organically from your premise. The world just starts to spin itself out. Whenever something new has to appear, you ask yourself what the material would look like. Some details you'll draw from real life, and some you'll imagine.

Your assignment: come up with a premise. Then, take some time to write up a detailed description of the world you'll be writing about. Draw it. Map it. Describe its landscape, its climate, its sky, its streets (if it has streets), its dwellings (ditto). Is it a totalitarian regime, or an anarchic utopia? Think about time, too: is this in the future, present, or past?

## Step 2: Create Your Character(s)

When you stop and think about it, caring about fictional people is really weird. Why do we care about Charlie Brown, who's not a lot more sophisticated than a crosswalk figure? The answer is that, to some extent, your brain believes that Charlie Brown is a real person, so he matters to you.

That's the writer's job. You're trying to trick someone else's brain into thinking a fictional character is a real person, so that he or she will care about them.

How do you do that? There's no one true way, but in general, it's a good idea to figure out who your main character is, and what he or she knows and doesn't know, and really stick to that consistently. Part of what makes dramatic tension is what one character knows and another doesn't, and one way to blow it is to have characters act like they know something they don't, like when a character expresses a

certainty about how another character is feeling. "I walked into the room, Janet was waiting for me, she'd been there for hours, she was internally furious." How do you know that? It starts feeling too made-up.

Your assignment: imagine a person who, for a reason that's entirely plausible, showcases the most interesting aspects of the world you'll be writing about. This is the person who'll be taking us on the tour of the world you've just created. Describe the person in concrete detail. What does he or she look like? What gets him excited? What makes her afraid? What's this person's best trait, and worst? How does she respond to authority? Who else is in his life, and how does he relate to them? What's her biggest problem, her greatest wish?

## Step 3: Bring Your World and Your Characters Together

Now you'll bring your elements together to start your story. The basis of pretty much every story is a person and a place with a problem and things are getting worse, but you don't need to get hung up on the details just yet. Start with one scene, and see where it leads you.

# CORY DOCTOROW'S TOP THREE TIPS

1.  *Write every day.* That's the one piece of advice I always assumed people were lying about, but I wish I'd learned to do it ten years earlier. Anything you do every day gets easier. If you don't have much free time, just set a minimal word target, like 50–250. Then: STOP, even and especially if you are inspired. Stop in the middle of the sentence, so you know what the first few words will be the next day. That way, you don't have to be creative to start writing the next day, and then the subconscious takes over.

2.  *Don't revise while you're writing.* This is really hard to avoid. There's a point when you become convinced you don't know what you're doing anymore, when your subconscious takes over and starts throwing in details and it feels like you're about to trip yourself up. That moment always occurs when things are going best. That feeling of vertigo means you're doing it right. Your subconscious is coordinating more than you can consciously. That's when we're tempted to reread and rewrite. I always want to reoutline, but that's the kiss of death. Just keep writing.

3.  *Don't write ceremonially.* Don't have a bunch of things you need to do before you write. Don't feel like you need to put yourself in the mood. I ended up with more and more conditions that had to be satisfied before I could write and it became really burdensome. Learn to write wherever you are. Don't write for inspiration. I don't believe in inspiration. The days you feel like you're inspired and the days you're not are related to your state of mind, and not to the actual work you're producing. Later, reading the work, you won't remember when you felt inspired and when you didn't.

# WRITING FROM EXPERIENCE

*by* STEPHEN ELLIOTT

1 SESSION, 2 HOURS

IN THIS CLASS STUDENTS LEARN TO TRANSFORM THE EVENTS OF THEIR lives—painful, funny, enlightening, embarrassing—into compelling fiction. The best part is that they learn something about themselves in the process. Their life experiences and how they respond to them create their unique literary code, and it's the greatest thing a writer has to offer. This class helps them get it down on the page.

The first thing I do is spend some time convincing students that borrowing from real life is okay. Students often feel that this is cheating—that in fiction, you have to make everything up. So we spend some time talking about all the great books that are based on real experiences, like *On the Road* and *The Bell Jar*. I bring up Charles Bukowski, who wrote 60 books directly from his own life. Bukowski was acutely aware that the reader is not the writer's mother and has to be won over with a good story line and compelling characters. He took real elements and transformed them, turning true events into great writing.

Which brings us to our next issue: Who cares? Who cares about your stories? Why is writing about your life important? My answer: because you learn so much about yourself just from doing it. That's a huge benefit, and it's much more valuable than being published.

Sometimes students are worried about writing from experience because they're afraid to offend people they know. I remind them that writing and publishing are not the same thing. The time to worry about other people's feelings is at the publishing stage. In the meantime, don't let it limit the story. Keeping that in mind really frees you up.

Once they're convinced we roll up our sleeves and get to work. The assignment: write a fictional story based on an event from your life. The handout will walk you through the process, from finding something to write about, to getting it down, punching it up, and revising it.

# HOW TO TURN YOUR LIFE INTO GREAT FICTION

### STEP 1: FIND SOMETHING TO WRITE ABOUT

Lots of students claim nothing interesting has ever happened to them, but that's just not true. Make a list of everything that has happened in your life so far. Now read the list over. What event brings up the strongest reaction for you? That's the one you should write about. It's something you haven't quite resolved, and it will have a lot of energy and life on the page.

### STEP 2: GET IT DOWN

Now that you have your topic, start writing about it. Get it all down on paper. Don't worry about whether it's good or not. Don't hold anything back. Just get it down. We'll go back and fix it later.

### STEP 3: PUNCH IT UP

Here's where we transform the true event into a really compelling tale. This is writing, not reporting, so we can make things up. Don't let truth get in the way of a good story. Let go and start creating. Look for ways to make it more readable. Condense characters or create new ones. Change the order of events or even their outcome. Change the ending if you want. This is your opportunity to live out the fantasy, to let the story end the way you want it to. What do you want to have happen to these characters? What are you curious about? Writing is like looking in a crystal ball. This is your chance to envision the future. How would it be changed if you'd done things differently?

As you punch things up, your priority is to keep the story interesting. That means you need to come up with ways to make your characters charismatic. An easy way to do it: make your main character intensely interested in something. When characters care about something—a person, a pastime, whatever—the reader will care about them.

### STEP 4: REVISE

In the rewrite you're exploring subtext. You're looking for themes, things you might not have put in there intentionally. Maybe your story about learning to ride your bike mentions your big brother a lot. Maybe the story is actually about how much you miss him now that he's moved away. In the revision, you want to turn up those moments. You're also looking for ways to punch up any conflicts. Ask yourself: Did I end this scene too soon? Should I keep these people in a room together longer? That can be a pressure cooker. People want to relieve the pressure, so they let one of the characters out of the room. Sometimes it's better to keep them there and let the conflict happen.

That's it. Turn it in and be proud of yourself.

# TOO MUCH MONEY!

## AN ETHICAL WRITING EXPERIENCE IN 10 EASY STEPS

*by* LOUANNE JOHNSON

**1 LESSON, 45 MINUTES TO 1+ HOUR** *(Time varies depending on number/age of students. Steps 4, 6, and 7 can be skipped to shorten the duration of the activity)*

**MATERIALS:**
*Student journals*
*Whiteboard/LCD screen/easel pad*
*Team cards*
*Timer and signal*

THIS LESSON INTRODUCES STUDENTS TO THE BENEFITS OF JOURNALING, using an ethical conundrum to keep them invested and involved.

**OVERVIEW OF ASSIGNMENT:**

Step 1: Think

Step 2: Quick Write

Step 3: Secret Vote

Step 4: Quick Discussion (optional)

Step 5: Team Task—try to reach a consensus

Step 6: Team Reports (optional)

Step 7: Whole-Group Discussion (optional)

Step 8: Second Secret Vote

Step 9: Journal Write

Step 10: (Optional) Informal Essay Assignment

# Introduction (5 minutes)

First, the instructor introduces the activity and explains that students who fully participate in this activity earn full credit, regardless of their personal opinions. The instructor also informs students that various segments of this activity will have time limits, and then demonstrates the audible signal that will let students know when the time has elapsed for those segments. The instructor may ask for a volunteer to be the Official Timer, using a stopwatch. A rain stick, chime, or other pleasant sound makes a good signal.

## Step 1: Think (1 minute)

The instructor presents verbally the following scenario to students and gives them one full minute to silently consider their first response: *If you buy something at a store and the clerk gives you back too much money by mistake, do you keep the money? Yes? No? Maybe?*

The instructor will also present the question in writing on the board/screen/easel for visual learners.

## Step 2: Quick Write (5 minutes)

Students have 5 minutes to write down their response to the question in their journals, along with their reasons. If they choose Maybe, for example, they should explain the criteria. (What would affect your decision? The amount of money? Whether anybody else would know? What would happen to the clerk?)

## Step 3: Secret Vote (1–2 minutes)

Students will place one hand against their chests, with their hands folded into a fist. The teacher will then take a secret vote, tallying the number of Yes, No, and Maybe votes on the board or easel so everybody can see the results.

## Step 4: Quick Discussion (3–5 minutes)

The instructor asks for a volunteer from each group (Yes, No, Maybe) to present his or her thoughts on the issue in less than one minute. This is meant to be quick, just to encourage thinking. Students will have ample opportunity to express their views in the next segment.

## Step 5: Team Task (15–20 minutes, including forming teams)

*Assign Teams (5 minutes):* The instructor distributes playing cards or cards with animal pictures or symbols, with 3–4 matching cards for each team. Team assignment should be quick and random to prevent "friendship cliques" from forming. The idea here is to mix it up. An effective way of forming teams quickly is to give students 30 seconds to find their team partners.

*Team Task (10–15 minutes):* Each team is tasked with discussing their ideas on this ethical question, with the goal of reaching a consensus during the allotted time. The instructor sounds the signal to end the team discussions.

### Step 6: Team Reports (5–30+ minutes, depending on number of teams)

One or two members from each team will have 1–5 minutes to present the result of the team's discussion: Were they able to reach consensus? If so, what did they decide? If not, why not?

### Step 7: Whole-Group Discussion (5–15 minutes)

Again, the instructor will ask for volunteers to present their points of view, especially those who may have changed their votes based on the team discussions.

### Step 8: Second Secret Vote (2–5 minutes)

Following the group discussion, students will return to their individual seats and the instructor will take another secret vote, again presenting a tally on the board/screen/easel for students to view.

### Step 9: Journal Write (10–20 minutes, depending on student ages and enthusiasm levels)

In their private journals, students will write about the exercise. This can be a free-write, but some students may ask for guidelines. For those who prefer guidelines, suggest that they outline their initial response to the question, give their thoughts about the team discussion, and explain why they changed their votes on the topic or why they didn't change their votes. They may also want to write their response to this activity overall: Did they enjoy it? Did they learn anything about themselves or other people? Would they like to do similar activities in the future? How would they "tweak" this activity, if they think it could be improved?

### Step 10: (Optional) Informal Essay Assignment

Instructors may ask students to take home their private journals and use them as the basis for an informal essay on the question of how to respond to Too Much Money! their votes on the question, their response to the team discussion, why they did or didn't change their votes, and their thoughts about the activity in general. For more mature students, the assignment might be on the general topic of personal ethics, with students choosing their own specific topics and format for the written assignment (Q&A, personal essay, persuasive essay, brief research paper, and so on).

*Note: This activity can serve as a springboard for further group discussions, team tasks, and journal writing/essays/projects on similar topics such as shoplifting, lying, or cheating on tests, or for issues that appear in the news media, such as insider stock trading, financial contributions to political parties, voter fraud, and so on.*

# THE TALK SHOW CIRCUIT

*by* ELLIE KEMPER

1 SESSION, 2 HOURS

WHEN I WAS SEVEN, I WROTE A BOOK called *Jenny Watching Too Much TV*. Our tragic heroine was a 7-year-old girl, Jenny, who watched too much TV. It was a really good book. Then, when I was 8, my ideas sort of dried up. What was left to write about? I was stuck.

My creative writer's block continued into high school. It wasn't that I didn't enjoy writing; I just felt that my stories weren't interesting enough. I used to agonize over English papers. What could I possibly have to say that hadn't been said before? I doubted my insight and my analysis. I had no personally tragic tales to tell, and no stories of triumph, either. Had my creative life peaked with Jenny?

Then, and this is embarrassing, I came up with an idea. I pretended that I was a guest on David Letterman. I have always loved David Letterman and his show; he is the best talk show host in the world. One night in ninth grade, I was working on a creative writing assignment. We were supposed to write an essay about something on which we were an "expert," and I was making little progress. What did I know about anything? Then, it hit me. I went into my closet, slipped on a pair of (very low) high heels, and put on some entrance music (undoubtedly The

Cranberries). Then I pretended that the computer screen was David Letterman, and I began to chat.

As I said, this is extremely embarrassing. It is also a very helpful exercise in brainstorming. For the most part, guests do not go on late night talk shows to tell deeply personal or tragic tales; save that for the daytime. On late night, guests go on to tell an entertaining story. They are not always successful. I think it's a very difficult feat to pull off. For me, thinking about a story that I could tell on a late night talk show is very helpful in coming up with short story ideas. They do not have to be big or brassy or heartbreaking. Personally, I think the more mundane the story, the better. My very favorite talk show guest is Amy Sedaris. I could listen to her tell stories about her cheese balls for hours. It's all in the telling of the story.

A good story does not have to be about something earth-shattering. Examining the boring or everyday happenings in life can often yield the very best stories. While *Jenny Watching Too Much TV* was an earth-shattering work indeed, the actual stuff of the story was something anyone with a TV, or named Jenny, could relate to. And that's why it was such a hit. Everyone has a good story to tell.

## Talk Show Exercise

Separate the class into pairs. Each student will have a chance to be the guest and the host. Entrance music and high heels optional.

To begin, both students spend a half hour or so individually brainstorming good talk show stories. Here are some tips:

1. **Keep the story simple.**

   Stories with too many characters, or inside jokes, or circumstances that a random audience would have trouble relating to are not good talk show stories.

2. **You should not be the hero of your own story.**

   What fun is it for an audience to have to listen to you bragging? The more embarrassing the story is for you, the better it is for the audience. That said, don't feel like you have to tell some deeply personal story that is genuinely mortifying to you. Just make sure you don't come out looking too good.

3. **Make sure that the story has some sort of build.**

   Ideally, your story will increase in action or circumstances as it goes on, not decrease. For example, if you are telling a story about cooking dinner, make sure that you save the part about food poisoning for the end, not the beginning.

4. **The more distinctive the flavor, the better.**

   A good talk show story, like a good short story, uses concise examples to give a very clear idea of who the character is. If the story is about you, try to find an anecdote that really gives the audience a sharp impression of who you are. Do you have something strange that you collect? Is there something unusual that you feel very strongly about? Is there an activity that you love or hate that defines you? You only have about 8 minutes to tell this story, so editing is very important.

5. **Anticipate and be open to the host's interruptions.**

   A good host will only help the story along, not derail it. Be prepared to answer his questions and let him or her help you build the story. If you end up using your story as a written story, you can use his or her "questions" as invisible guidelines on how to further the action of the story you are telling.

———◆———

After you have finished brainstorming, exchange your ideas with each other. Think of the other person as your own segment producer. As a segment producer, you must choose which stories from the guest will be the most entertaining to the audience. Work together to figure out what will create the best show. Once you have narrowed each other's stories down to three (or two, or even just one longer story), you are ready to change from "segment producer" to "host." (Again, each student has a chance to play both parts.)

As a host, work with the guest to create the best build for the story. Make a list of questions that the host will ask. The guest will be ready for the questions, and will frame his or her story accordingly. In an actual talk show, the very best parts, in my opinion, are the unscripted and spontaneous moments that come from just being present and alert. Make sure that the host and the guest *are listening to each other.* There is nothing worse than a talk show segment where a guest says something really funny, but the host is so focused on the next question that he isn't even listening to what was actually said. And vice versa. Remember, at the end of the day, it's just a conversation. Don't be afraid to go off script.

Now you are ready to "tape" the segment. You can either perform the interviews in front of the class, or tape them at home and bring them in. But no fair taping over and over again. As in an actual talk show, you really only get one chance. That is why spontaneity is so valuable!

Then, for a creative writing exercise, students should take their talk show stories and write them down. Try to keep the essence of the "live" interview present in the story. Use an "invisible" host to push the story along, if necessary. Or, perhaps even use an actual interviewer in the story to create a written interview format. The principles of the talk show segment remain the same: be concise, sharp, selective, and flavorful. Try not to alienate the reading audience in your story. I think that any story that goes over well in a talk show setting would make an excellent short story. Think about Joaquin Phoenix; hello? He could write an entire book of short stories from his brief 15 minutes on David Letterman as an insane person. On second thought, don't think about him; think about Amy Sedaris. She actually has written a bunch of books. And they're really good. A good talk show guest knows how to tell good stories.

# THE FIRST DRAFT IS MY ENEMY

## REVISIONS

*by* SARAH VOWELL

1 SESSION, 2 HOURS

WHEN I WAS IN HIGH SCHOOL I WAS ENTHRALLED WITH THE BEATS AND spontaneity and things happening in the moment. I wouldn't revise or pore over a paper because that would make it fake, dry, professional. Also, I didn't have to. The teacher would mark it up, and then we'd never fix it.

Now I treasure making things better, going over the nineteenth draft, making it funnier and shorter. That only happens with patience and time and doing it again and again. In this lesson plan we learn to do exactly that.

The assignment: take a paper you've already turned in and fix it. Picking a paper you got an A on is cheating. Choose something that needs work. Polish it up and spit-shine it into something better. The following handout has eight tips to make the project easier.

# HOW TO REVISE: SARAH VOWELL'S EIGHT BEST TIPS

### TIP #1: READ YOUR PAPER ALOUD

The best way to figure out what works and what doesn't is to read your paper aloud. The parts you cannot wait to get through are probably really boring. That's a red flag saying you need to make it shorter or funnier or gone. The parts that you find yourself looking forward to reading are generally okay.

### TIP #2: LOSE THE TOPIC SENTENCE

The first sentence is really important, but it shouldn't tell what the thing is about. That's just bad poker playing. You don't want to open with a topic sentence. Topic sentences spoil the mystery. A first sentence should be a lapel grabber. Maybe it's your jerkiest sentence, or an exclamation point of an idea, or some jarring piece of dialogue.

### TIP #3: THINK *BEHIND THE MUSIC*

Your paper probably has to convey some facts. The trick is deciding which facts are relevant and interesting and which are just deadweight. Imagine you just read something and now you're telling someone about it. What would you tell this person about this topic? What were the weird things, the cool things, the things that made you mad, or made you want to learn more? Include whatever facts or figures or anecdotes make you want to phone your best friend and say, "Get *this*."

I call this the *Behind the Music* approach. *Behind the Music* leaves out the drudgery to focus on the juicy details, the drama, the embarrassments, the setbacks. There's something human about failure and quirks, the stuff that would never be mentioned in a eulogy or a travel brochure.

### TIP #4: OUTLINE ON THE RUG

In school, they always told us to do an outline, and I never, ever, did, because of course I wrote everything at the last minute. But now, what I do is use my living room rug. I get index cards, and I make a note of every joke I want to tell, every anecdote I want to recount, every idea I want to get across, every fact I need to convey, and then I lay them out on the rug and move them around, sometimes for days, once or twice for weeks, trying to arrange them in some kind of logical narrative form. When you know where you're going, it's easier to get there.

### TIP #5: SHENANIGANS

Sometimes you've got something really great, some funny joke or bizarre anecdote, and you don't know where to put it or what to do with it. I call those "shenanigans." You can't have too many of them but you have to allow yourself a few. That's part of what's fun about being a writer—throwing in some random cool thing. If you're disciplined about it, your reader will allow and enjoy the digression.

## TIP #6: CUT THE CLUTTER

Watch out for clichés and tired phrases. If "don't even go there" appears in your essay, cut it immediately. Replace any words that are so overused they've lost all meaning, like "crazy" or "amazing."

## TIP #7: SPELL CHECK

Some of the best writers are some of the worst spellers. Don't be a hero. Use spell check and a dictionary.

## TIP #8: ENDINGS ARE HARD

Beginnings are hard, but endings are harder. There's something sad about every ending, even happy ones, because something's over. An ending should be poetic. If you've said all you have to say, your last thought should be philosophic or poetic or pretty. There should be a graceful little moment at the end, something melancholy or reflective. It shouldn't be another person's quote if you can help it. Ending with a quote is the easy way out. Your last sentence should be your own.

If you're stuck for an ending, you may have already written it. Somewhere in the middle of your paper, maybe, you've got your best sentence or paragraph. It has a kind of wisdom and finality. Move that to the end.

# SEE YOU AGAIN YESTERDAY

## PLAYING WITH TIME

*by* AUDREY NIFFENEGGER

1 SESSION, 2+ HOURS

PLAYING WITH TIME IS A GREAT EXERCISE for a beginning writer. It relieves the pressure of having to begin at the beginning, which not everyone is suited to doing, certainly not me. My own work tends to start off with a phrase or an image, and I don't necessarily know what it means. In the case of *The Time Traveler's Wife,* I started out with that phrase, and then had an image of an elderly woman with her cup of tea, waiting. And from there, eventually, it became a novel.

Nontraditional time lines work in almost any genre of literature. It doesn't have to mean science fiction time machines. For me, the time travel was mimicking memory. Memory isn't all that tidy and doesn't come in strict chronological order, so often a jumbled chronology can give a more naturalistic story.

Sometimes playing with time is done in an obvious way, and sometimes it's subtle. The nice thing about an atypical approach to time is that it allows you to give and withhold information in ways that heighten the reader's experience of suspense. Often in mysteries and suspense novels the author starts with the end or the climax—he or she flash you a jolt—and then in chapter one you go back and see how you get to that point. It's done so often it doesn't even sound like time travel.

In this lesson students practice playing with their own nontraditional time schemes.

## Exercise 1: Scramble a Story

Have students write a story in which every sentence starts with "And then." Then, have them put the sentences back in a different order for a different outcome. The fun thing is to write a bunch of unrelated sentences. Then it gets very surreal. It's great to have the students read these aloud.

## Exercise 2: Write a Story Backwards

A harder and more interesting thing to do is to start a story at the end point and work backwards. It's sounds simple, but it's not the way we're used to thinking.

## Exercise 3: Write 100 Unrelated Sentences

One of the things that's makes playing with time such a great exercise for a writer is the underlying principle of unfamiliarity. It jars you out of your habits and habitual way of looking at things, which is always good for creativity. So I do a lot of exercises that force people into peculiar juxtapositions. In this one, I have students write 100 unrelated sentences. After the first 20, it gets surprisingly hard. But when the students are done they have a grab bag of stuff they can use all semester.

## Exercise 4: Begin and End with Two Random Sentences

Once the students have their 100 sentences, I'll have them write a story that begins with, say, sentence #74 and ends with #22. The results are typically hilarious, but the work they're doing, getting from point A to B, is worth doing. Obviously you can connect any two points if you write long enough, but usually these are timed, in class. That's another thing: giving yourself finite time periods to write is REALLY helpful.

## Bonus Exercise: Character Development

Managing character development when your character is going backward and forward in time can be tricky. It's hard to remember what your characters already know, what's going on in their lives at a given time, and especially all the little details that make them who they are. I like to give my students a questionnaire to help them keep track of all that (see handout). It's a combination of basic facts and things you'd ask at a party, plus much more intimate questions. Once it's filled out you'll have a pretty good idea of who your characters are, where they've been, and where they're going. What we do in class is share the characters, and then we have the characters interact, at which point students start to write dialogue. It's a nuts-and-bolts way to get up and running. I've found it useful for myself for continuity.

# CHARACTER DEVELOPMENT

What's the character's name?

_____

_____

How old is he or she?

_____

_____

Where does he or she live? Who else lives there?

_____

_____

Where is the character from originally? If he or she is from some other place, why did he or she leave?

_____

_____

What sort of family did he or she come from?

_____

_____

What is this person doing for a living?

_____

_____

What job would he or she prefer to be working at?

_____

_____

How much schooling has this person had?

_____

_____

How smart is this person?

_____

_____

Does he or she have any pets?

_____

_____

What is at stake for this person?

_____

_____

What does this person care about?

_____

_____

Whom is he or she in love with? (If this love is in the past, what happened?)

_____

_____

What has disappointed this person?

_____

_____

What is he or she proud of?

_____

_____

What is his or her biggest vice?

_____

_____

What is he or she insecure about? Why?

_____

_____

How do other people see this person?

_____

_____

Describe this person's physical appearance.

_____

_____

What does this person smell like?

_____

_____

What are the dominant moods of this person? Does he or she seem sad, cheerful, resigned, insane? Does this person's interior match his or her exterior?

_____

_____

What does this person dream about?

_____

_____

What is his or her earliest memory?

_____

_____

Does your character enjoy thinking about his or her life, or is he or she trying to forget? Is he or she nostalgic for anything?

_____

_____

Is this person waiting for something?

_____

_____

# LOOK SMART FAST

## COLLEGE APPLICATION ESSAY BOOT CAMP

*by* RISA NYE

1 SESSION, 3 HOURS

*RISA NYE HAS BEEN AN APPLICATION ESSAY reader for one of the nation's largest and most prestigious universities. Her insider tips have been invaluable to our students. In this lesson plan, she shares them with yours.*

Because the hardest part of writing a college essay is just getting started, I like to help students get some ideas on paper right away. Here are three techniques to jump-start the writing process and generate first drafts.

### Thinking Inside the Box

☛ Ask students to take a piece of paper and draw two lines down and one across, creating six boxes on the page. Like this, but bigger:

☛ Now ask them to label each space with some aspect of their lives: everyone can be a son or daughter, some will be a brother or a sister. From here, everyone can fill in the spaces with other things: computer geek, diva, tap dancer, class clown, or cat lover.

☛ When all six boxes have a name, the students are then asked to come up with five story ideas about being a banjo player, a big sister, a Trekkie, and so on, until they have a grand total of thirty possible essay topics.

☛ At this point, students may see how several of these ideas might be woven together into one essay. Ask for volunteers to copy one of their boxes onto the board. Students can then "pair share" their ideas and brainstorm the best combination of topics, asking some probing questions to bring out details. ("When did you take up the accordion?" "Why?")

☛ Students can now take 10–15 minutes and free-write an essay that answers the question "Tell us about yourself," using some of their favorite story ideas.

## The Keyhole Essay

Building on one of the story ideas from the box exercise, this kind of essay starts with something small, and then uses that small beginning to show the reader the larger picture . . . kind of like peeking through a keyhole and looking around a room.

☞ Students are asked to think of an object that is important to them, come up with a way to introduce it to the reader, and then use this object as a way of showing some of their qualities and characteristics. For example: "The velvet painting of Elvis is the closest thing to an heirloom my family has," or "I don't care what anyone thinks, I always wear the lucky dinosaur socks I got for my birthday when I take a test," or "I found the old bowling trophy in a thrift store, and I often wonder about the guy who won it." In each example (painting, socks, trophy), the object opens up many possibilities.

☞ By describing a treasure or personal ritual or things to wonder about, the writer lets the reader peek inside the keyhole too. Ask students to try this out with the first thing that comes to mind, and take 10 minutes to free-write about it. (Find good examples of this technique in a short story anthology. Students may like to hear a few before they start.)

## The List That Is More Than a List

An essay may ask for a list of things you would take to a desert island, or put into your own personal time capsule—or bring to college! Students have an opportunity to highlight what is important to them, while also letting the reader see how they define their character and personality. So if you start off with "I could never choose just one book to take," the reader gets a clue that you love to read. Likewise, if your essential items include a Giants hat or a package of marshmallow Peeps or some Star Wars action figures, that tells a story too. The more detail you provide, the more the reader learns about you. This can work very well for essays that ask you to come up with your own question and answer it! (For example: "If you were leaving Earth to live on another planet, what would you bring? And it has to fit in the overhead compartment of your space craft!")

☞ Ask students to come up with a question that could be answered with a list that is more than a list—that tells something important about them as a person—and then let them go for it! (It might be fun to read a few out loud and see if the kids can guess who wrote them.)

Students will now have buckets of great essay ideas . . . and the handout will help them avoid common college essay pitfalls.

# WRITING THE COLLEGE ESSAY: SOME POSITIVE POINTERS AND A FEW MAJOR NO-NO'S

The strength of your essay may set the tone for how the rest of your application is read, so make it sparkle!

- Choose a topic you are really passionate about, whether it's making paper airplanes or collecting buttons. You can make anything sound exciting if you believe it is.

- Read the question and instructions carefully first.

- Write in your own voice, using words you don't need to look up in the dictionary.

- Tell the story ONLY YOU can tell, by showing the reader details and observations from your unique perspective.

- Be thoughtful and reflective as you conclude your essay. If you have learned a lesson or gained an insight from the experience you have written about, the reader needs to understand how you got there.

Experienced admissions officers are familiar with the common pitfalls students inadvertently fall into when writing college essays. Most are avoidable, but if you don't know about them, you might tumble into the Cliché Crevasse or the Bottomless Pit of Banality.

Some topics just don't work on a college application. Some are simply inappropriate, while others are extremely popular topics that make admissions officers' eyes glaze over. For example:

1. Your relationship with your girlfriend or your boyfriend (or how it ended)
2. Your religious beliefs (unless the question asks you to write about them)
3. Your political views
4. Sex
5. How great you are
6. The importance of a college education
7. Placing the blame for your academic shortcomings (if any) on others
8. Big ideas that you have not given much thought to before
9. "The Best Game of My Life" or another athletic incident written in glib style
10. Your trip abroad, unless truly noteworthy

There are always exceptions, however, and some students can create enough context and detail that the reader comes away with a sense of knowing something important about the writer—which is the point of writing this kind of essay!

## YOU SHOULD AVOID CLICHÉS LIKE THE PLAGUE

Especially:

"My hard work really paid off."

"It (or he or she) made me who I am today."

Or starting your first sentence with alarm clock sounds ("Brrrrrrrrrrrring!!!").

## OVERUSED WORDS: "PLETHORA" AND "EPIPHANY"

(On a related note: any word that sounds plucked out of the thesaurus should be thrown back. Use vocabulary that is in your comfort zone.)

## MAJOR PITFALLS

1. Writing about the death of a distant relative you didn't know very well for the dramatic impact.

2. Writing about a relative you did know well, without saying anything about yourself.

3. Writing at a superficial level and not from the heart.

4. Letting anyone else add another "voice" to your writing. (This means parents, aunts, uncles, your college-age neighbor, or your seventh-grade English teacher.) Ask for and accept feedback, but always use your own words.

5. Choosing a deeply personal topic to write about (parents' divorce, coming out in high school, any kind of abuse) without getting feedback from a trusted adult. This is the hardest thing of all—knowing when a topic is just too personal and revealing, although it is of great importance to you.

6. Not answering the question or following directions (very important!).

7. Use of humor: Are you funny? That is, "funny ha-ha"? Always run this by someone who understands the difference between funny and not funny when it comes to college essays. College folks do appreciate creativity and wit, but they also have to read an awful lot of essays, so don't write backwards or in Pig Latin or use crazy fonts. If you have a natural sense of humor, though, let your writing reflect this—it's part of who you are!

8. Perhaps the biggest pitfall ever is blowing off the essay because you think, "No one really reads them." Not true! A good essay can make a big difference on an application that may not otherwise stand out in a field of highly qualified and competitive applicants.

And finally, your essay may be the only chance you get to let the person reading your whole college application hear "your voice." Ideally, the reader should feel that he or she knows you after reading your essay. For the best feedback, ask, "Does this sound like me?" Yes? Congratulations! You have written a successful essay!

# WRITING ABOUT PAINFUL THINGS

*by* PHOEBE GLOECKNER

I FLUNKED OUT OF SCHOOL FOUR TIMES. I'M NOT A GOOD STUDENT. EVERYTHING I do needs to be open-ended. If I have it all planned out, it becomes an assignment. So this lesson plan doesn't have a plan or an assignment beyond the simple direction to write about a painful experience. You won't turn it in, and you won't be graded. Do this at home, for yourself. Protect it, and share it when you're ready.

There are a lot of good reasons to write about the things that hurt you. I can only speak for myself, and the reason I do it is because if I didn't, I would be dead. That sounds like a cliché, but it's absolutely the truth. Writers write what they know, and this is what I know. People always ask if it's therapeutic. I don't think it is. I've gone to therapy, and that's a very different experience. Writing is hard. If you're going to tell kids writing is fun—it's fun sometimes, like when it's done, and you think, "Look what I did!" But while I'm doing it, it's torture. It hurts, and every line feels wrong.

Here's why it's worth it: writing is about love. It really is. It's about loving life, and wanting to preserve it, cling to it, understand it. You want to distill experience, and make it like the earth makes diamonds from coal: you want to compress it until it's this moment in life that people can understand. Not necessarily understand you—just understand something. When my work is done, it's not me. If it has any life at all, it's because of people who read it. Writing is all about love, and feeling happy to be alive, but being aware all the time of life's fragility and impermanence.

Your assignment: write, or draw, or write and draw one scene. It should be based on a painful experience you feel the need to explore, but it doesn't have to be factual or literal. You can change whatever you want.

Don't do it in a workshop. Don't do it at school, so you don't have to show it to anyone or be graded on it. Do it at home and hide it under your mattress. Don't post it online. It's weird to have immediate feedback. If I'd done my early work online I probably would have lost it all because I would have forgotten the password. You lose continuity—you have it in all these different places and in the end it's in no place. I recommend notebooks. It's good to write.

If you show your work to your friends, they'll compare it to pop culture and your work will become more derivative and your friends will want you to draw Sailor Moon or whatever. So at first, keep it secret. Don't post it online. Protect that little seed. Incubate your talent in the dark until you're ready to show it. You'll know when that is. Then, when you're ready to show other people, you'll already have a body of work. If you start when you're 14, by the time you're 16, you'll become a good judge of your work. And it will be your story entirely. No one will have said, "It didn't happen that way." You know how it happened. More than anything, writing about yourself makes you vulnerable. And when that kind of writing is strong, it makes you stronger.

Here are some things to keep in mind while you're working, to protect yourself when dredging up the hard stuff, and ultimately make the work better:

☞ **Get some distance.**

A lot of girls write to me that they want to tell their own story but they're afraid to say the truth. And I think: What do I tell them? Even if I look at my own early work, when you have a difficult personal story to tell, often you'll tell it through some kind of code. Because you can't tell the truth, because you are going to get in trouble, or risk something in your actual life. So you either act really tough, or you create some distance.

For *Diary of a Teenage Girl: An Account in Words and Pictures,* I had to separate from the protagonist, who was me, so I could love her. I had to make her a character. I have to reach a point of schizophrenic dissociation, where I become a character, and with that distance, I can write about it.

☞ **It's OK to change the story.**

Remember this: autobiography is not the truth. You're fictionalizing truth because it's the only way you can understand a story. Even when we're just telling a story to ourselves, we have to restructure it, rearrange the order, cut out the stuff that's not relevant. To make a story of your life in any way you have to alter and distort it because you're not after the literal truth, you're after some emotional truth, and if you just vomit it up on the page you're not going to get that.

There's so much craft involved. You have to be brutal, because when it's your own life, it's all precious to you. But some of it is extraneous. It's hard to know what to cut because it all feels equally important, but keeping it all would make the story too confusing. You're changing it to get the most three-dimensional story you can, by collapsing space and time and reshaping it. I have to build or rebuild a whole world. It's an alternate universe that's very real when you're creating it.

☞ **Even in painful stories, not everything is painful.**

Autobiography is often associated with things that are negative or sad, but that's not always true—some of it is funny.

☞ **It hurts less when you let yourself, and the other characters, be complex.**

It hurts you less if you don't see yourself as a victim, and if you can see the other characters as three-dimensional, it helps you understand them. It's calming—you see you haven't been attacked by a big monster. You have to understand all those points of view. It doesn't make the story happier, but it protects you in the sense that you can accept others making mistakes when you can see them as human, and it helps you accept yourself.

Autobiography has this flavor of the literature of victimhood, but I think for myself it's always important to think of yourself as a full human being, and a victim has no agency. We ALL have agency. It's always a mistake to oversimplify yourself, and when you're really young, that sometimes happens, because people tell you you've been a victim. That causes you to think of yourself in this one-dimensional way, and if you sit down to write about it, it becomes one-dimensional too. But really, there's this tangle of emotions, and you have to constantly remember and acknowledge every other feeling that you have. You may love the person who hurt you, and you may hate that person at the same time. To embrace those feelings doesn't mean you're bad, or that something bad didn't happen to you. It means you're a person.

# MUTANT SHAKESPEARE

BY KYLE BOOTEN

4 SESSIONS, 1 HOUR EACH

MATERIALS: *Handout that you have prepared of one scene from a Shakespeare play with random words omitted, Mad Lib–style (first exercise)*
*Magazines, scissors, and glue sticks (third exercise)*

WHEN A RADIOACTIVE SPIDER BITES YOU, YOU TURN INTO A SPIDER-MAN. When a radioactive Shakespeare bites you, you turn into a Mutant Shakespeare.

Shakespeare's poetry and plays can be intimidating, boring, and frustrating even to the most enthusiastic readers. His language is no doubt difficult to parse, but part of the difficulty comes from the way we often talk about literature as if it were a math problem; you either "get it" or you don't. The point of this class is to leap over this problem by erasing the boundary between reader and Shakespeare, replacing both with a mutant combination of the two.

The class consists of exercises that permit and encourage participants to splice themselves with Shakespeare. I've supplied four starting points here.

## 1. Text-Splicing

Romeo:
Draw, Benvolio; Beat down their weapons.
Gentlemen, for shame—if you stop, I will give you both ice cream.

We have split into two groups, each of which will perform the same scene from Romeo and Juliet—a friendly *Romeo and Juliet*—off. When we look at our scripts, however, words are missing—a few here, a few there, even some whole lines. One of us mentions hearing something on the news about a computer virus that targets printers, making them unable to print classic literature. We must be the latest victim. Our scripts look like Elizabethan Mad Libs, and we are filled with despair.

But someone else speaks up, suggesting that we try to complete the script as best we can. Okay, why not? We already have roles assigned, so each person focuses on filling the holes in her character's lines. Because these lines interweave in dialogue, we have to work together too. In the process, we realize that *Romeo and Juliet* never did have enough references to Pokémon. We perform the two versions and compare them.

## 2. Literary Telepathy

Asides are those moments in the script when a character briefly comments on the scene to the audience, revealing an inner thought or emotion. As Lady Capulet rants against Romeo for killing Tybalt and calls him a "villain," Juliet must go along with her mother, yet she shares her real thoughts with the audience:

> Villain and he be many miles asunder.
> God pardon him! I do, with all my heart;
> and yet no man like he doth grieve my heart.

As it turns out, new chemicals added to the water supply have given us all literary telepathy, the ability to read characters' minds. We divide into groups and pick characters. Then we supply new and frequent asides for our respective characters. We perform the scenes and compare our asides...

> Romeo: Farewell, farewell! One kiss, and I'll descend!
> Juliet: (aside) I've got to send a pigeon to my BFF about this!

## 3. My Boyfriend's Eyes Are Like Twin iPods

Shakespeare's Sonnet 130 ("My mistress's eyes are nothing like the sun") is a sarcastic take on the *blazon,* a poem that describes somebody (usually a beloved) by metaphorically comparing different parts of her face and body to other things. Eyes can be like stars, lips like roses, ears like ermines. It is a verbal portrait made of a collage of similes.

"Collage" is a magic word. Just to think it makes lots of arts and crafts supplies appear before us: old magazines and books, scissors, pencils, and glue sticks. We like Shakespeare's Sonnet 130, but we think we can do better. We each cut objects out of magazines—a chair, a tree, a flashlight, a smoothie, a sports car, a moldy sandwich—and assemble these objects into the face of somebody we admire but have difficulty describing. (It's best to draw the shape of a face first.) After that, we compose our own blazons based on our portraits.

## 4. Time Travel: Secret of a Sonnet

One of the chief reasons that Shakespeare's sonnets can be confusing is that they address a person or situation that remains a secret to the reader. Scholars divide the sonnets into those to a Fair Youth, a Dark Lady, and a Rival Poet—but whether or not these characters existed in real life remains a matter of debate.

Good thing we have the power to warp through space and time. Using this power, we go back in time to sixteenth-century England and hang out with Shakespeare for a day. We ask him about his friends, his enemies, his loves. We take notes on little things too: the weather, the color of the birds outside his house, the songs he hums, the taste of his food.

When we get back to our modern-day classroom, we write down the story behind the sonnet, explaining exactly what was going on in Shakespeare's life when he wrote it.

## Alternate Version

Exactly the same as the last exercise, except Shakespeare is the time traveler. He comes forward in time to hang out with us. We show him around our town, take him to the skate park or the mall, play him our favorite songs, and talk deeply with him about life. As he leaves, he gives us one of his sonnets, remarking that it was inspired by the time he spent with us. Winking weirdly, he suggests that the poem contains many references and details drawn from things we saw or did or talked about. Back in class, we write down the story of our time with Shakespeare, making note of all the things that inspired Shakespeare to write his poem.

# HOW TO WRITE A ONE-PERSON SHOW ABOUT A HISTORICAL FIGURE

*by* KRISTEN SCHAAL

4 SESSIONS, 1 HOUR EACH

THIS IS YOUR OPPORTUNITY TO LEARN EVERYTHING YOU CAN ABOUT YOUR favorite historical celebrity and embody him or her in a one-person show. Why do a show? Because everyone can write a paper about Ulysses S. Grant, but not everyone gets to be that burly drunken beast for half an hour! (At least for a grade.)

## Select Your Subject

Pick a person. This might be the hardest part! There are so many fascinating people in the world. I would try to narrow down your search to people who have had at least one or more biographies written about them. And anyone with an autobiography has just made your life easier. But a lot of the most intriguing people never wrote about themselves.

Try to go with a person that you feel passionate about—someone that you feel connected to, or inspired by. Politicians, writers, artists, entertainers, scientists, entrepreneurs, humanitarians: the list is vast. It's okay to choose someone notorious, but remember you have to soak up his or her essence. The majority of notorious people can be annoying.

They don't have to be dead either. Believe it or not, there are some interesting people with heartbeats that rival some of our dead heroes. Or at least make a good case for hanging out with them.

## Research

You should try to research everything you can about your subject. Read at least two biographies.

If your subject was involved in other media, then get your hands on those materials.

---

*Note:* Based on a class Kristen attended at Northwestern University taught by Dwight Conquergood.

## Write Your Show

Write a time line of that person's life in its entirety or up until now. What, in your opinion, are the key moments in that person's life that brought him or her to your attention? Pick three.

Now you have the three centerpieces of your show. Write an intro, as the person, explaining who you are and what you have done. Then describe the events that created the person's legend. In first person. Here is where you are allowed to be creative. You want to use the person's own words, especially if they are available. But if they are not, then you get to fill in. You have researched the person enough now that you should have a sense of what he or she was feeling, and what thoughts were going through his or her head when these things happened. Paint the picture for your audience. Try to bring them there as much as your historical figure would allow.

Whether it was leading the soldiers to battle, recording a top 10 hit, or holding his or her first child, these are the moments that you are going to describe to your audience as the person.

The person's life might even have a theme that he or she has unconsciously harbored. If you stumble on this, exploit it in your show, and use it in your closing remarks.

## Acting

Uh-oh! This is the scary part! Well, believe it or not, after doing a month of research on your figure, you are more prepared than some of the greatest thespians of your generation. Don't forget what drew you to that person. Was it his or her courage, or humor, or recklessness? These are the things that you can play up in your performance. If your character has an accent, give it a go. If your character has a limp, so do you! You are that person telling this story. And after the journey that you went on together, put your butterflies aside and give your character's story the integrity that it deserves, and that the audience deserves to hear.

Don't forget to put thought into the person's costume, including props to use onstage.

## The End

Everyone is clapping, and they learned so much! You tell me you'd rather write a paper?!

# WRITING FOR GAMERS

*by* TOM BISSELL

1 SESSION, 90 MINUTES

THERE ARE PLENTY OF STUDENTS WHO ARE MORE INTERESTED IN VIDEO games than in writing—and that's not necessarily a bad thing. Video games offer an entirely new way to provide and experience narrative. In traditional forms of writing a lot of the rules are already established—that party's over. But with games, there's still room to do things that few have thought to do before, which is what is most exciting about video game narrative.

What makes games so compelling is that sense they often provide of walking into a traditional storytelling environment—there are characters, setting, and all the trappings of a cinematic storytelling experience—but with an added, unfamiliar feeling that you have agency in this world. It's the feeling of traditional storytelling running alongside something much more novel. It's an unfamiliar sensation that, once you experience it in a game that really does it well, feels profound and often transformative.

Games, unlike novels or films, are thoroughly interactive. Games will probably never provide the kind of interiority that novels have, or the dramatic compression you see in films, where everything is important, everything is arranged, and everything adds up to something intended. What games can do is provide you with an experience that may be a little slower than movies, a little more external than books, but that is also founded upon personal discovery. This feeling of "discovery" gets its own pace, one dictated by the player and not the author. Drama is nothing but ruthlessly imposed pace, but in games, drama comes at you in different ways. In certain kinds of ambitiously open games, the narrative changes in response to the player.

The role of narrative in video games is mostly to give the player a space in which he or she can have an experience. It's not guided. The creators aren't dictating nearly as much as they would in other media, and they're not necessarily leading the player through a linear story. They're giving the player an array of things to be concerned about or interested in. Games are at their best when the designer finds a way to decorate a game space with really intriguing things, so that players can then have an experience that feels unique to them while also remaining consistent within the game's greater storytelling flow. It's not telling a story, not exactly—it's creating an environment that gives players a chance to create their own story.

In this lesson, students use the elements and narrative conventions of video games to create stories of their own.

## Exercise 1: Imagine the Opposite

Pick your favorite game and your favorite character, and imagine the character doing the exact opposite of what he or she usually does: instead of fighting, for instance, walking along a seashore. (And don't make the character think about fighting or kill everything he or she sees—that's not the point.) Write a scene about this character in an entirely new situation.

## Exercise 2: What's Behind the Door?

A lot of games, for technical reasons, have places that are blocked off, doors that are closed, paths that are obscured by obstacles, to create the illusion that there is more "space" in the game world than there actually is. In this exercise, explode a cliché of game design, and have students write a scenario in which they try to account for why these blockages exist. Is it for political reasons? Geographical ones? What might be behind these closed doors and blocked paths?

## Exercise 3: The Emergent Story

As homework, ask the students to play a game and analyze the differences between the story they're being told by the game and the story they create as a player going through the game (the "emergent" story, this is called). To encourage them to think beyond what they're playing and doing, you have to get them to think about fairly complicated stuff. So, for instance, with Halo, the story they're being told is that the Halo machine has been set up by the Covenant, and you're fighting to stop them. But what is *the player's individual* story? You're the guy with the gun running over the hills: what is happening to you? How does it feel? What can you see? Write that down.

# HUMOR WRITING

## AN EXERCISE IN ALCHEMY

*by* DAN KENNEDY

1 SESSION, 2 HOURS

*(FOR GRADES 9–12. AND FOR ESPECIALLY* bright or troubled eighth graders as well. Also for seventh-grade savants.)

There are a handful of misconceptions about humor writing, the first being that it must involve waiting around for a funny idea. The fact is, if you wait for a funny idea to come, you will most likely never get around to writing something funny. So picture that. You and your students, alone in a room, waiting for funny ideas to make themselves known and instead only being visited by the humorist's bedfellows Depression, Anxiety, and Restlessness—ha-ha, very funny, right? Here's something I wish I would've known when I was a young student: feelings of apathy, depression, and restlessness are often the best starting point for writing humor, especially satire. Once I understood that you didn't necessarily find yourself in a funny mood before writing something funny, I realized there is hope. And potential! We the quiet or bored, the seemingly uninterested, the long faces and short attention spans, the energized and dead tired—we could have a laugh and even change a few things sometimes in the process. There was only one teacher who recognized that kind of hope and potential where I went to school.

## Lesson Plan

On the chalkboard, a very subversive piece of media if there ever was one—in that anything you write on there can be made to disappear—write a list of three subjects and Thought Starterz™®. Actually if by now schools have replaced the chalkboard with lasers or holograms, please disregard my use of the word. I guess now that I've dated myself, I would like to say that Def Leppard's "Pyromania" rocks. Also: No Nukes. OK, so . . .

### SOME DISCUSSION TOPICS TO COVER

☞   Fake memo from authority figure (Principal? Boss?)

☞   Humorous version of school newsletter

☞   Acceptance speech

Then go over the following with the class, hand out the handouts, and watch the comedy magic happen.

## Fake Memo

The fake memo from an authority figure can be about anything. You've seen some of the memos issued in the so-called modern world. A world of semi-effective managers drunk on the combination of the illusory power of title and middling jurisdiction...they're a treasure trove of possible satire! My favorites to write are fake memos from chain restaurant managers that I used to work for in my twenties, fake vanity e-mails from competitive, self-absorbed peers, fake dispatches from mayors or councilmen, and the like. You might type up a "MEMO FROM THE DESK OF_____" starter sheet with an opening line for students to follow up, or use the "Memo" handout here. I like to open with painfully honest corporate sentiments, such as "While I love Mr. Myers's comedic endeavors, as the manager of McCormley's Seafood Shanty I need to issue the reminder that I do NOT see humor in employees referring to me as Dr. Evil. During yesterday's lunch shift... (students pick up here in the lined writing space you provide).

## Humorous Version of School Newsletter

I think in a perfect world, this assignment could maybe even lead to a student's first writing job: making the school announcements more fun to read or listen to. Maybe they could staff the whole thing like another yearbook gig. To get started, take the latest edition of the school newsletter or student body newsletter and copy it into a new Word document. Keep the original set-up portion of each item and leave space for students to finish the remainder in their own words. Here, I'll do an item from one of my old high school's newsletters:

> Attention athletes: All spring sport pictures are in the Student Store now. Please pick them up before we box them up and remember that you only need to do this if you're an Athlete/Jock. There are no pictures of loners at the Student Store, only athletes, so freshman and sophomore misfit types can continue

hanging out on the stairs and nurturing the denial that is keeping us alive and sane here at PHS. Let's not fight instinct when it attempts to preserve us, you guys. But anyway, athletes: you should pick your pictures up.

## The Acceptance Speech

This is wide-open territory. Any award a student can dream of. Oscar, Grammy, Best Human in the County, State, and Possibly Universe—you name it. All of the fun (and I might add, bolstering of self-esteem) lies in students being assigned to dream of bigger things and then deciding whom they would thank or NOT thank for helping them accomplish these feats, whom they would admit to their kingdom of success and happiness . . . and whom they would remind to please stop calling! You can start the speech off with a few of the stock lines from celebrity thank-you speeches we've all had to endure while figuring how much money we've made off of coworkers or loved ones in the wager pool. If you like, you can get them started with the "Acceptance Speech" handout.

> This is great . . . thank you. Wow, I really . . . wow . . . God, OK . . . I would like to thank my family— except my brother Gary—for believing in me and giving me their love and support. I would also like to remind Mr. Folley from second period Algebra to please stop calling my assistant trying to act like you and I are friends in hopes of being invited to certain events. That is simply not going to happen, Mr. Foley. It is weird that you call like this. And sad that you insist on attempting to contact me daily in hopes of finding yourself admitted to parties or festivities taking place at my summer home. Thank you everyone, except Gary. Thank you.

Good luck and lots of laughs. I'm sure there's always one kid who's going to fill in the blanks with stuff like *Metallica rulez and this assignment sucks it!* But, you know, applaud even that kid. I mean, if you're anything like me something like that would make you laugh, and at least that student is saying something he or she honestly feels with some degree of conviction, which is more than you can say for a lot of the so-called adults on the planet. Anyway, I don't need to tell you that these kids are our only hope. Now more than ever, if it's up to the adults, we're up a creek.

# A MEMO FROM THE DESK OF

A MEMO FROM THE DESK OF

# ACCEPTANCE SPEECH

I promised myself I wouldn't cry . . .

_____

_____

_____

_____

_____

_____

_____

_____

_____

_____

_____

_____

_____

# ON PINING

## WRITE A VERSE TO MAKE THEM STAY

*by* THAO NGUYEN

1 SESSION, 20–30 MINUTES
MATERIALS: *A live flamenco guitar player or recorded dramatic romantic music*

MY MAIN OBJECTIVE WHEN WORKING WITH TEENAGERS IS TO GET THEM to loosen up. This was originally a creative songwriting lesson designed as a warm-up, to encourage students to emote and be silly and abandon some of their finely honed reservations . . . to encourage self-expression, and have them express themselves outside their own experience.

Another objective of this exercise is to write succinctly and evocatively—enough to hypothetically win a heart.

Everyone talks and cries about love some time. And even if the student has not personally dealt in love, imagining oneself in the throes should be feasible enough. In this exercise, they do exactly that.

1. Set a scene. Please be overly dramatic—set a tone for freewheeling silliness and passionate expression: The love of your life is about to sail away. You have messed up! BIG TIME! You have four lines to make him or her stay.

2. Explain that the lines have to be good enough to convince the person you have wronged to stay and give you a second chance. The lines should also sound good being delivered. "But I like you" might not read as well given the high drama and tension of the moment. Basic rules: no clichés, no poems that start with "Roses are red, violets are blue."

3. Give the students ten minutes to compose their verses. Rhyming is optional.

4. Ask a student volunteer to stand on a chair or desk or any kind of raised platform. Tell the student that he or she is at the edge of the ship's deck. Provide a handkerchief to wave. Ask the student to try tearing up, or at the very least to look sad and disappointed.

5. Cue music.

6. Ask for another student to step forward and deliver his or her lines. Encourage passion and emotion. Maybe have the student take a knee. Turn up dramatic romantic music so he or she has to plead and woo over it. We have had great success with students clutching their verses to their hearts and fake sobbing.

7. If the student on the ship is not compelled to stay, please invite the next volunteer to pine and profess.

# ADDING INSULT TO POETRY

*by* NICHOLAS DECOULOS

1 SESSION, 1½–2 HOURS

ANYONE CAN SAY, "SAME TO YOU, BUDDY!" In this workshop, you'll learn why it's not wise to cross a poet; they will write clever and unflattering poems about you that may become famous! Learn to use the blazon form to make sure your next comeback has a certain sophisticated burn.

This workshop is meant to teach high school students about understanding humor and its boundaries, as well as forms of poetry that can be written to express humor.

The workshop begins with a short icebreaker of perhaps some funny personal story that happened to a student. (Best to start with one of your own.) It can also be a joke the student might know. (*Note:* Unfortunately, because they are high school students, it may be hard to censor the story or joke that the student might tell, but this can be an opportunity, as the lesson is designed to help understand the boundaries of humor, what is funny, what is just mean, and the problem of going too far. More on that later.) This becomes a jumping-off point to then discuss . . .

What makes a story funny? Many students might answer: "A punch line." But then we have to pull specifics. A lot of times a joke is funny because it's either hyperbolic or simply unexpected. And even if it seems inane, a great example of this is "Why did the chicken cross the road?" Even though we may not laugh now because we know the joke, it was once funny because it was just simply unexpected to the person who first heard it.

Next, the teacher selects a poem that contains humor, something easy to decipher—preferably with puns. Read the poem aloud with the class and you may hear laughs. Once the poem is finished, ask those students who laughed why they did. Have the students really try to understand where that laughter stems from.

Then have the class read a more difficult, but still humorous poem. The best example is Shakespeare's Sonnet 130. This poem is riddled with the unexpected and hyperbolic. This one could be more challenging, so you may want to read it twice. Afterward, ask those students who laughed why they did. If they didn't, ask why they didn't. See if they can find what should have been funny or why this might have been humorous at one time.

After finding the "funny" in two separate poems, ask the students how the two poems compare. Often, the poems are about a person. You can share that Sonnet 130 is known as a blazon. This style of poetry doesn't always have to be humorous but sometimes is, listing, for instance, the physical attributes of someone. Next, ask the students to write a joke or a short poem in the styles they've talked about or seen in the class. To prevent hurt feelings, you can tell the students they should write about someone they don't know personally, like a celebrity. Then have the students share what they've written.

Students will get the hang of it as they hear each other's jokes or short poems.

The next step is to have students expand their jokes or short poems into longer ones—perhaps like the blazons they've read today. Some students may find it easier to write multiple short poems. In this case, suggest other styles of poems, like the haiku. This can challenge some students to make a joke in only three rather short lines.

Throughout this workshop you may find students playing with boundaries a bit. Ask students to use discretion toward the person they are writing about—and if they must, to change a name and to never directly hurt anyone's feelings. Once students understand that humor doesn't have to derive from making fun of anyone and can come from hyperbole and the unexpected, it will be easier for them to recognize wittier humor and make it more accessible in their creative writing.

Ultimately, this workshop should help students understand different styles of poetry better and also understand how to develop humor or jokes in a way that perhaps doesn't offend or cross lines that aren't worth crossing. This workshop can prove to be an important tool for knowledge of poetry, social skill development, and experience in creative writing.

# BAD WRITING

## BY NEAL POLLACK

WHEN IT COMES TO *READING* ASSIGNMENTS, you should expose students to only the best literature. "Best" is subjective, of course, but if you're trying to get your students to understand *literature,* you're probably going to have them read Shakespeare and Hemingway and Willa Cather, not Andrew Lloyd Webber librettos, pulp Westerns from the 1950s, or romance novels featuring characters from popular *telenovelas.*

There's nothing easy about teaching literature to high school students, but writing is even harder to teach. You can't give a student a copy of *The Great Gatsby* and say, "Go home and write something like that." Your best student could read *Crime and Punishment* six times in one weekend and still not come up with anything that remotely resembled Dostoevsky. And she would also come back to school frustrated, saying that there's no way she could ever write that well.

On the other hand, if you sent your students home with *Clan of the Cave Bear,* or a bodice-ripper about ancient Egypt, or even, if you're oriented that way, one of the *Left Behind* books, and said, "Write like this," the student might actually produce something that vaguely approximates literature. It will be bad literature, but literature nonetheless. Clichéd, melodramatic stories with clunky prose, far from being literary

anathema, are actually the building blocks of all literature, and they provide an excellent writer's education.

I first was inspired to write by John Jakes's *The Kent Family Chronicles,* a turgid eight-part series of historical novels that features lines like "Amanda, meet Abraham Lincoln." From there, I graduated to the vast plains of James Michener, and *The Thorn Birds,* and *The Winds of War.* My early inspirations weren't comic books or sitcoms or *Star Wars.* They were bad books, the kinds of books that I could see myself, with a little experience, producing. I wish someone had challenged me to create something like that.

## Lesson Plan

So here's how the class should go. The entire plan can take a long time, spaced out over weeks, or could be condensed into several longer sessions.

☞ You assign a photocopied reading of four or five of the purplest pages imaginable from a literary howler (preferably epic in scope), of your choice. Along with that, you assign four or five standard "analysis" questions, of the same type you'd give on a *Hamlet* quiz. Play it totally straight: "When Ayla says

Jondalar's rippling muscles give her a 'special feeling that she'd never felt before,' to what is she referring? What is Jean M. Auel's purpose in creating this scene?"

☞ You will then discuss this passage from the book of your choice at the next class, for, say, 10–15 minutes before showing your hand and telling the class that this is a lesson in Bad Writing. Explain to them that bad writing contains nothing like the universal truths and subtle beauties you've been discussing all year. It's all clichés and warmed-over historical research written in melodramatic prose with no subtlety.

☞ Then ask them to turn on a dime and discuss the clichés and warmed-over historical research. Have them figure out, for themselves, the essential elements of bad writing. In some ways, Tolstoy's maxim applies here: "All good writing is alike. Every piece of bad writing is bad in its own way." So there are no universal qualities to a bad piece of writing. Just try to decide what those are in the passage you've chosen.

☞ Next, drop another bomb. Tell them that by the end of the lesson, you want to see a piece of bad writing from all of them. Length is up to you.

☞ Have a list of twenty or so "bad" novels available in the classroom. Tell them to read bits from as many of them as possible. Have discussion groups to share clichés and historical howlers. Immerse the students as fully as possible in the language and rhythm of bad fiction of any genre.

☞ After that, tell them to choose a "quality" piece of literature that they've studied, either with you or with another teacher or on their own, and ask them to redo it as "bad writing." Make sure to recap the list of clichés and general characteristics of bad literature, both in terms of style and content.

☞ Tell them to have fun with it. There's no pressure. After all, the worse the writing, the better they'll do on the assignment. By the time it's over, they should have a pretty solid idea of what separates bad writing from good.

See the handout for a few short examples of good writing transmuted into bad writing. You can have the students use it as a starting point. Good luck!

# GOOD LITERATURE GONE BAD

*CRIME AND PUNISHMENT,* **BY FYODOR DOSTOEVSKY**

Raskolnikov loved Russia. He loved the way it smelled in the morning after a heavy rain, and the way everything went quiet after a heavy snow, and he loved its women more than anything. "There's no doubt in my mind," he said to himself that fateful morning, as he ate a bowl of thin gruel that his landlady had reluctantly prepared for him, "that Russian women are the finest in the world. This fire in my loins will never be extinguished."

*THE SUN ALSO RISES,* **BY ERNEST HEMINGWAY**

Jake Barnes knew he could never be the man the bullfighter was. He had no chance with Lady Brett. His war impotence hung heavy on his soul that fateful morning as he downed his third *café con leche.* How he longed for freedom, freedom of his soul from its terrible bondage of memory!

*DEATH COMES FOR THE ARCHBISHOP,* **BY WILLA CATHER**

The Archbishop was going to die. He could feel it in his bones. But when, he thought to himself that fateful morning as he finished off his bowl of *posole,* which is a kind of Mexican stew. When will death come for me?

*DON QUIXOTE,* **BY MIGUEL DE CERVANTES**

Don Quixote was not his real name, but regardless, he loved tilting at windmills. Sancho Panza felt powerless to stop him. "What can I do?" Sancho thought to himself that fateful morning, as he fed breakfast to the donkey that doubled as the Quixote's magnificent steed. "The man has quite an active imagination, after all, and I am just a simple peasant."

Just then, The Quixote came running out of the house.

"Sancho!" he said. "To arms! Hurry!"

"What is it, sire?" Sancho said.

"Dulcinea's in trouble! We must save her!"

*MACBETH,* **BY WILLIAM SHAKESPEARE**

"What's troubling you, honey?" asked Lady Macbeth of her brooding husband on that fateful morning. But Macbeth didn't answer. For he'd just killed his best friend. Nothing could help him now. Those witches had lied to him!

# WHERE STORIES COME FROM

*by* JULIE ORRINGER

1 SESSION, 90 MINUTES
MATERIALS: *Photographs,*
*newspaper clippings, poems*

MOST STUDENTS ARE ACCUSTOMED TO having clear-cut assignments; the freedom of short story writing may be overwhelming at first. This lesson can help students get words onto the page.

First, show students where other writers get their ideas. One of the best sources I've found for this is the back section of *The Best American Short Stories (BASS)* series, where writers are asked to contribute a paragraph or so describing the origins of their selected stories. I like to copy some of these brief explanations and have students read three or four of them. Here are some stories that took their inspiration from photos, magazine clippings, newspaper headlines, poems, and other forms of writing:

☞ Elizabeth Graver, "The Body Shop," *BASS* 1991

☞ Alice Fulton, "Queen Wintergreen," *BASS* 1993

☞ Robert Olen Butler, "Jealous Husband Returns in Form of Parrot," *BASS* 1996

☞ Chris Adrian, "Every Night for a Thousand Years," *BASS* 1998 (picture, letter)

☞ Heidi Julavits, "Marry the One Who Gets There First," *BASS* 1999 (photo essay)

☞ Kathleen Hill, "The Anointed," *BASS* 2000 (childhood memorabilia)

☞ Stuart Dybek, "We Didn't," *BASS* 1994 (a poem)

☞ Rick Moody, "Boys," *BASS* 2001 (a sentence)

☞ Jim Shepard, "Love and Hydrogen," *BASS* 2002 (a children's book)

To help students start their own stories, assemble three collections of materials:

1. *Photographs:* Snapshots or magazine cutouts work well. The photos can include human beings, but they don't have to. Photos of interesting settings work well too. Very old photographs are great, if you have them.

2. *Newspaper clippings:* General news can work; wedding announcements, obituaries, and science news are all good sources.

3. *Poems:* I like to use excerpts from John Berryman's *Dream Songs,* Pablo Neruda's *Residence on Earth,* Rainer Maria Rilke's persona poems, and Gabrielle Calvocoressi's *The Last Time I Saw Amelia Earhart,* for example.

Bring the materials to class. Pass them around after the *Best American Short Stories* discussion and let students take a few minutes to choose a few pieces they find particularly compelling. After they take some time to examine the items they've chosen, have them free-write about one item for 10–12 minutes. Then they'll move on to another item and free-write about that.

Before they begin writing, give them some pointers:

☞ If you're writing from a photo of a person, write from the point of view of one of the people depicted. Try to imagine a situation around that person and his place within it. What is he worried about? What does he care about? What's immediately at issue at that particular moment? Try to imagine the person's life outside this photo. What concerns are driving him? If you're writing from a photo that doesn't depict a person, or in which the person is less interesting to you than the setting, what is it about this place that's particularly compelling? What might you imagine happening there? What objects can you see, and what activities do they suggest?

☞ If you're writing from a newspaper article, don't bother taking the time to read the entire article; instead, look for a line or an image or a detail that captures your attention. Then try to imagine the human situation behind this article. Who is involved? What are the main players like? Choose one of these people, and free-write from that person's point of view. How did he or she get into this particular situation? What's at stake here?

☞ If you're writing from a poem, take a few minutes to read the poem completely and hold it in your mind. What images does it evoke? What kinds of characters does it suggest? What mood does the poem create? As soon as possible, put pen to paper and begin free-writing.

From their free-writing, students should begin to see stories emerging. Ask them to take the idea they find most compelling and develop it into a full-length piece.

# WORD KARAOKE

*by* MATTHUE ROTH

1 SESSION, 2 HOURS

SOMETIMES, YOU WANT TO SAY SOMETHING AND YOU'RE NOT SURE EXACTLY how. Sometimes, there's a song or a poem that you think is better than anything you could ever write—or, maybe, there's a song or a poem that you could do better.

That's the jumping-off point for Word Karaoke, a way of getting students inspired when they say they're not. Karaoke is the ancient Japanese art of singing along with prerecorded background music. Singing along with the radio is karaoke. Singing in the shower can be karaoke. When hip-hop MCs rap over a beat—well, don't tell them, but that's karaoke too.

We start by asking the students, "What's your favorite line from a song?" Get some suggestions. Write them on the board. Offer some of your own. Encourage more generalized, ambiguous responses; "Oops! I did it again" works much better than "My name is Shaa-dy"—although, for the purpose of this exercise, any suggestion is useful.

Writing, and especially music writing, is about using the listener's expectation and then turning it on its head. Using samples is a way to do this. When Eminem sings, "Stop—pajama time," he's borrowing from the briefly popular eighties rapper M. C. Hammer when *he* sang, "Stop—Hammer time." Sometimes, too, songs can use samples to express an idea. When dealing with the death of a friend, P. Diddy chose to use the feeling of the old song "I'll Be Watching You." He changed one word in the chorus, and ended up with a moving tribute called "I'll Be Missing You."

Once we've got their brains grinding (they will probably start out slowly, then, as they realize what's going on, produce a maelstrom of suggestions), call for a halt—a *temporary* halt—and separate the class into pairs. Make sure each student has a pencil and paper. Then, ask every pair to write a short poem or song (one side of a page is plenty) using one of the lines on the board, or their own idea. (The handout provides a format.) Suggest that they use their original line in another context—"Oops, I spilled the paint again," or "My name is mud." Get them to understand the idea behind karaoke: that, given a line of a song, they can create or change the meaning to whatever they want. They can start their verse with the "sample," or alternate that line with their own lines, going back and forth like a call-and-response.

Afterward, as time allows, students can perform their verses together. Encourage creative methods of presentation—one person can recite the sample line, and the other can recite the rest of the verse, or one can recite while the other performs an interpretive dance (be careful when offering this option to certain classes).

As an additional exercise, or for homework, students can write a new piece, either using the same verse from class with a different idea, or coming up with their own, new piece. For a real twist, get students to listen to one of their parents' songs and rewrite it from their own viewpoint!

# BECOME A HIP-HOP LYRICAL GENIUS

Song lyrics can come from anywhere—from things we say, from things our friends say, or even from having a deadline to hand in an assignment. For this exercise, we're going to take one line from an existing song and turn it into an all-new song—well, an *almost* all-new song.

Here is my sample line:

_____

_____

_____

_____

_____

_____

from the song _____ by _____
(don't forget to give props to the masters!)

Now, use that line in a poem or song of your own. It can be the title, the line that starts your song, the line that closes it, or a chorus that the poem or song keeps coming back to. Use the back of the page if you need more space. Most importantly, try to add your own ideas to the sample—if people wanted to hear the original song, they could always just run to a record store and buy the album! Make them buy YOURS instead!

_____

_____

_____

_____

_____

# TALL TALES AND SHORT STORIES

*by* STEVE ALMOND

1 SESSION, 90 MINUTES
MATERIALS: *Index cards, lollipops*

THERE ARE TWO COMPETING IMPULSES WHEN YOU'RE WRITING. ONE IS THE feeling that everything you do is awful, and when that takes over, you get writer's block. The other is the unchecked belief that everything you do is great. This exercise tries to shoot the gap between the two, by bringing things back down to earth and lowering the stakes. When you tell students to write fiction it's kind of crushing—it seems such a grandiose mandate. This exercise turns that mandate into play. You're just trying to fool some people, not write the Great American Short Story.

Start by passing out three-by-five-inch cards. Instruct the students to write down three strange and unusual facts about themselves. Two must be lies. One must be true.

"I once fell down a waterfall."

"I sat on Jerry Garcia's lap."

"I've seen Kevin Costner in his underwear."

One by one, the students read their three strange facts aloud and then face an interrogation session. The class gets five minutes to ask questions, trying to figure out which of the statements is true. "How big was the waterfall? Did you get hurt?" "Where did you meet Jerry Garcia? What did he smell like?" "Boxers or tighty-whities?" Meanwhile, the student in the hot seat lies as best he can (like a good politician) trying to keep the class from figuring it out.

Some tips for beginning liars: you shouldn't make everything up. Pull some details from real life, from something that happened to your cousin, or that you read about in the paper. Believe it or not, this is how stories usually get started. I hear some strange true story, and I start thinking, "And then what? And then what?"—trying to come up with background, imagining the scene.

To make the exercise more interesting you can keep score, having students vote for the statement they think is true, and rewarding the student who fools the most people. I usually provide suckers for the winner. (Get it?)

After a little while the students start to notice things. They see what makes a story believable and what rings false. A short story is just an elaborate improvised lie, and the way you establish its veracity is by including lots of compelling details. You have to sound very sure of them, and you have to be loose enough to just riff. This game jump-starts your "lying faculties."

Once we're warmed up we get down to work. For the second part of the exercise, students turn one of their statements into a short story. It can be true or false as long as it's interesting. Ideally, the interrogation allowed them to figure out which of their statements was most compelling. What story was the easiest to elaborate on? Which one got the biggest reaction? What made them jump out of their seats? Write about that.

# WELCOME TO THE FUNHOUSE
## WRITING FUNNY SCENES
*by* MARK O'DONNELL

*12 SESSIONS, 1 HOUR EACH*

THIS CLASS PROVES THAT ANYONE CAN learn to write funny scenes. Each week, we practice writing a different comedy scenario. Try these out with your students, and in no time at all your class will be a regular Friars' Club. Thank you! I'll be here all week!

We get in the mood with some funny viewing and reading. We start with video clips of Daffy Duck, W. C. Fields, John Leguizamo, *The Kids in the Hall, Strangers with Candy, The Upright Citizens' Brigade, Monty Python and the Holy Grail,* and *Raising Arizona.*

We follow up by reading aloud from Chekhov's "The Evils of Tobacco," Robert Frost's "Grass," Philip Larkin's "This Be the Verse," W. H. Auden's "As Poets Have Mournfully Sung," Frank O'Hara's "Lana Turner Has Collapsed," Bob and Ray, Bruce McCall, and Steve Martin, and, if they're willing, the submissions of several brave and instantly popular students themselves.

Once we're warmed up we get to work writing the following scenarios.

## Scenario #1: The Great Made Small, the Small Made Great

You're pretty much guaranteed laughs when you make a mountain out of a molehill or vice versa. Reduce an epic! Conversely, make a big anguished deal over a triviality. Make a fairy tale repulsive. Parody anything pretentious. Imagine the royal family getting drunk; Lilliput having a military parade, or a wart in Brobdingnag; the Plumber of the Year Award ceremony; The Royal Order of Raccoons; *Star Trek's* U.S.S. Enterprise as a revolving seafood restaurant on *SNL;* a Kid in the Hall anguishing over his missing ballpoint pen; South Park's mayor, teachers, and Jesus; Zeus's furtive affairs; Monsterpiece Theater; chimpanzees reenacting *Titanic;* people fighting over a turnip.

**Suggested reading:** Anything from the *Onion;* James Thurber's "Fables for Our Times"; Charles Portis's *Masters of Atlantis;* P. J. O'Rourke's *Give War a Chance* and *Holidays in Hell;* Candide; *Don Quixote.*

**Assignment:** Write the script for a news report that either makes a huge deal out of a little event ("Area Man Can't Decide Between Vanilla and Chocolate") or deflates a huge story ("End of World Announced. Details to Follow 11:00 Rerun of *Friends*").

## Scenario #2: A Tale Told by an Idiot

Here, the speaker is unaware of his own awfulness or stupidity. Maybe he's a boor. Maybe she's a terrible snob. Either way, his or her complete lack of self-awareness makes for some great material. Think of Ring Lardner's senile teller of "The Golden Honeymoon" and dizzy teen of "I Can't Breathe"; Charles Portis's stoic cowboy *Norwood*; Eudora Welty's "Why I Live at the P.O."; Twain's naive narrator of *Huckleberry Finn*.

**Suggested viewing:** *Gentlemen Prefer Blondes, The Search for Intelligent Life in the Universe.*

**Assignment:** Write a scene in which a completely clueless person holds a position of power.

## Scenario #3: The Wrong Person for the Job

Competence is not funny. Instead, get a load of: Inspector Clouseau; Tom Sawyer; a skunk who thinks he's a great lover; well-bred gophers; a clumsy dentist; a mad psychiatrist; Monty Python's harmless Inquisitors ("The comfy chair!"). Think antiheroics and silly villains: Austin Powers; Dudley Do-Right; Don Quixote; the moronic messengers in *Dumb & Dumber*; Gilbert and Sullivan's *The Pirates of Penzance*, who are, in fact, nice.

**Suggested viewing:** *Take the Money and Run, The Pink Panther.*

**Assignment:** Write a scene about someone who takes on a job he or she is completely unqualified for—an irresponsible guidance counselor, a skittish bomb squad expert, and so forth.

## Scenario #4: Overlooking the Obvious

"Er—I don't see any elephant!" Ignoring the unignorable is usually pretty entertaining. Think Ingrid Bergman in *Gaslight*—he's clearly trying to kill her, but she doesn't notice. The new ambassador is a gorilla; Godzilla's in the bedroom; the cat is in the goldfish bowl. Also funny: complete denial (ironing during the apocalypse, chatting as the Titanic sinks); and selfishness without self-awareness (saving the Pekinese but not the children).

**Assignment:** Write a scene in which somebody is missing something HUGE that's completely obvious to the reader.

## Scenario #5: The Monkey in the Palace of Heaven

As per the Chinese folk tale, order leads to disaster. In Native American myth, Coyote messes up the gods' orderly rows of stars to create our splashy Milky Way. Things fall apart; chaos runs roughshod over stuffed shirts. Think of Eddie Murphy at an Embassy Ball, the Three Stooges in the courtroom, Bugs Bunny doing Wagner's Ring Cycle, Jim Carrey in *Dumb & Dumber*, the Blues Brothers destroying an entire mall, *A Connecticut Yankee in King Arthur's Court*, a dog on the table, a dull orchestra learning to swing it.

**Suggested viewing:** *Dumb & Dumber, Animal House, A Night at the Opera.*

**Assignment:** Set up an important scene (wedding, formal poetry reading, surgery, and so on) and then have everything descend into chaos.

## Scenario #6: Defending the Preposterous

Sticking to your guns can be very amusing when your guns are completely and obviously wrong. Best is deadpan nonsense: You say that *Bikini Beach Bingo* is the best movie ever made? Satan is a sweetheart? Lassie was a human in a suit? Your neighbor is sending solar-derived brainwaves to drive you mad so he can steal your spoons? Shooting fish in a barrel is actually very difficult? People over age ninety go through a "rebel" phase? Barney is a menace to children? There are aliens in your soup? Tell us more!

**Suggested reading:** Robert Benchley's "Treasurer's Report," Jorge Luis Borges's *Ficciones.*

**Assignment:** Write a scene in which a character defends a ridiculous idea (such as "all dogs and cats are secretly married") with careful logic.

## Scenario #7: Slang and Language

This is the poetry of comedy. It can be highbrow (Bertie Wooster's "That's exerting the old cerebellum, Jeeves!") or low-brow (Bill and Ted's "righteous and bodacious" surfer-ese, *Wayne's World*'s "babe-osity"). Think of beatnik slang, teen talk, hip-hop argot, workplace lingo ("Adam and Eve on a raft, wreck 'em!")

**Assignment:** Write a scene in which all the dialogue is slang. It can be real, or you can make it up.

## Scenario #8: Confusion, Delusion, and Mistaken Identity

We know something they don't know. The duchess is mistaken for a maid, the bum for a billionaire, the gay man for the straight, Jack Lemmon and Tony Curtis in *Some Like It Hot.* Think of *The Comedy of Errors, Twelfth Night, Much Ado About Nothing,* and just about every episode of *Three's Company.* The possibilities are endless. A vain man thinks an indifferent woman loves him. The spies are after the wrong guy. Someone isn't as smooth as he thinks he is.

**Suggested viewing:** *The Gods Must Be Crazy.*

**Assignment:** Write a scene in which trouble follows when someone either misunderstands or refuses to believe what the situation really is (for example, "I'd be scared of this burning building if it weren't a hologram!").

## Scenario #9: Things Happen Too Fast

A relationship begins, grows, and ends in the space of an elevator ride; human history happens at a lightning pace. Think of the Marx Brothers, the Keystone Kops, any farce. The action fast-forwards or jump-cuts. Allegiances change in a second if money, love, or violence enter into negotiations.

**Suggested reading:** Martin Amis's *Time's Arrow.*

**Assignment:** Show a romance begin, grow, and fail in one minute, or show us fifty years of a family epic in two minutes.

## Scenario #10: Ridiculous Ambition

Show tiny people with godlike projects. Greed and competition escalate among idiots or even geniuses. Think of Pinky and the Brain; *Dexter's Laboratory;* SpongeBob's Plankton nemesis; Yertle the Turtle; the highfalutin' poseur brothers Niles and Frasier on *Frasier*; any game show; all money-grubbing inheritance farces. This is the small made great, the great made small again.

**Suggested viewing:** *The Adventures of Baron Munchausen; Time Bandits; It's a Mad, Mad, Mad, Mad World;* Blake Edwards's *The Great Race.*

**Assignment:** Write a scene about a fool with a cosmic plan.

## Scenario #11: Exaggeration/ Grotesque

This is cartoonish comedy: caricatures, gross-outs, tall tales, bad luck surpassing belief. Think of Homer Simpson's thick-headedness, or Itchy and Scratchy's horrific overkill; Monty Python; *Sunset Boulevard* and *Whatever Happened to Baby Jane.* Write hyperbolically. Characters aren't just dumb, but the dumbest people in the world; not simply poor, but so hard-up they live in a puddle, carve a pea into fifths, or eat pictures of food. Imagine the wildly fidgety man at an auction; the glutton who literally explodes in *Monty Python's The Meaning of Life;* a really, really dense cowpoke in the city; an impossibly prudish aunt.

**Suggested viewing:** *Strangers with Candy.*

**Assignment:** Write a scene about the dirtiest, or the cleanest, or the weirdest, or the richest, or the unluckiest, or the sweetest people on earth.

## Scenario #12: Try a Little Tenderness

Comedy can also be delivered with tenderness and strong, true emotion. Think Woody Allen's *Annie Hall, Radio Days,* and *Manhattan;* such comedies as *Diner, When Harry Met Sally, Raising Arizona, My Life as a Dog, The Rules of the Game, The Truth About Cats and Dogs;* Shakespeare's *Much Ado about Nothing, Twelfth Night, As You Like It;* and all of Chekhov.

**Suggested reading:** Frank O'Hara's *Lunch Poems.*

**Assignment:** Write a tender and loving reminiscence about something dumb you did when you were younger, but survived.

# LOOK, KIDS! FREE BONUS SUGGESTIONS

**PARODY**

The best way to start. Write a parody of your favorite TV show, movie, novel, or play. The fastest shortcut to originality is imitation.

_____

_____

_____

_____

**KWIK 'N' E-Z**

Write a commercial, a game show, or a foolish trailer for a nonexistent movie.

_____

_____

_____

_____

**QUIRKS AND ANNOYING HABITS**

Write a scene about the worst guest; the nut on the subway; the compulsive liar; the giggling spinster.

_____

_____

_____

_____

**OLD HABITS DIE HARD**

Nature will out; beasts will be beasts. Write a scene about the impatient man (Yosemite Sam, say) trying to hold his temper; the lady on the Titanic lifeboat wondering when the Funny Hats contest will resume; the gentleman being dainty while the cannibals cook him.

_____

_____

_____

**AN IDIOT CON MAN**

He wants to cheat you, but his ploy, disguise, and alibi are all obvious and lousy. Think _Dirty Rotten Scoundrels_. Write a scene in which he gets his just deserts.

_____

_____

_____

**LOOK DOWN ON EVERYONE**

Write a scene in which everyone is bad, or even the virtuous are stupid and ridiculous.

_____

_____

_____

**THE DOPEY-OF-THE-SEVEN-DWARVES SYNDROME**

Include one character who just doesn't get it: the out-of-sync dancer, the hungry fool at the philosophers' salon, the high-strung guy in Shangri La, the drunk who doesn't notice the earthquake. Think Penny in John Waters's _Hairspray:_ "I got a nosebleed!" "I missed the bus!"

_____

_____

_____

# VOICEMAILS FROM MY FUTURE SELF

*by* MARK SIPOWICZ

4 SESSIONS, 2 HOURS EACH
MATERIALS: *GarageBand software or digital recorder*

THIS WORKSHOP HAS BEEN AN EXCITING exploration for both my students and me. One student said at the end of the second session that she didn't know when she had last felt "so calm and so stimulated" at the same time! The goal is to get students interested in their inner voice and offer them a safe and educational environment to honor their subjectivity. The idea of a voicemail is intriguing and different; the idea of a future self speaking to you is mysterious and alluring. Who is that voice? Where does it come from? And what can it tell me about my future? This class helps students to trust themselves and their inner wisdom, opens the door to conversations regarding their inner life, and gives students a broader palette for their creative endeavors.

## Session 1

Most students either have too literal a sense of where they're going, or, on the other hand, almost no idea. This workshop will help us find a middle ground between those extremes.

The first session is inevitably devoted to discussing (1) what is this mysterious subject, (2) why does it matter, and (3) how can we make this a safe, comfortable, and inviting environment for writing and sharing. Inner voice, or whatever else you might prefer to call it, is the bedrock of this workshop, and so some of the following questions should get put on the table from the start: What is the inner voice, what isn't it, where does it come from, what does it sound like and look like, what are its concerns, its interests? What kinds of dreams, people, animals, and other stuff hang around with your inner voice? Assuming your inner voice is different from your outer voice, is it more mature, nobler, more innocent, less so, and does it ever push or pull you along?

I like to bring in some outside material to help with the atmospherics, like the Nalungiaq (Inuit) invocation/poem "Magic Words." It begins in a magical time in the past where, "The human mind had mysterious powers. A word spoken by chance might have strange consequences. It would suddenly come alive and what people wanted to happen could happen."

Finally, we do a fun in-class writing exercise. Tell the students to imagine they've just completed the workshop and it's been a total success. Ask them to write a letter to someone they know well and tell him or her about what they've learned in this experience about themselves and their inner voice. Remind them they got an A+ in the class. They really learned a lot!

## Session 2

Ask the students if there is any material that came up since you last met that reminded them of their project here. A student might talk about hearing her inner voice while walking in a crowd or wondering about all the other inner voices in a crowd. You definitely want the conversation to wander and percolate. Students might share bits of reading or music that they like or wonder about. You also will want to be open to a discussion or suggestions of other names for the inner voice. Then, as with any of the writing assignments, if there is time I ask them to either discuss the material as a group or break into small groups or pairs—possibly responding to writing with two favorite lines, a suggestion, and a question. Here we might discuss the A+ writing exercise from last class before moving on.

Next I guide the students through a visualization that offers them a contemplative way to explore their inner landscape. I walk them through relaxing their breath, mind, and body. Then I invite them to visualize their own mountain, meadow, river, room, house, or other location: welcoming what is interesting and calmly saying hello and goodbye to that which is distracting or off subject. There could be many other ways of doing this. We talk afterwards about colors, images, and feelings that we experienced.

Then I ask the students to write a pledge, meditation, chant, poem, or song that welcomes their inner voice to be heard. This is a chance for them to let go of resistances and welcome discovery.

The next activity is called Finding Your Personal Hall of Fame. I ask students to identify three or four living, dead, or fictional people that they admire—people that they can't imagine the world without. Together we discuss the top two to three qualities that people associate with these figures and whether the students share any of the same qualities. Finally, we narrow the list of qualities to a top three or four and ask the students to explore the potential for those qualities within themselves! This is fun and quite often revelatory for everyone.

Next, we tackle a rough draft paragraph speculating on the events, interests, concerns, questions, and truths of the inner voice. Then the students reduce the paragraph to a sentence, then a word or phrase. Of course, finding a way for them to share these rough images of their inner voices will help move them along toward the final voicemail.

Finally, at the conclusion of this busy session, we discuss the difficulty of pinning this material down and the diversity of voices that exist in the world. Here I introduce a William Stafford poem, "The Way It Is," and his metaphor of the thread as a possible additional metaphor for our inner voice. "There's a thread you follow. It goes among things that change. But it doesn't change. People wonder about what you are doing. You have to explain about the thread."

## Session 3

I start with a chance for students to share anything that came up for them between classes, and so at this session I might ask: Any surprises, interesting images, questions, or voices this week? Did you think about the thread, see it, or feel it? Then I have the class read the Stafford poem a couple of times, in different voices.

Time for a writing exercise. Using Stafford's poem, write about a page of responses to the following questions: What are the qualities of your thread, where did the thread come from, what is it made up of, what does it sound like, look like, feel like, do you have any instincts or intuitions about the thread, what does the thread say to you? Can you be the thread?

Find a safe way for students to share what they've written. Reading to each other in pairs, or students spontaneously reading a single sentence popcorn style (randomly) to the group can work well in a smaller group.

Then offer another guided visualization, seeing what new ideas, images, or shifts occur. Try to encourage the students to return to the same imagined location unless they had some specific problems getting into it.

Next we brainstorm or write a series of "Questions for the Quest." Most students identify with or get excited by the life as quest metaphor. Introduce the idea that a question usually starts the quest. Share a few choice quotes like, "The obstacle is the path," or "The problem, if you love it, is as beautiful as the sunset," and start collecting questions from your students. What are they seeking, what do they hope to learn about themselves?

## Session 4

Throughout the workshop, and especially here at the end, I try to honor the students in a meaningful way for taking a chance on exploring a hidden and often unseen part of themselves and for having the courage to do it with others. This is usually a good time to write up a collective inventory of all the names we've given our inner voice. A few of those have included: conscience, destiny, soul, higher self, best self, creative self, iceberg below the surface, intuition, the thread, instinct, new eyes, like a kid hanging on to the back of your shirt, or the one that keeps you on track.

Then ask the students to look back at what they've done, with an eye toward what calls to them most strongly and what needs to be heard. Give the students 20 minutes to look over their notes for each of the exercises and fill at least a single page with all the best parts that still ring true. (Obviously here it is worth noting that the best way for students to undertake all the writing exercises is to include them all in an ongoing small journal or notebook.) Then read a few prompts to set them on their way scripting the final voicemail from their future self. Here are a few of my prompts:

☞ Your future self is the thread pulling you, guiding you. What are some of her primary concerns, her interests, her advice?

☞ You've lost your way and your future self is giving you a call to help you navigate. "I hope you get this message. I'm over here. I miss you. Where have you been?"

☞ Your future self has never gotten in touch with you directly before. Here is his message after so many years . . .

☞ She calls all the time; this is just her latest message for you . . .

When your students have finished a draft have them read to each other in pairs or triads. Ask them to respond to each other with two favorite parts and one theme or line you suggest they expand. Then have them edit and rewrite a final time before recording.

We record our final voicemails on the GarageBand software (or a digital recorder) and include introductory messages like, "You've reached the voicemail of . . ." and then devise a beep of some sort. If you have the time and the group dynamic has flowed well you could arrange a special group listening to all the recordings. Most audio software also makes it easy to send the students their recordings in an e-mail attachment. In the end, I tell the students this isn't the kind of work you can ever really complete, but that it is a door they've courageously opened or a pathway they have successfully widened to which they will want to return as often as they can throughout their lives.

# HOW SHORT IS SHORT?

*by* VENDELA VIDA

2 SESSIONS, 90 MINUTES EACH

IT'S NOT UNCOMMON FOR A WRITER TO APPROACH A SHORT STORY WITH A sense of trepidation: What if I spend weeks (or months) working on it, and it amounts to nothing? Sometimes the fear of time wasted gives way to stalling—or at least provides a good excuse for it. The goal of this class is to help students realize how much they can accomplish in short, intense bursts.

We start by reading some short short stories (loosely defined as being under five pages), such as "Snow" by Julia Alvarez and "Girl" by Jamaica Kincaid. The students are then asked to write their own stories using each of these works as a prompt. For example, after reading "Girl," which is told in the second person, the class is given 20 minutes to compose a short short story in the second person. After reading "Snow," about a girl who comes to America from the Dominican Republic and sees snow for the first time, the class is given about 15 minutes to describe what snow or thunder or an earthquake could look like, or be mistaken for, by someone who had never seen any of these things before.

In the next class, we delve into selections from Issue 13 of *McSweeney's*. For this issue of the literary journal, a number of authors were asked to write a story in 20 minutes. It's both interesting and inspiring to see how different writers approach this challenge, and the students feel encouraged that maybe they, too, can produce something publishable in a restricted period of time. For her entry, the novelist Jennifer Egan wrote an outline for a story, which, in effect, is the story. The students then try their hand at writing an outline that reveals something about the narrator—for example, a shopping list. Or a to-do list. As with all in-class exercises, the students share their works aloud when the allotted time period is over.

Another submission to *McSweeney's* 13, one by J. Robert Lennon (next page), also serves as a great writing prompt. His story is composed entirely of subjects and verbs. After reading and briefly discussing it, the students are given twenty minutes to write a story in a similar vein. Without adjectives and adverbs, they're forced to really think about the power of verbs. It's easy to get lazy and grab the plainest, blandest verb: go, want, ask. But in the resulting students' stories, the characters stumble, pray, plead. And more.

He noticed. He stared. She noticed. She smiled. He approached. She rebuffed. He offered. She accepted. He said, she said, he said, she said. They drank. They said. They drank. He touched. She laughed. They danced. He pressed. She kissed. They left. They did. He left. She slept.

He called. He called. He called. He begged. She refused. He called. He wrote. He visited. He called, called, called, called. She reported. He arrived, shouted, vowed, departed. He plotted. He waited. He visited. She gasped. He demanded. She refused. He grabbed. She screamed. He slapped. She ran, locked, called, waited. He panicked. He fled, hid, failed.

She accused. He denied. She described. He denied. She won, he lost. They aged. She wed, reproduced, parented, saddened, divorced. He bided, waited, hardened. Fought. Smoked. Plotted, planned. Escaped. Vanished.

They lived. She thrived, he faded. He wandered; she traveled. They encountered.

He sat, she sat, they ignored. He noticed. She noticed. He gaped. She jumped. She warned, he assured. She reminded, he admitted. She threatened, he promised. She considered. She sat. She asked. He told. He asked. She told. He smoked. She smoked. He apologized. She cried. He explained. He begged. He pleaded. She considered, resolved, refused. He stood. He clenched. He perspired. He spat. She flinched, paled.

He stopped. He slumped. He collapsed. She stood. She pitied. She left.

They lived. They forgot. They died.

—J. Robert Lennon, March 28, 2002,
9:05–9:25 am, Ithaca, NY

The How Short Is Short? class runs for several sessions, and the students end up with some great short pieces. Often, they're so good that students want to expand on them, so I encourage students to pick their strongest story (or two) to flesh out into a longer work. As for the exercises they're not as fond of, well, they only spent 20 minutes on them. And who knows? Maybe the prompts planted the seed for something else.

# 26

# COMIC COMPOSITION CHALLENGE!

*by* STEVEN WEISSMAN AND JORDAN CRANE

**1 SESSION, 1 HOUR**
**MATERIALS:** *Timer*
*1 piece of paper for each player*
*Enough pencils or pens for everyone to draw with*

THIS IS A GREAT LESSON FOR STUDENTS WITH SHORT ATTENTION SPANS AND students who don't think they like to write. It uses comics and games to get them thinking about dialogue and narrative. The writing is done in fast-paced bursts, so they don't have time to get bored.

We call this exercise the 5-Minute Cartoon Challenge. Everybody loves to read comics, and everybody thinks he or she has a great idea for one. Three or more players will have to use their imagination and drawing skill in concert to create the best comic strip possible.

Divide the class into groups of three to six students. Distribute blank pieces of paper, then have each player divide his or her sheet of paper as shown below into three equally sized panels (if six or more students are playing) or four panels (if four to five students are playing). This can be done by folding or careful line drawing.

## How to Play

### First Round

When the 5-minute timer starts, each player will draw the first panel of a comic strip on his or her sheet of paper. The first panel will contain a title, one or more cartoon characters, and enough scenery to establish location. Any narration, dialogue, or action is up to each player. At the end of 5 minutes, players must put down their pencils and pass the comic to the left.

While the timer is reset, players will have an opportunity to read the comic they've been handed. Players may ask for clarification during this period.

### Second Round

During the second 5-minute period, players continue the action from the first panel they've been given. Players must take care to keep both the storytelling and drawing style consistent with the first panel. The second player may introduce more characters, "write out" existing characters, add conflict, movement, action, and so forth. As before, at the end of 5 minutes, players must put down their pencils and pass to the left.

*Note: If playing a four- or six-paneled game, the same rules of play apply to period(s) 3 (for four panels), 4, and 5 (for six panels).*

### Final Round

After the rest/reset, the final panel is begun. This panel will conclude the comic strip, and must do so satisfyingly. Comedic "punch lines" are encouraged, but a tragic end is also acceptable. The final player on each strip must resolve the action as he or she sees fit.

### Rules of Play

- ☞ All text must be legible to all players.

- ☞ Players may not contribute to more than one panel per strip.

- ☞ Players are obliged to match narrative tone and visual style. Characters introduced in the first panel must maintain their design elements. Transitions in story direction must be considered (for example, "Elsewhere, a different character participates in an unrelated activity").

- ☞ At the end of 5 minutes (one period), pencils must be put down. No drawing or writing is allowed outside the timed limits.

- ☞ Players must draw for the entire 5-minute period.

- ☞ Dream imagery is allowed, but it may not be identified as being or having been "all a dream."

## Tips

☞ Keep pencils sharp for clear details and handwriting.

☞ Players often have differing skill levels when it comes to drawing. This challenge is about consistent storytelling with pictures and words. No points are awarded for a panel that "blows away" others in the same strip.

☞ If you're not having fun drawing it, nobody will have fun reading it.

☞ What we're trying to do here is build a narrative. To that end, when presented with a story direction, go with it rather than against it—take what is on the page, and build on it.

## How to Win

Each comic strip presents its own challenges. Players are encouraged to discuss and award the most valuable contribution to each strip and award that contributor one point. In the event of a tie, everybody wins.

# MY BORING LIFE

*by* MICAH PILKINGTON

3 SESSIONS, 1 HOUR EACH

IT'S BEEN OUR EXPERIENCE THAT ALL TEENAGERS THINK THEIR LIVES ARE TOO boring to write about, and they couldn't be more wrong. Whenever we give them a prompt, they come up with some amazing stuff. The students in this three-session class knocked our socks off. We're sure yours will too.

## Session 1

The workshop leader begins by telling a gripping true story. In one class, the instructor relayed a traumatic event from her past involving a show tune performed in sixth-grade choir. She told the story, sang the song, and demonstrated the absurd choreography. We're sure you have a great story of your own. We identify the main events in the story we heard, then ask for a show of hands: Who else has done something embarrassing in public? Did anyone have a hard time adjusting to middle school?

We retreat to a big dry-erase board and ask the class a more general question: What are some changes that can happen in a person's life?

After we fill the board with ideas, we ask the class to write down everything they remember about three specific times their lives changed. Before we ask for volunteers to share their work, we introduce the Story Monkey, a friendly creature with special powers. (If your students are too old, or too cool, for stuffed monkeys, just substitute another object.) Whoever possesses the Story Monkey has the room's undivided attention. We've heard some great stories from the holders of the monkey, from a rumble with a petting-zoo goat to memories of a beloved babysitter who died of cancer. When everyone has had a turn, we add a second step to the exercise: write down some problems you've encountered as a result of changes in your life. We end by discussing how conflict is the center of every story.

## Session 2

In our next class, we start by writing a few sentences of the most boring story we can think of on the board, then ask the class to fix it. We discuss different ways to do this:

- Does the story improve if we add details?
- How about adding action?
- Maybe more descriptions of sights, sounds, and smells?
- What about dialogue?

Now what does the story look like?

After students improve our story, we return to the work done in the previous session. Students each pick one of the events they wrote about and rewrite it using the techniques we practiced on the board. We like to take a decent amount of time for this part, so the instructor provides snacks and checks in with each writer, giving direction and encouragement.

We finish this session with the Story Monkey. We ensure that all students get specific feedback on their work from both the instructor and their peers, and we encourage them to reread and revise on their own. We send the students home with a little bit of homework: to give their pieces a final polish.

## SUPERTEACHER BONUS ACTIVITY

Because these stories are so incredibly un-boring, we think they deserve an audience. Superteachers may want to organize an afterschool reading and invite the students' friends and families to hear their wonderful work. Photocopy fancy invitations to send home with the students, and schedule a practice or two to make sure the kinks are worked out.

## Session 3

The last session is our reading. It can be in class or, even better, after school, before an audience of friends and family. Before we begin we remind the students how important it is that no one have any fun. Readers should speak in a whispered monotone, preferably while staring at the ground. We also caution against laughter, and advise the reader to glare at the audience if he or she receives any. After a few minutes of this, we admit that having fun is actually pretty important, as is making sure the audience can hear you. We reminded one class how they were subjected to the instructor's very bad singing, and anything they did would be an improvement over that.

Before we begin, we ask if anyone has suggestions on how to shake off nerves. Yoga? We do some as a group. Jumping jacks? Sure! A spazzy dance with your eyes closed? Awesome. We're ready. The reading begins, everyone is blown away, and off the students go, to continue their non-boring lives.

# COLONEL MUSTARD IN THE LIBRARY WITH A CANDLESTICK

## HOW TO WRITE A MYSTERY

*by* JULIANNE BALMAIN

**1 SESSION, 90 MINUTES**
**MATERIALS:** *Miscellaneous objects (keys, costume jewelry, cups, photos, and so on)*

MYSTERY STORIES ARE FUN TO WRITE BECAUSE THEY HAVE A WELL-DEFINED beginning, middle, and end. This also makes them especially satisfying to read. Finding the answer to a perplexing question feels good. Once you know who drank all the milk and why, you don't have to stay up all night wondering about it. The world is full of nagging questions that never get answered. In mysteries, we finally get to know the truth.

Most mysteries begin when the main character, often a grizzled detective but sometimes just a person who is excessively curious, discovers a question that urgently needs answering. This question is usually, Who perpetrated this terrible crime? It can also be, What happened to this lost but very important object (such as a rich man's last will and testament) or person (such as the French Ambassador to Peru) or pet (such as the beloved parrot from the local café)?

The middle is when the detective or curious person is on the trail, hunting for clues. Often one clue will lead to the next clue and so on until the mystery is solved. Very often, near the end, the detective runs out of clues and is temporarily stumped. This is a good time for the detective's sidekick or some other subordinate character to accidentally provide a hint. For example, the curious person's mother could leave a note saying, "Jimmy stopped by to see you today." If we know it couldn't possibly have been Jimmy since Jimmy was with the main character the whole time, and therefore someone must have been pretending to be Jimmy, it's definitely a clue. What's more, whoever was impersonating Jimmy is a suspect.

Once the driving question of the mystery has been answered and all other "loose ends" have been tied up—a loose end is a minor mystery within the mystery—the story ends and everyone saunters off to have tea and biscuits, or whatever readers like to have at the end of a good story.

Ready to give it a shot? To prepare, collect several objects and display them on a table at the front of the room. They can be ordinary objects, such as a key, a feather, or a coffee cup, or special items, such as a satin glove, a diamond brooch, an antique photograph, or a treasure map.

You may also want to assemble a cast of three to five suspects using photographs cut from newspapers and magazines. Alternatively, choose several volunteers and decide the basic attributes of their characters as a group. Then distribute the handout, let your students loose, and watch the mysteries unfold.

# WRITE YOUR OWN!

Using the objects on the table as clues, write a mystery story with a beginning, middle, and end.

## STEP 1: WHERE

Imagine a setting. Where would you like your story to take place? An exotic locale such as Mexico or Paris can be intriguing, but your own neighborhood works too. Mysteries happen everywhere.

## STEP 2: WHO

Who will investigate the mystery? It can be any kind of person you like, but using a detective makes things particularly easy, since it's in his or her nature to go around asking questions. If you pretend you are the main character and tell your own story, you will write from what's called the *first-person* perspective. If you want to tell a story about what happened to someone else, you will be writing from the *third-person* perspective.

To get the story started, write a sentence or two establishing who and where the main character is, and what he or she is doing. For example:

> *Sabrina opened the window overlooking Puerto Vallarta. She was glad to be on vacation, far from her job as a detective.*

## STEP 3: WHAT HAPPENS

Now all you need is a crime. Think of ways to bring your detective in contact with the crime and the objects on the table. For example:

> *Across the street, a man was stuffing an enormous bag overflowing with bills into the trunk of a tiny car. Sabrina had never seen so much money. Where could it have come from? As she watched, he jumped into the car and sped away. Another man ran up after him, cursing loudly.*

## STEP 4: CLUES AND SUSPECTS

Look around for clues. Is there any evidence to suggest what might have happened? Are there any witnesses? Who might have a reason to be involved in the crime? Have your detective question suspects to see what they say. Could they be lying? Does something they say lead to the next clue or suspect?

**STEP 5: RESOLUTION**

The best part of any mystery story, and the hardest part to come up with, is the final insight that triggers the "aha" moment, when the detective finally knows what happened. How does your main character discover the truth?

You may want to finish by finding a way to prove your detective's guess is correct. Does the guilty party confess? Is he or she caught in the act of committing another crime? Does this person make a mistake that reveals his or her guilt once and for all?

**Alternate Method:** You could also try writing a story by going in reverse, starting with your resolution and working backwards.

**Extra Credit:** Create a pseudonymous author name. Like an alias, a pseudonym is a false name mystery writers sometimes use to make themselves seem more mysterious. Write a brief description of your pseudonymous persona—similar to the author bios you see in books—including where your authorial residence is located, what you like to do in your spare time, what qualifications you have for writing the story, and anything else notable.

# CREATING CHARACTERS

*by* JONATHAN AMES

1 SESSION, 3 HOURS

THIS CLASS HELPS STUDENTS CREATE STORY CHARACTERS THAT ARE WELL rounded and compelling and vivid.

There are four basic building blocks to create characters, and all of them are essential and should be used almost as a checklist when reading over one's story:

1. The first thing you need to do is describe characters physically. As soon as they appear on the page, quickly let us know what they look like, how old they are, and so on. Look at your favorite books and see how the writer gives a quick thumbnail description: "Amy entered the room. She was short with brown hair, and she'd just turned 17." Mention an odd characteristic, like a crooked tooth. Graham Greene would do this, and would return again and again to that detail. You can spin a whole character out of one little thing. That one detail will bring to mind the entirety of the character in the reader's mind. It's like being able to clone someone from a strand of hair.

2. The second thing to consider is the way they speak. Make your characters' dialogue distinctive. Do they use slang? Are they rude? Vulgar? Are they taciturn or garrulous?

3. Next, enter their mind. Are they secretly nervous, but act bold? Are they angry or timid? Show their thoughts, their secret ways of looking at the world.

4. Finally, have them take action. Do they run from trouble or lash out? Do they cry, steal, help others? The actions they take will reflect the kind of people they are.

Then we practice.

## Exercise 1: Creating a Toolbox

Give the students 5 minutes to write down the first and last names of every person they have ever known. It should be in paragraph form, with names separated by commas, not a linear list.

When they're done, ask them what the experience was like. Most people say they started with friends or family, and then this led to other groups of people, which in turn led to other groupings. That's exactly the point. I tell them that's half the reason we did this—it mimics the act of writing itself. We begin with an idea and then something else occurs to us. We start off describing a tree and then we end up talking about the bird nest in its branches. Writing is an association game.

The other reason we do this is that it provides everything you need to write stories and create characters. Here's your toolbox. The people you listed have all these different aspects, all these individual traits—red hair, missing teeth, shyness, big feet, bad breath. Like Dr. Frankenstein, you can draw from the different people in your life to build a new character. These people all have incredible stories, about luck and problems and divorce and death, and you can take bits and pieces of their stories and make your own stories out of them. Hemingway said, "Write what you know." And what we usually know in life are people. So in this list are the people you know and you can learn from them. They have all the ingredients one needs for stories: courage, heartbreak, loss, love, humor.

## Exercise 2: The Elevator

Ask your students to pretend they're alone in an elevator. One other person comes in—someone completely different from them. Give them 5 minutes to describe this person in as much detail as possible. Then, after that, have them skip two lines, and do it again switching places—pretending they're the other person, describing *them*. The first part is a great way to practice describing other people physically. The second part helps you learn how to get in another character's mind.

## Exercise 3: Profiling

Have your students write an honest description of someone in their life. It can be a friend or a parent. Parents are usually very strong characters in our lives and that translates to the page and can make for a powerful piece of writing.

# HIGH SCHOOL CONFIDENTIAL
## HOW TO WRITE A YOUNG-ADULT NOVEL
### *by* MATTHUE ROTH

**2 SESSIONS, 1 HOUR EACH, PLUS HOMEWORK**

YOU'D THINK THAT WRITING ABOUT YOUNG ADULTS MIGHT BE THE EASIEST thing for a young adult to do. But, for a non-teenage instructor, teaching young adults how to write for young adults takes a certain kind of chutzpah—and a certain amount of deference. After all, they know way more about what they're doing than any teacher or writing coach does. Anything you do is basically backseat driving.

On the other hand, writing a young-adult story is going to require your students to become backseat drivers themselves. Salman Rushdie said, "The only people who see the whole picture are the ones to step outside the frame." He wasn't specifically referring to writers, but he might as well have been. We don't have a good perspective on our own lives. We're in the middle of it. The aim of this exercise is to encourage students to step outside that frame, and write about their own lives.

One note: young-adult novels are usually short. There's a reason for that, and it's not (usually) laziness. It's immediacy. First, step outside the frame. Take a good, long look at what's happening, and write your book. Then jump right back in. Writing from the mind of a teenage character is hard mostly because there's so much LIVING involved in being a teenager. You have to write fast, because life happens so fast.

During this exercise, we're going to write a novel—or, at least, start one. Instructors can approach this as the beginning of a novel, or as a loose outline for one. You can also do the exercise as a two-page short short story and call it a day. Call that one living *really* fast.

We'll start by creating a toolbox with the "Toolbox" handout. In the first part of this exercise, students will fill up their toolboxes. In the second session, distribute the "High School Confidential" worksheet, and let the students put it all together.

# TOOLBOX

## TOOL 1: WRITE ABOUT YOURSELF

Well, not *exactly* yourself. Change one major detail. It could be writing about a girl instead of a guy, or about a guy instead of a girl, or that you're the exact same age and race and height but you're secretly a vampire, or a Liechtensteinian spy, or an alien who's been raised among humans.

But remember: you're still basically writing about yourself. So, when you talk about your alien superpowers or how much you miss your native Liechtenstein, it's not some weird superhero speaking—it's *you,* with your voice and your feelings. What kind of music did you listen to on Neptune? How do you feel about having to assassinate that hot guy who sits next to you in chemistry class?

Jot down a few lines here. They can be anything—what your guy or girl looks like. A few lines of dialogue in the way you think your character would talk. His or her secret desires. The one thing he or she is afraid of.

## TOOL 2: WRITE ABOUT SOMEONE WHO ISN'T YOURSELF

Often, people think young-adult books don't have antagonists or villains. THEY DO. In some stories, the entire world antagonizes the main character. In others, the main character meets a lot of minor antagonists who build up, either getting more annoying or more formidable—think about the succession of people Holden Caulfield runs into during his night in New York City in *The Catcher in the Rye*. Or sometimes it's an antagonist, but not an evil one. In Coe Booth's novel *Tyrell,* the main character's father, though away in prison, is responsible for several of his unfortunate circumstances—or, at least, Tyrell thinks he's responsible.

The antagonist can be anyone or anything. The big question is, how will the antagonist antagonize? How will he/she/it/they annoy your character and drive your character to the extremes of both their personalities? List a few ideas.

## TOOL 3: LOCATION, LOCATION, LOCATION

Every story has plot, setting, and characters. In the best stories, all three devices are sending the same message. Believe it or not, the setting of your story can be the best way to drive home the story you're trying to tell. Think of a great story, and its setting probably relates pretty strongly to the characters. The message of *Buffy the Vampire Slayer* was, "High school is hell," and they took that literally—Buffy's high school was next door to the Gates of Hell. In *Twilight,* Bella is emotionally isolated from other teens—and she's living in a town in the middle of nowhere where she doesn't trust anyone. *The Catcher in the Rye* is the story of Holden Caulfield realizing that he doesn't have the priorities that society wants him to have, and the entire story is narrated from inside a mental hospital.

With that in mind, pick a setting for your character. It doesn't have to be original—it could be as simple as "an attic," "a graveyard," "a club"—but there should be a reason why your character finds himself or herself there. Describe it. Describe the things inside it.

# HIGH SCHOOL CONFIDENTIAL: THE NOVEL

Now it's time to start your story using the worksheet. Don't write it all right now. This can be a summary, or it can be the beginning of your story. Start with one of your tools. (It doesn't have to be the character who's basically you; you can start off describing your mortal enemy, or the world where this all takes place.) Throw in the next tool when you can. It doesn't have to be when you reach that place on the paper—it can be sooner, or later. That's the best thing about writing teen fiction. The first rule is that you have to break all the rules.

And you don't have to cram your whole story in here. We've added prompts to guide you, so that a line or two before the setting shows up, you can write about your main character stumbling out of his bedroom into an alien world, or an alien chemistry class.

**1.** [Introduce the character who's basically you]

_____

_____

_____

_____

**2.** [. . . and an antagonizing character]

_____

_____

_____

_____

**3.** [. . . and tell us a little bit about where they live]

_____

_____

_____

_____

. . . and now you've started your novel. The hardest part is done. All you have to do now is just keep going.

# GET YOUR HAIKU ON

*by* DAPHNE GOTTLIEB

SOMETIMES IT'S HARD TO LOVE POETRY. Some of it is really stuffy, some of it is really abstract and hard to follow, and some of it is so quaint it's cringeworthy. But there's one form that never lets us down—it's precise, it's snappy, and it sounds as contemporary as anything even as it's a traditional form thousands of years old.

That's right, we're talking about haiku. Haiku, with its traditional Japanese form: the first line has 5 syllables, the second has 7, and the third has 5, for a total of 17 syllables. Before you know it, you're done with one and on to the next.

You can drop all sorts of language from the world around you into haiku form, from the instructions on microwavable food to classified ads from the newspaper to the most important: your own life. Students are often somewhat

turned off from writing poetry because it's effeminate or stodgy or snooty. But by bringing in everything from song lyrics to shampoo instructions (*lather, rinse, repeat / lather, rinse, repeat, lather / rinse, repeat, lather*), the mundane takes on the sublime. And can be ridiculously funny. We have been surprised time and again teaching workshops—by high school weightlifters writing about pushing it to the point of failure in the gym; by after-school cooks giving us recipes on how to make the whole world better; by all the writers telling us about what's outside the window, in their day. That's the point of poetry at its best. That's why we love it.

Ready to get your haiku on in your own classroom? The handout has four haiku variations for your students to try: group haiku; speed haiku; an un-haiku haiku; and a haiku battle. Enjoy.

# THINGS TO DO WITH HAIKU

Given the short form of haiku, it's possible to take 10 to 15 minutes and have a bounty of poems result. The key to writing, sometimes, is finding permission to speak—song lyrics and shampoo bottles sort of grant that these haiku are everywhere and hey! anything anyone writes will be better than those! What do you see every day that people need to know about?

## 1. THE TANKA
Honoring the old tradition of *tanka* (see "A Brief History of Haiku," below), each student writes a haiku (5–7–5) and passes it to another student for the *tanka* (7–7) addition. You could stop here or keep going, and pass it to yet another student for the 5–7–5 *hokku,* then to another for the *tanka,* and so on. This is a traditional *renga,* in which one completes another's work.

## 2. THE 3-MINUTE TOPICAL HAIKU
Begin the day with haiku. Write a topic on the board (like "lunch menus," or "P.E.," or a current event). Everyone writes a haiku on the topic. These can be posted in a blog, in a chapbook, in whatever collected form is interesting.

## 3. WRITE A HAIKU FROM . . .
Advertising. A cereal box. From something in the newspaper wanted ads. From your iPhone. From your math book. From a love note. From your wildest dreams. Once you know how to find poetry, it's always there.

## 4. THE HAIKU BATTLE
Three flags. Two haiku. Two students come up and do an MC-style haiku battle. After hearing both, the flags vote. Whoever gets the most flags wins. The haiku battlers are replaced with two more students, and the flags are passed to other students.

## A BRIEF HISTORY OF HAIKU

In addition to being a formal form of poetry, haiku also depicts a certain moment—that of a world in transition. Originally about the observation of nature in flux (as in the case of great masters Basho, Buson, and Issa, in Japan's Edo period, 1600–1868), haiku originally derived from the form of *tanka,* which had a structure of 5–7–5–7–7. Between the ninth and twelfth centuries, one person frequently would write the first three lines, then pass the poem on to another writer for completion. The first part was called *hokku,* or "starting verse," and became what we know as haiku. Americans, as we are wont to do, co-opted it and changed it. When the beat poets found haiku, they threw the 5–7–5 out the window when they needed to, as well as the examination of the natural world, and focused in on what they saw. When they wanted to make the syllables work out, they'd add an "er" or an "um." This is not only legal but applauded. Make up the rules. What changed you today? What's important to say? You've got 17 syllables. Go.

# THE ESSAY

*by* MEGHAN DAUM

1 SESSION, 1 HOUR

LET'S FACE IT, "ESSAY" ISN'T THE MOST EXCITING WORD OUT THERE. (OK, IT'S more exciting than "rhombus," but not by much.) Still, I'm weird enough that I've gotten my thrills out of essays since I was in high school. Why? For one thing, I figured out in tenth grade that it was easier to insert "profound" rock and roll lyrics by the likes of Sting and Elvis Costello (yes, I'm that old) into essays than into short stories. For another, I discovered that if you can summon the courage to write honestly and frankly about what you're really thinking, people will read it and say, "Yeah! I feel the same way. I just couldn't figure out how to express it."

As you may already know, the word "essay" literally means "to try." When you write an essay you're not so much stating indisputable facts as trying to make sense of the world around you. There are lots of ways to do this; you can write about something you've experienced personally; you can document a specific event, such as an election or a political dispute or even a sporting event, and use the facts to arrive at a broader conclusion; you can write about another person (it can be anyone from your best friend to your favorite musician—you don't have to know him or her personally) and talk about why that person is important to you. You can write comedy. That's right, stand-up comedians are essayists in their own right. Anyone who ever had their own HBO comedy special knows a thing or two about the essay form, even if they don't use the word "essay." We can learn a lot from comedians.

I once wrote an essay called "My Misspent Youth." In it, I talked about how when I lived in New York City when I was in my twenties, I managed to get into a lot of debt even though I had a pretty good income and never seemed to buy expensive things. On the surface, this essay was a chronicle of how I managed to accrue this debt—student loans, rent, too many dinners out with friends. But that's only part of the story. What I really set out to do was use my own life as a way of talking about bigger ideas. Most of those ideas had to do with certain glamorous ideas many people have about living in New York. After living there for several years I eventually noticed that the stereotypical "starving artist" life we read about in books and see in movies isn't quite possible anymore (unless you actually want to starve; and that's not what "starving artist" really means). Due to economic forces, cultural shifts, and plain old real estate prices, it had become almost impossible to live the life of a genuine bohemian or artist in New York City. So my essay, even though it told my personal story and included many small details about my own life, was really about a larger phenomenon that affects many people. Yes, it's about me, but it's even more about New York City and, by extension, people all over the world who dream about living there. "My Misspent Youth" is an example of a personal essay. Even though it uses the word "I" a lot, it's not a memoir. The following handout explains that in more detail.

# ESSAY FORMS FOR YOU TO TRY

## 1. THE PERSONAL ESSAY

When you go into the bookstore, you usually don't have to take more than eight steps before you get to a book that looks a lot like it could be someone's diary. These are called memoirs, and it used to be that they were written by famous people or, at the very least, people who had been alive for a long time and had done strange or interesting things. In the last ten years or so, even people in their twenties have started publishing memoirs. Like all books, some of them are good and some of them aren't, but as an essayist, I'm always reminding people of this:

*A personal essay isn't a memoir!*

A personal essay is bigger, more complex, often harder to write, and, in my opinion, a lot more fun than a memoir. The reason people sometimes confuse them is due partly to that pesky article "I." When you use "I," it can seem like you're talking entirely about yourself, but the truth is that "I" is a useful tool for talking about other stuff. When you use your own experience as a starting off point for talking about other things—politics, movies, sports, music, whatever—you're using your mind to engage in the outside world.

For example: say you go to the mall to buy a pair of jeans and everything you see is just dumb looking, gross, over-designed, tragically trendy, whatever. In an essay you can not only talk about the frustration of not being able to find jeans but use the piece as an opportunity to think and write about why designers and marketers have to change their styles every ten seconds. You could write about what it's like to be a member of the jean-buying public and how people who design and market things to teenagers get it wrong (or maybe they get it right; you can talk about that, too). In other words, a personal essay takes a small moment in your own life and uses it as a springboard for a discussion about bigger things in life. A pair of jeans turns into thoughts about marketing. A breakup with a boyfriend or girlfriend turns into an exploration of the changing rules of romance in society, or the irrational nature of jealousy, or the problems of communication. With personal essays, you're using yourself, the "I," as a vehicle for talking about something that lots of people can relate to.

## 2. THE REPORTED ESSAY

You can also write an essay that involves going out and collecting information, doing interviews, researching historical events, and learning about new things. Then you can weave all that stuff into an essay in which you express your opinion, too. This can sometimes be a little tricky, but it can also be really satisfying when you're done. Why? Because after you write a reported essay, you realize that not only do you know lots of new facts, you also know what you think about them. A lot of writers say they write in order to know what they think about something. That may sound strange—after all, don't you have to know what you think before you start writing?—but it actually makes sense. Writing is sort of an extreme version of thinking. So say you wanted to think really hard about something in your school, like a class election or the cafeteria food or how certain cliques got to be the way they are. You could just write about it from your own perspective (that would be a personal essay), or you could do some reporting (find out where the word "clique" came from, identify the different cliques in your school, interview members of the different cliques) and then write about it in a way that conveys the information and also incorporates your own opinion. You can use the "I" if you want, but you also don't have to. For instance, you can say, "I think it's sad that people feel compelled to organize their entire social lives around the types of music they listen to," or you can say, "It seems sad that people feel compelled to organize their entire social lives around the types of music they listen to." Pretty simple, huh?

### 3. THE HUMOR ESSAY

Like I mentioned earlier, many stand-up comedians function as de facto essayists (*de facto* meaning they're creating essays without necessarily meaning to). But when you think of what it takes to stand in front of an audience and string together a series of thoughts that makes sense as well as makes people laugh you see that it's a lot like what an essayist does. Often, the hardest part about writing a humor essay is getting started; once you find your "comedic voice," you're rolling. So start with something that seems hilarious or absurd to you. Then don't be afraid to go a little crazy. Does the term "Pythagorean theorem" strike you as demonic? Then imagine it *was* a demon. What would it look like? What kind of mayhem would it inflict on the world? What kind of ritual would be necessary to purge it of its evil spirits? In a humor essay, you can be as off-the-wall as you want. You can speak from your own point of view or, as though writing fiction, take the perspective of the subject you're writing about. And one very important thing: when you're poking fun at things, it always works better when you poke fun at yourself even harder. So poke away!

# THE STORY OF ME

## WRITING ABOUT YOUR LIFE AND YOUR FAMILY

*by* JASON ROBERTS

1 SESSION, 2 HOURS

HERE'S THE THEME OF THIS WORKSHOP: *You don't have to wait until you're really old to write your life story!* You've already seen many surprising and memorable things, and a lot of people, events, and ideas have helped shape who you are (and who you're becoming). This workshop helps kids discover how fun it is to connect your experiences, your influences, and your family history, and see how it all adds up to the story of you.

We usually begin not with introductions, but with a deliberately provocative exercise: the facilitator announces that he is the new alien overlord of Earth. Each participant is commanded, in turn, to explain why he or she should be allowed to stay on Earth to continue his or her life in progress, rather than being shipped off to the salt mines in the Glorgg Nebula. This exercise prompts students to immediately start thinking of themselves in terms of their qualities, actions, and affinities, rather than as a little bundle of biographical data. It starts them thinking about *what* they are, not *who* they are.

Next, we ask a simple question: *What is your earliest memory?* This tends to bring forth some particularly vivid imagery—indeed, one's first memory is usually little more than a vivid image.

We then proceed to place that imagery in an emotional context, asking for more details:

- What feelings come attached to that memory?

- Who's hovering outside of the scene? Where do you think your mom/dad/sister/brother were at that moment?

- Can you remember any vivid sensory images from this event? A smell, a taste, music, something you saw?

- Why do you think you remember *that particular moment,* and not something from the day before or the day after?

This last question typically sparks a lot of introspection—it's a new idea, the concept that there's a reason this specific memory has stuck in their head. Sometimes, there's no clear reason; it's just a pretty image. But more often than not, the participants can be encouraged to see it in the light of their own emerging personality. A first memory about, say, coveting an older sister's toy might lead to a cascade of anecdotes about growing up in the shadow of a sibling.

By now it's time to start writing these memories down. To help their essays take shape, I encourage the participants to imagine their Story of Me as a sort of recipe: *these* people plus *these* events made it possible for me to be who I am, and who I'm becoming.

Here are some of the other questions I regularly pose during the workshop, to help the process along:

- ☞ Can you think of some decisions your parents and grandparents made, long before you were born, that helped shape who you are?

- ☞ If one or more of those decisions hadn't been made, what kind of person might you have been instead?

- ☞ Did luck and chance play a part in their stories? What accidents of fate put them on a path that resulted in you?

- ☞ What are your biggest interests now? Can you trace the birth of those interests?

- ☞ How are you different from your parents?

- ☞ How are you alike?

- ☞ How are you different from who you were five years ago?

- ☞ If the kid who was you five years ago showed up in your room for a day, what would you do with her or him?

- ☞ What would you tell him or her?

- ☞ What things did you believe when you were younger that you know now to be wrong?

- ☞ Where you ever unjustly accused of something you didn't do?

- ☞ Did you ever do something you shouldn't, and not get caught?

- ☞ Did you ever unintentionally hurt someone else's feelings? When did you realize you had made a mistake?

- ☞ What's the most trivial thing that, for some reason, means a big deal to you?

- ☞ If you could relive a single day, which day would it be?

- ☞ If you could erase a single day, which day would *that* be?

# MEET YOUR PROTAGONIST!

*by* RYAN HARTY

**1 SESSION, 90 MINUTES**

HERE'S A LESSON I LIKE TO USE NEAR THE BEGINNING OF A COURSE. STUDENTS like it, and it gets them thinking about sophisticated fictional elements like character and plot—often without even realizing it! Most of the time, it encourages them to write good, engaging stories in which important things happen.

I begin with the discussion of a good, engaging published story in which important things happen—maybe something the whole class has read. As we discuss, I raise the question, *What does the main character want?* (In almost all good stories, of course, the protagonist wants something.) Another question: *What is the main character afraid of?* (Again, this should be evident.) You can talk about whether the character gets what he or she wants in the end; whether the character avoids the thing he or she is afraid of; how students feel about the outcome. (If they like the story, they'll have plenty to say.) Then I ask, *Why might desires and fears be important to consider when writing a story?* Invariably they know: it makes the story exciting; it gets us involved; it makes us want to know what will happen; and so on. They're thinking about conflict, narrative drive, plot, and the like. (And in fact with older students, upper-level high schoolers, say, it can be an opportunity to introduce this kind of vocabulary.)

Now we discuss the main character in further detail. *How does the writer make us know who she is?* With descriptions, they say, with dialogue, with the character's thoughts and actions. (They are becoming experts on characterization.) *What are the most important things we know about the character?* They shout them out: her parents just got divorced; she has a pet Chihuahua; she's afraid of Amanda Petruzzi, the class meanie; she loves the color purple.

Now it's time to create our own character. We do this first as a group. Here's the template:

2 desires

2 fears

1 secret

8 very important things

I start with the basics. *How old is the character? Boy or girl?* (You might want to do a boy *and* a girl, so all students can identify.) *What's his or her name? Where does he or she live?* These are not your eight very important details, just basic facts.

Now have students come up with desires and fears, encouraging them to be as specific as possible. For example, it might be interesting to know that the character has a crush on a boy at school; but if we know that she's in love with Rodney Rapunzi, a quiet boy who knows all the answers in math class, we know a good deal more about her (and we have a better idea of what her story will be like). Likewise, whereas most boys worry about being humiliated in class, if our guy is worried about his new corrective eyeglasses, or his embarrassing cousin Dmitri from Lithuania, we get a better sense of what his world is all about.

Fill in the important details. Ask students about the character's family, friends, teachers, school, and so forth. Write down what they shout out, again encouraging them to be specific (and asking clarifying questions, if necessary). Write down more than a dozen details, then have students pick the eight most important ones.

Secrets are essential. They create a sense of intimacy between character and reader, and they often point to the heart of a story. *What do we know about this character that no one else (or almost no one else) knows?*

So now you have a character. Here's an example, this one based on an upper-level high school class (middle schoolers will have much sillier characters, which is great):

- ☞ Matilda Gleeson is 13 years old and lives in Redwood City, California.

- ☞ She wants a new Guess watch to replace the one she recently lost.

- ☞ She wants to see her father more often than she does (which is almost never).

- ☞ She's afraid she might be losing touch with her best friend, Amanda.

- ☞ She's afraid she's going to have her mother's (large) nose.

- ☞ Her secret is that she sometimes goes to the neighborhood where her father lives with his new wife and her kids.

- ☞ She is smart, but she doesn't try hard in school (she's afraid her friends will think she's a loser).

- ☞ Her favorite teacher, Miss Alvarez, once read one of Matilda's short stories aloud in her English class.

- ☞ She loves her little brother, Matthew, but is sometimes mean to him when her friends are around.

- ☞ She has a pet cockatiel named Charlie.

☞ She likes to stay up late at night reading the Narnia books (though she thinks she's too old for them).

☞ A few times, since the divorce, she has heard her mother crying in her bedroom.

☞ Her grandmother lives two blocks away; Matilda likes to visit, because Grandma is fun and never pries.

☞ She dreams about moving to France and becoming a photographer.

Ask students what kind of story they'd like to read about this person. See how sharp their instincts are. In most cases they'll know right where the heart of the story lies. They might want to see the girl spying on her father's family, for example. They might want something to happen with the brother, or with the best friend, or with the mother. *Where should the story begin?* They'll have lots of ideas. Depending on how old they are, you might take a few minutes to discuss writing scenes versus summary, showing versus telling. Or you may just want them to write. You can have everyone write about the character you've created, or students can create characters of their own, using the template (this is what I usually have them do). If they create their own characters, you can have two or three of them read theirs aloud, if time permits.

# EVENTUALLY DIE"

READ OUT LOUD

AFTERWARDS, EVERYONE SHOULD WIPE THE SWEAT OFF EACHOTHERS' BROWS + WRITE AN INSPIRATIONAL QUOTE ABOUT **COURAGE** OR **WHATEVER**! It's GOOD to BORROW other people's QUOTES, UNLESS they're CONVICTED FELONS ON "60 MINUTES," BUT it's WAY MORE FUN to MAKE UP your OWN + go AROUND QUOTING YOURSELF in the THIRD PERSON. I MADE UP "ALL WITNESSES EVENTUALLY DIE" to KEEP MYSELF FROM WETTING MY PANTS OUT OF FEAR ALL the time. GOOD LUCK!

--ERIKA "MAD DOG" LOPEZ

CUT THE TRUTH ALONG THESE LINES

R.I.P. "THE GUY WHO SAW WHAT YOU DID LAST NIGHT"

# 36

# WICKED STYLE AND HOW TO GET IT

*by* MICAH PILKINGTON

2 SESSIONS, 2 HOURS EACH

MAYBE YOU'VE NOTICED—TEENAGERS agonize about style. The same anxiety that goes into finding the exact right pair of sneakers goes into their writing. In our workshops they often ask us: How do you find your own authentic voice? This class helps them do just that.

## Session 1

On day one, we warm up to the topic by examining a few different writing styles. We read passages from a diverse group of books, from slangy (*The Catcher in the Rye* is a good one) to comic (maybe some David Sedaris) to more formal (Henry James). We ask: Which do you like? Which doesn't work for you? Which do you identify with? Which puts you off and why?

Next we read the first paragraph of Jonathan Lethem's novel *Motherless Brooklyn* and an article from the *Onion* titled "Area Mom Freaking Out for No Reason Again." After the students read them, we discuss the ways the style and the content of each work together to make a great piece. Lethem's novel is about a detective who suffers from Tourette's Syndrome. The first sentence could simply state the facts: "My name is Lionel, and I have a neurological disorder that is characterized by recurrent involuntary tics involving body

movements and vocalizations and often has one or more associated conditions, such as obsessive-compulsive disorder." But instead it takes us inside his head, giving us a vivid first-person account of what it feels like inside his colorful, uncontrollable brain. His disorder is a character in the story. He describes where it comes from, what it does, what it wants, and what happens when it's upset. Because Lionel is obsessive-compulsive, he is driven to describe things from all possible angles in order to understand them. He uses five different metaphors to describe how other people see him. When he's talking about Tourette's, he can't stop listing things it does.

We ask: Would *Motherless Brooklyn* be as effective if it didn't rely on stream-of-consciousness? Would the *Onion* piece be as funny if it weren't deadpan? Then we ask: How can you use style and content to make your own writing better? What kind of word choices can you make? How do you structure your sentences? What kind of imagery can you use? We take suggestions and write everything down on a dry-erase board.

Enough talk; it's time for a writing exercise. We ask everyone to choose a scenario and describe it using an "inappropriate" style. We use the example of narrating a three-alarm fire using a slow pace and flowery language:

It was Sunday afternoon in the firehouse. Time for my tea. I just love tea, don't you? It's so fragrant and rich—it makes one feel like the Emperor of China! As I was saying, I was just about to have a cup of tea, when the alarm went off. Three of them, in fact. But before we get to that, let's talk about this: Earl Grey. Earl Grey is my very favorite kind of tea. I like it because you can enjoy it with breakfast, lunch, or dinner, or all on its own. It goes especially well with cookies, especially the rich buttery ones favored by the Scottish.

Students are invited to share their work, and the results are often thoroughly enjoyable and surprising. We were once treated to a pencil-sharpening scene reminiscent of Greek tragedy.

We end the first session with an out-loud reading from Charles Dickens's *Oliver Twist,* of the scene where Oliver first meets the Artful Dodger. Noting the difference between the narrator's voice, Oliver's voice, and the Dodger's voice, we send the kids home with an assignment: combine two voices in one scene and bring it in next time.

## Session 2

On day two, ask the students to read their homework piece aloud. In one class, we got to hear a lively conversation between a businessman and a large, angry puppet. Next, we hand out two important short stories: Ernest Hemingway's "A Clean, Well-Lighted Place" from *Winner Take Nothing* and Scott Stavrou's winning entry from the annual Imitation Hemingway contest called "Across the Suburbs and into the Express Lane" (see www.scottstavrou.com/hemingwayaward. html). We read the first paragraph of each and discuss the choices made by the faux Hemingway and how they differ from, say, those of someone imitating Virginia Woolf. Then we ask the kids to write a quick description of their own writing style, citing influences, techniques, and things they'd like to try in the future, such as, "I'm a modern Jack Kerouac with touches of Joyce Carol Oates. I'm into stream-of-consciousness narration, and I'd like to try my hand at magic realism."

Our last exercise as a class is a really fun one. On three separate pieces of scrap paper, each student writes down a character, a setting, and a line of dialogue. We gather each category and mix it up, then pass them back out. Now we write a scene using all three elements in any way the author chooses. We read the results out loud, and usually it's so much fun that we to do the exercise all over again.

At the end of class, we make a list of recommended reading. We hear great suggestions, including *Tender Is the Night, The House of Sand and Fog,* and *How the Garcia Girls Lost Their Accents.* Stylish!

# PRESIDENT TAKES MARTIAN BRIDE

## WRITING TABLOID FICTION

*by* ALVIN ORLOFF

**1 SESSION, 90 MINUTES**

SURE, THEY'LL NEVER WIN A PULITZER, BUT TABLOIDS HAVE THEIR USES. THEY teach us to believe (Elvis Lives!), to better ourselves (The Amazing Ice Diet!) and to have compassion (Bat Baby Needs Your Help!). They can also teach us to be better writers. This lesson plan uses tabloids to explore what makes good writing good and bad writing bad, and why the latter can be much more fun.

You can start this lesson by passing around a few easily obtained supermarket tabloids, preferably with humorously salacious headlines. Then, discuss what makes a paper a "tabloid," making sure students are aware of the key elements of the tabloid:

**Malicious Celebrity Gossip.** Tabloid readers love to feel like they're invading the privacy of larger-than-life celebrities, but it's not enough to say that movie star X has been spotted canoodling with pop singer Y. There has to be an outlandish twist, preferably one that allows for bit of schadenfreude—taking joy at another's misfortune. Readers love hearing about the faults, foibles, and failures of celebrities, particularly those of the obnoxiously rich and beautiful, though the just plain annoying will do. Ask students why they think people want to hear about celebrities' private lives.

**Shocking, Tell-All Confessionals.** Everybody's family is a little bit weird, we all know of a strange neighbor or two, and most of us, at some time, worry about our own normality. Tabloids make readers feel better by relating stories so lurid that everybody gets to feel well adjusted by comparison. This aspect of tabloid news has been somewhat superseded by trash television, but still persists. Ask students what makes a personal story so freakish that it becomes of interest to others.

**Absurd, Improbable, or Supernatural Events.** Bigfoot, space aliens, Elvis Presley, ghosts, and the like all make their appearance in the tabloid world with amazing frequency. In this way the tabloids are carrying on ancient folkloric traditions, relating the sort of tales grandma used to tell in hushed tones late at night as the family huddled by the fireplace. Urban myths of the alligators-in-the-sewers variety are also a key component of the tabloid cosmology. Ask students what urban myths they've heard of and how they know they're not true.

**Clichés.** Authors of nontabloid fiction go to great lengths to avoid clichés (words or phrases that have lost their effectiveness through overuse), but tabloid stories revel in them. In tabloid land, every "ordeal" must be "grueling," and no story of romance can be complete without "sex kittens," a "love nest," or a "two-timing hussy." Ask the class to think up as many tabloid style clichés as possible.

**Hyperbole and Alliteration.** Tabloids are positively addicted to the tacky tricks of alliteration (the repetition of initial letters of adjoining words) and hyperbole (deliberate and obvious exaggeration used for effect). Good writers do their best to avoid these, but tabloids thrive on them. Not much to discuss here, but students need to be aware.

Society in general, and literary people in particular, look down on tabloids, so to finish up the discussion, it might be nice to give another perspective. Realism (lifelike representation of people and the world without any idealization of fantastical invention) is only one way to tell a story. Many writers feel that just stating facts only gives readers one side of reality, one that doesn't convey the actual lived experience of the human mind. By inventing things, authors of fiction let readers see life as someone else sees it. Some genres of fiction, like magic realism and surrealism, use fantastical invention that isn't, on the face of it, that different from tabloid fiction. Plenty of general fiction, too, employs elements of the tabloid style: histrionic narrative voices, improbably or impossibly zany plotlines, and depraved celebrities. This can be done for humorous effect, with a wink and a nod to let the reader know one is appropriating tabloid style, or with complete deadpan seriousness, as in million-selling trash novels sold at supermarkets.

Discussion finished, it's time to let the students have at it! The handout will help them create their own tabloid masterpieces.

## SUPERTEACHER BONUS ACTIVITY

Compile all the students' articles into a tabloid authored by the whole class, and distribute it to the school at large.

# WRITE YOUR OWN PIECE OF TABLOID FICTION

Good news—tabloid fiction is supposed to be fun for the reader, and the best way to make it that way is to have fun writing it. Remember to use lots of alliteration, hyperbole, and clichés for that tabloid style. Still, as with traditional or real news stories, you're going to want to quote sources and answer the basic questions of journalism: Who? What? Where? When? and Why? Remember, enquiring minds want to know!

Here are six choices for your tabloid fiction project. Your finished story should be about a page long.

## 1. MY CHRISTMAS WITH A BIKER GANG
Write a first-person story about a shocking experience. You can exaggerate something that really happened to you, or make something up. Your tone can be either confessional (you're sorry for whatever you did and want to warn others not to make the same mistake) or defiant ("I don't care what anyone thinks, I love my husband even if he is a space alien!").

## 2. BIGFOOT TRIES OUT FOR THE DODGERS
Write a news article about a nonexistent creature. Remember, it's the interaction of the everyday and the fantastic that captures people's attention, so make the parts of your story that don't deal with the imaginary creature as realistic as possible. Put yourself in the creature's position and try to imagine what it would say or think about things.

## 3. BRAD PITT AND HIGH SCHOOL SENIOR CALL IT QUITS AFTER 72-HOUR MARRIAGE
Imagine a quickie Vegas wedding between you and your favorite star, and write it up either as either a news story or a tell-all memoir. Remember, celebrities don't live the way regular people do. They're apt to go around bathing in champagne, flying in specialists to groom their eyebrows, and having fresh orchids delivered daily to their pet Chihuahua.

## 4. EGOTISTICAL STAR MAKES FANS RETCH WITH DISGUST
Real newspapers try to deliver stories from an objective point of view. Not so with tabloids! Write a story about a celebrity, real or imagined, in which you display an obvious bias. You could be worshipful, be mean, or (and this is particularly nasty) pretend to feel sorry for the star.

## 5. GREAT-GRANDMOTHER WINS SNOWBOARDING COMPETITION
Tabloids occasionally serve up heartwarming tales of triumph. These usually involve the last person you'd expect winning a contest or saving the day in some manner (rescuing a puppy from under a steamroller, raising enough money to pay a mortgage on the orphanage by knitting socks). If you make the story ridiculously sweet enough, it can even become funny.

## 6. SHORT STORY
Write a short story using elements of the tabloid style. Let your imagination run wild, but remember to contrast the preposterous parts of your story (celebrities, fantastic events or beings) with the mundane (everyday). If everything in the story is unbelievable it becomes fantasy, which is another genre of writing altogether.

# LYING FOR FUN AND PROFIT

*by* EMILY KATZ

1 SESSION, 2 HOURS

WE CAN ALL TELL LIES. BUT TELLING a good lie requires thought and creativity. It requires the people involved to have personalities, dialogue, and character traits. It requires movement, setting, and plot development—which makes it a lot like good writing. In this class we learn to turn lies into literature.

It helps to begin lying right from the start. As I arrive, I heave down my belongings and greet students with, "You wouldn't *believe* the mess I just went through," or "Guess who I just ran into?" These are both, of course, lies—the trip that regularly brings me to the classroom is perfectly ordinary, and nowhere near as interesting as the story I'll tell them now.

Next, it's the students' turn to fib. For the duration of the lesson I give students the option of going by a different name and creating alternate identities for themselves. We go around the room and students each say a few sentences about who they "are." This can include likes or dislikes, what they did right before class, their favorite band, and so forth. Then we jump into writing exercises. Spend 10 minutes on this first prompt:

Make a list of things that are true.

When that's done, if you like, you can spend a little while having the students read aloud from their lists. Then, have them spend 10 minutes writing on the next prompt:

Make a list of things that are lies.

These will probably be a little more fun to share. The lies they create can be outrageous or simple. A few of the best ones I've heard come out of this exercise are: "I am the walrus," "When my older brother eats, he gurgles," and the cryptic "Enough is enough." (This one provoked a lot of oohs and hmms.)

Finally, we move on to our last prompt:

Make a list of truths *and* lies.

They do not need to designate which is which, and in this exercise students begin to recognize how the two can run together to make great stories. Lies very often begin with a grain of truth, and even after they turn into great big whoppers, you can usually spot a little truth in there. We talk about how the fluidity between truth and lies can make us better writers. I remind the students that they don't have to be intimidated by the prospect of inventing characters and plotlines, because they can begin simply with what they know, and can then move in any direction they like.

This is a good point to sit together and read some examples of authors who use lies quite successfully. I like to read a passage from the novella "Honda" in the book *Not a Chance* by Jessica Treat, in which the main character, a compulsive liar, gets caught up in her own thoughts, which are a web of humongous lies. She creates a really detailed, intricate story that is very far from reality, but ends up seeming kind of real because of the great lengths she goes to make everything work out right. I ask the class if they think this story began with a lie, and what the lie might have been.

Next we break up and work independently. The students pick an item from their lengthy collection of lists and build a story. Some students opt to begin their thinking with a "spider map," putting their own lie right in the center and brainstorming parts of the story visually. I remind them that the goal is to make the stories complete, outrageous, and as detailed as possible. They can include dialogue, characters, distinct personality traits, and, of course, a setting and movement. I emphasize the importance of plot and remind them that they can just make one up, and they can make the ending up too. It doesn't matter if the end results are long or short, as long as they are imaginative and bald-faced.

# HOW TO FINE-TUNE YOUR FALSEHOOD

**1. BORROW DETAILS FROM PEOPLE YOU SEE.**
You can base a character on someone you saw one time on the bus, or someone that you can't imagine living his or her own life. A lot of students say they can't imagine their teachers doing anything but standing in the classroom (what, they have homes?!). What does that girl with pink hair you see walking down Market Street eat for dinner? Whom does your teacher tell about her day when she gets home from school?

**2. THE SETTING YOU CHOOSE CAN BE COMFORTABLE TO YOU WITHOUT BEING DULL.**
It is always nice to use a story setting that you know personally because it helps you to add rich detail, and might make the reader trust you more. If you don't want to set your fabricated story in outer space, that's okay. If you want to set it in the same city that you live in now, sure, go ahead. But perhaps instead of the plot unfolding on 24th Street, where you've lived your whole life, it can take place in another neighborhood, across the city, that you've driven through but haven't gotten to know that well.

**3. USE AN OUTRAGEOUS PIECE OF DIALOGUE.**
Your character is allowed to say things you would *never* say. Something outlandish. But fairly clean, please.

**4. TAKE A REAL-LIFE SITUATION AND IMAGINE HOW IT CAME TO BE. OR, TAKE A REAL-LIFE SITUATION AND IMAGINE WHERE IT COULD GO.**
Fantasizing about the past or the future is a great way to get writing. In fact, that's much of what creative writing is based on: using a situation we've come to know, or a person we just can't understand, and figuring out *why* through creative thought. It is important not to let your conclusions rest—push them further, open more doors. Challenge your thinking, and imagine what might happen if things unfolded in a completely different way.

# THIS CLASS SUCKS

*by* KAZZ REGELMAN AND ANDREW STRICKMAN

4 SESSIONS, 1–1½ HOURS EACH
MATERIALS: *Sea salt, kosher salt, and table salt*
*Reviews from newspapers and magazines*
*A CD and its published review*

THIS CLASS DOES NOT, IN FACT, SUCK
at all. It's one of our very favorite workshops here
at 826 Valencia, and not just because it involves
food. It introduces students to different forms of
criticism, preparing them for a swag-filled life as
a reviewer. Here are the activities we do in class,
all designed to help students be better critics and
critical writers.

## 1. The Good, the Bad, and the Ugly

This short activity is a helpful introduction to
critical and descriptive writing. Most students
at this point understand that adjectives are the
building blocks of description. But not all adjectives are created equal. As a group, brainstorm
about adjectives that are overused, underwhelm-
ing, and slangy: "good," "bad," "awesome,"
"cool," and "sucky," for example. These are just
a few of the many "four-letter" words of critical/
descriptive writing. It shouldn't take more than
5–10 minutes, at most, to come up with a list of
words that should be banned from most critical/
descriptive writing (except perhaps when used

ironically, such as in the title of this class). Ask
your students, what does the word "interesting"
really tell them? Or "different"? Different from
what? "Unique"—unique how? "Nice," "good"—
could these words actually help a reader visualize
the subject?

## 2. When Is Salt Not Salty?

This exercise can be (and has been) used in *any*
writing class to stimulate the use of descriptive
language, but it evolved out of a session on food
writing we did with our students. We created
a multicourse tasting menu for the students
that consisted exclusively of salt. We used three
different types of salt: sea salt, kosher salt, and
table salt.

Students sample the salts one by one by placing a few granules on their tongues. Encourage
them to play with the salt in their mouths, to
appreciate fully the tastes and textures. Students
tend to make funny faces during this exercise
and moan and groan when the sharp tastes are
revealed. Make sure you have some water to
drink between each tasting. Encourage them

to use as many of their senses as possible. What does each one look like, feel like, even sound like, as well as taste like?

After each tasting, the students should spend 5 minutes writing about each salt—encourage them to use similes, metaphors, and descriptive writing—and the only rule is that they cannot say the salt tastes *salty*. After each salt has been tasted and described, one last writing exercise has the students compare and contrast the salts. As salt "critics" which would they recommend and why?

## 3. A Four-Star Exercise

After the students have done some writing of their own, we like to bring everyone back together for a group activity. Before class, we've gathered some professionally written reviews and made copies to hand out to the students. We kept a teacher's copy that was complete, but on the students' version, we had whited-out the letter grade (or number of stars, or whatever system is used). We used movie reviews from *Entertainment Weekly,* because they are brief but just meaty enough. You could use reviews of restaurants, movies, CDs, books, art, performances of any kind, even consumer products like cars, food, or clothing. Present a mix of reviews— some that pan the subject, others that praise.

Let the students discuss what grade they think the reviewer gave. Did the reviewer think it was well made? How about the service? Was the product a good value for the money? What is the target audience that will like this product? The writing in a well-written review should reflect the grade given (and vice versa), but this will not always be the case in the reviews you read. You'll be surprised at how students interpret the writing in the same review: some will swear the reviewer loved the film and gave it an A, while others will swear it got a D. From your key, tell them how the reviewer really rated it.

It also can be very interesting to read two contrasting reviews from different sources about the same subject. Why did one reviewer love it, while the other hated it? Who would you believe and why? Which writing was more convincing?

Choose reviews that are appropriate for the age of the students, of course, both in terms of content and difficulty. Some helpful sources to start with include national magazines like *People* or *Entertainment Weekly* that have numerous graded reviews meant for popular consumption. Also, local papers (and their online publications) are fantastic sources of reviews on everything from restaurants to film, music, and performances of all sorts. Don't feel limited to local papers, either; check out the *New York Times,* the *Boston Globe,* the *Chicago Tribune,* the *Los Angeles Times,* or any major city paper.

## 4. Moving Outside the Comfort Zone

One of the most challenging things about writing criticism for a newspaper or magazine is that you are often not given the choice to only write about things you like, or that you know. This, of course, requires an open mind and, occasionally, some level of research to be successful and to craft a strong piece. So we talk a little bit about the responsibilities of the critic, and the qualifications a critic should have. Do you have to be a dancer to review dance? Do you have to be a chef to review food, or do you just need taste buds?

The exercise begins with a discussion about the special challenges of writing both negative and positive reviews. The best criticism *explains* what is wrong, or right, with a particular piece of art (be it music, film, literature, theater, food), which frequently comes from a base understanding of the intent of the piece. A critic must understand the intent and context of a piece to judge it effectively and honestly. A critic cannot condemn something just because it falls outside of his or her own personal taste, or because it seems "cool" to be cynical. Each subject must be judged on its own merit.

The exercise then moves into a bit of show and tell. A piece of music is played that most students would not like—perhaps opera or avant garde jazz. The students then talk about what they heard. Was there *any* part of it that they liked? Could that appreciation be used to build an effective piece of criticism? Whether or not they liked it, did they feel it was skillfully executed? The next step is to have them use the Web to research the style of music and the performer or composer.

After they've spent some time researching, they should write a two- to three-paragraph review of the piece (playing it for them again now that they are educated on the style of music). Give them cues to listen for, or places where they might need help hearing the nuance of a certain instrument or voice.

The final step in this exercise is to then show them a review of the piece they heard. How did a professional writer interpret the music? Do they agree with the writer? Where do they disagree?

# SCREENWRITING

*by* NOAH HAWLEY

1 SESSION, 3 HOURS

SCREENWRITING IS VERY DIFFERENT FROM EVERY OTHER FORM OF WRITING, and not just because there's a possibility a famous actor will say your words while viewers stuff their faces with popcorn. Screenwriting requires an economy of language. There's no time to linger—you have to keep it moving. In novels, the rule is "Show, don't tell." But in movies, that's *exactly* what you have to do. This class teaches you to do it well.

Screenplays can take a long time to write, so we do the fast version. The assignment: have each student create a list of characters and a script outline, then pitch their movie to the class. Pitching is actually a really important skill. So much of the movie business is about the pitch. It's really rooted in the oral storytelling tradition, and it's a great way to practice storytelling skills. If you want the real Hollywood experience, let the whole class give feedback.

The handout shows you how to put a pitch together in three easy steps.

## SUPERTEACHER BONUS ACTIVITY

Have the students write a script for a 2-minute movie. They can collaborate or write their own. Then film it!

# HOW TO PITCH A MOVIE IN THREE EASY STEPS

**STEP 1: CHARACTERS**
The first thing you need to figure out is who you want your movie to be about. A bank robber? A spy? A cheerleader with a secret?

You also need supporting characters: friends, an antagonist, and maybe a love interest. Create a list of all the characters, with a brief description of each.

For all your main characters, you want to figure out who they are, why they do the things they do, and why we're dropping into their lives at this particular moment. Why now? The more a character seems to be in crisis, the more vital the movie becomes. A movie about a bank robber on the day he has to get a bunion removed probably wouldn't be very interesting, but on the day he risks everything for a heist, you're pretty much guaranteed some excitement.

A final note: never name a character Jack. There are way too many Jacks in the movie already. Bob, Bill, Randy, fine—but no more Jacks.

**STEP 2: OUTLINE**
Once you've figured out who your characters are, figure out their story. This means making an outline. In novels, you can sometimes skip this step, but screenplays really have to be outlined first. Outlining helps you see how each scene moves the plot forward. Unlike fiction, every scene in a movie has to be there for a reason.

The basic screenplay structure is three acts. In Act I, you want to introduce all your main characters and make us care about them. Introduce the problem, and end the act on a high point, with things going either really well, or really badly. As the movie proceeds, it's like bringing water to a boil. The energy and stakes have to go up. You're always dealing with setbacks. So in Act II, the tension builds. There are more and more problems. The end of Act II is the biggest setback of all, the crisis. Act III brings the story to a resolution.

Each act breaks down into many scenes. So your outline will be approximately 6–10 pages long and look like this:

**ACT I**
*Scene 1:* Joe, a down-on-his-luck bank robber trying to go straight, is finishing up a hard day at work as a school janitor. On the way to the parking lot he says hi to a student in worn-out clothes—they seem to be friendly—and gives him a couple bucks.

*Scene 2:* Joe tries to start his car, an old beater, but it's dead.

*Scene 3:* Joe tries to take the bus, but realizes he's out of cash—he gave his last dollar to the kid.

*Scene 4:* We see Joe finally arriving at his run-down apartment, obviously exhausted from a long walk home. On the door is a notice for eviction of nonpayment of rent. Joe looks like he can't take one more thing.

. . . and so on. You'll probably need sixty or so scenes, depending on length.

Each scene breaks down into "beats." "Beats" are the moments, the actions in the movie: this happens, and then this happens, and then this happens. Those are your beats. So in our bank robber movie, he has a hard day at work (beat). He picks up after some rude students and mutters to himself, "I used to make $10,000 for an hour's work" (beat). We see his prison tattoo (beat). We see him be nice to a kid (beat). Each beat establishes something.

As you create scenes, it's important to think about *why* your characters do what they do, or else their actions will ring false. What's the backstory on these characters? What's their motivation? If your main character is going to rob a bank, we need to know why. What does he need the money for? Is he just in it for the thrill? What's worth such a big risk?

The other important point to remember is that you have to keep things moving. In each scene, you want to drop in as late as you can and get out fast. You don't need to show your protagonist driving to the bank, looking for a parking spot, locking the car, and so forth. Just cut in at the latest possible moment. The viewer can fill in the rest. Less is more, especially when it comes to dialogue. Audiences get stuff really fast. Sometimes a glance can replace a whole speech. And you don't have to have a character explain that she's a scientist if you just show her working in a lab.

As you do your outline you'll figure out the overall arc of the story. You start off with characters who are trying to accomplish something, and you need to decide if they'll succeed or fail—they rob the bank and get away, or they get caught. Endings are tough in any medium, but especially in movies, which tend to be more black-and-white. Your movie needs to resolve itself, but it doesn't have to end happily, and it doesn't have to end the way we expect. What you want is the resolution for the character. So even if our bank robber doesn't get what he thought he wanted—he doesn't get the money—his internal crisis is resolved when he realizes that he'll take the girl over the money. It's sort of amazing what you can do when people care about your characters. You don't have to satisfy their fondest wishes. He doesn't have to get rich if he's going to be happy.

**STEP 3: PITCH IT!**
Once you've got your characters and your outline, it's time to prepare your pitch. A good pitch will make others love this movie as much as you do.

Your pitch should be 3–5 minutes long and should start off with a bang. You need to hook the listeners in right away with a character we care about. Keep them interested with a mystery, a problem, an exciting possibility. Using your outline, give the movie's story, but in the most interesting way possible. You probably don't need to mention the scene where the bank robber sits in his car, casing the Savings & Loan. But the scene where everything goes wrong (the alarm is going off, the bank employees are not cooperating, and the thief is having an asthma attack) is definitely something you should mention.

Screenwriting is a very collaborative medium, and you generally get a lot of input on your work. Sometimes it's beneficial. Sometimes it's frustrating: "I love your bank robber movie. What if it wasn't about a bank robber?" People will rewrite your work, and your ego has to live in a different place, but sometimes the criticism is helpful. You have to be flexible. That doesn't mean you compromise on what makes the movie what it is, but sometimes criticism will lead you in an unexpected, better direction.

And if you end up with a pitch that the class loves, maybe you should think about turning it into an actual script. Good luck.

# HOW TO WRITE A GHOST STORY

*by* LISA BROWN AND ADELE GRIFFIN

1 SESSION, **90** MINUTES

GHOST STORIES MAKE GREAT WRITING EXERCISES, BECAUSE THEY'RE EVEN better when they're short. Their creepy otherworldliness counteracts the boredom of everyday life. That's why people want to believe in ghosts. It makes life more exciting. It's also incredibly freeing. If you've decided to believe in a ghost, you've decided to that the world is full of things you can't easily explain.

Another great thing about ghost stories is you don't have to worry too much about a seamless plot. Ghost stories can be successful if they just concentrate on setting and atmosphere. And you don't have to worry too much about the ending, either. It's better if you don't. The best ghost stories don't have a cut-and-dried denouement or explanation; they're unresolved.

A ghost story is *not* necessarily a horror story. In a horror story there's a lot more physical violence and there's usually a resolution. In good ghost stories there's more ambiguity, and the drama can be more psychological than physical. In other words: inner thoughts, not innards.

Ghost stories are certainly about fear, but they're also about hope. A ghost story, after all, is a life-after-death story. With all our technology, we've had no breakthroughs on death. Death is still as terrifying now as it was thousands of years ago. Ghost stories are an author's attempt to come to terms with that.

In this lesson plan students will practice writing their own terrifying ghost stories. First, they'll need a few things, detailed on the following handout. Then they'll do the exercises below. Now, turn the page . . . if you dare.

## An Exercise

Ask your students to share a real-life ghost story. Not something they heard around the fire at summer camp involving a serial killer, but something that actually happened, to them, a friend, or a family member, something that no one can quite explain.

What makes it scary?

What could you change to make it scarier?

## Another Exercise

Invite the students to imagine that they are ghosts. Ask them: What would you do if you needed to get a message to somebody? What would be important enough that you would need to make contact with the living?

## Now That Everyone Is Properly Spooked . . .

. . . it's time to write your ghost stories. Distribute the student handout on the following page to get them started. Turn them loose, then come back and share frights.

# WHAT EVERY GHOST STORY NEEDS

**1. A SETTING**
When and where does your story take place?

It's fine to start with an ooky-spooky house. You can begin with those old clichés. It's a great opportunity to bring in creepy and fun historical elements, too.

Remember, in many cases you might need two separate settings, one for the ghost, and one for his hapless, haunted victim. There's even nice time-travel-y feeling when you juxtapose an old ghost with a modern locale; an old tragedy existing at the same time as a contemporary setting.

**2. THE GHOST**
Who is he or she? How did he or she die? Why would he or she need to come back and haunt someone? (Or, to put it another way, What does this ghost want?)

**3. THE HAUNTED**
Who is he or she? Why is he or she being haunted? Is it simply because he or she is in the wrong place at the wrong time, or is he or she being haunted for personal reasons? Did he or she do something to make the ghost angry, either in life or in death?

**4. LIMITATIONS**
Your story will be more focused if you set parameters for your ghost. A ghost is more interesting if he or she isn't all-powerful, but exists within a circle of specific abilities. Here are some creepy limitations:

The ghost can be seen, but not heard.

The ghost can be felt, but not seen.

The ghost can be heard, but not felt or seen.

The ghost only appears in photographs.

The ghost only appears reflected in mirrors or glass.

The ghost can move little things around.

The ghost can move things around that are too heavy for humans to move.

The ghost can leave messages on paper or chalkboards, or by tracing words into the dust on old furniture.

The ghost can be heard, but only says the same thing over and over again.

The ghost can be heard, but only makes noises like screaming or crying.

The ghost can appear in dreams.

## 5. A PLOT

Believe it or not, a good ghost story doesn't always need a beginning, middle, and end. It's more important that it has a creepy setup, a ghostly event, a nervous reaction, and a (partial) explanation.

An example: A girl goes away for the summer to an old house in the country owned by a grumpy uncle. She begins to hear crying in the middle of the night, and finds messages scrawled in lipstick on the mirrors. Her uncle refuses to believe that anything out of the ordinary is going on. One of the lipstick messages tells the girl to look in the garden. When she does, she finds the skeleton of her uncle's old fiancée, presumed missing for thirty years.

OK, that's very simple, but you get the picture.

## 6. SOME GOOD SCARES

Now, think about what kinds of things scare you. Some hints:

*Details are scary.* Start with things that exist in real life, then twist them. Slightly. The closer your story feels to a "real" account, the scarier it will seem. Details build tension, and details have their foot firmly planted in the real world. Stephen King understands this—he tends to create an almost hypernormal world—so that when something is off, you're so immersed you barely notice it. The more normal the world is, the more upsetting it is when something out of the ordinary happens.

*Uncertainty is scary.* Things are most definitely scarier when they are unexplained. If you have too good an explanation for all the ghostly goings-on, it becomes less frightening. It takes a certain amount of self-control to write a good ghost story. It's easier and more tempting to explain things, but it's usually better if you don't.

*Almost-but-not-quite is scary.* Think about how scary it is to see something out of the corner of your eye, or to reach out and touch something that you can't see and can't identify.

*The natural world not working the way it's supposed to is scary.* Cold when it shouldn't be cold, hot when it shouldn't be hot. Being able to look through something that should be solid, or seeing shadows without anything there to cast them. It's also good when things are just a tiny bit off (see "Almost-but-not-quite," above). Not completely off—you're not in a sci-fi or fantasy world. You're in the real world, but something is a little odd.

*Unexplained knowledge is scary.* Someone knowing something that he or she could not possibly know unless the ghost has whispered in his or her ear is very unsettling.

*A narrator with bad judgment is scary.* It makes the reader tense, which is a good thing. It's like shouting at the movie screen. Don't open that door! Don't go in that creepy house! A narrator in a ghost story is constantly doing ill-advised things.

*You are scary.* Well, not really, or at least not all the time—but when deciding to write about something spooky, you should take a trip through your own imagination and figure out your most vivid "point of departure." What gets your heart beating? An enclosed space? A choppy sea? A box of broken toys? Remember, a ghost story is just another way of handing off your worst nightmare to others. Kind of like the flu.

*Flipping expectations is scary.* Or fun, at least. Lead your readers down a path, letting them believe in one thing, and then get the jump on them with an entirely different outcome.

That's all you need to get started. Now go! What are you waiting for? You're not scared, are you?

**BONUS FUN**
Set part of your ghost story in the historical past.

Write a letter to or from a ghost. Then answer it.

*For a group:* Find an ordinary object and imagine that it has a mysterious past. Pass around the object, with each of your friends contributing to its lore.

Write page 128 of a ghostly tale.

List off ten things that make a perfect ghost recipe: a dining room table, a broken mirror, a love letter, a lost marble, an attic, a chandelier, a blind boy named Percival . . . whatever you like. Can you invent a story with all of these elements?

# 826 UNPLUGGED

## SONGWRITING

*by* CHRIS PERDUE

1 SESSION, 2 HOURS

MANY OF US REMEMBER HOW PASSIONATE we were about music in our teens. Everything is changing so fast, your parents have no idea, you're too shy to talk to that girl or guy, and you feel like you're the first person in the history of this wretched earth to feel so confused and misunderstood. That is, until a certain song or album or artist says it all for you. You and Morrissey are right . . . *there.* Music can express feelings in a way that's unparalleled by any other medium. But getting started writing songs can be hard on your own. Students usually have the opportunity to do a fair bit of creative writing in school, and there are music ensembles, but there aren't so many chances to take a shot at writing a song, and to get good feedback on your creation. To be sure, although the desire to learn is definitely there, it can be challenging to get students to open up and participate in a songwriting class. Sharing your writing can be a big step in itself, but the idea of *performing* a song in front of your peers can be pretty frightening.

This lesson is designed to help students get over all of that. One of the most important things to learn with songwriting, as with a lot of things, is to not take it too seriously. As a group, we'll come up with lyrics and melodies together, so no one is in the hot seat for too long.

First, the lyrics. We use a writing exercise called the Exquisite Corpse (see Lesson 45 for another lesson plan that uses this method). On a blank sheet of paper, someone starts by writing a phrase at the top. The next person writes his or her phrase below it, but before it's passed, he or she folds the paper over so the next person sees only one line before. And so on, until everyone writes a line. The exercise gets its name from a verse that originated one of the first times the game was played: "The exquisite corpse will drink the young wine." It often makes things more interesting to write sentence fragments that the next person has to complete. Or, devise a rhyme scheme: number the lines, and specify that every even-numbered line has to rhyme with the odd-numbered line before it. Obviously, the finished product will most likely be all over the place. That's okay: the point is to have a lot of imagery and lyrical ideas with which to work.

Now, the students will split into groups. Groups of three to five will probably work best. Assign each group a key for their song, or let them decide for themselves. This will depend on the level of musical experience of the groups; for students with little musical experience, just stick with C major.

Next, each group writes down everyone's phone number. They then translate these numbers into the musical notes of their scale. For example, if your group is in the key of C, 1=C, 2=D, 3=E, and so on. For zero, use the leading tone—in this case it's B; 9 is an octave above 2. So, in C, the phone number 867–5309 would be C-A-B-G-E-B-D. The groups should play each melody to see which ones they like, and then they can start working on setting the lyrics from the Exquisite Corpse exercise to these melodies. At this point, you can help each group build chord progressions for their song based on their chosen melodies and their experience level.

The students should be well on their way. This exercise will supply them with plenty of seeds for their song, and they can take it in any direction they like.

## SUPERTEACHER BONUS ACTIVITY

Record the songs, and issue a class CD!

# SPORTSWRITING

## THE LIFE

### *by* SAM SILVERSTEIN AND JASON TURBOW

3 SESSIONS, 2 HOURS EACH

THE CAREERS OF PROFESSIONAL ATHLETES are measured in years, perhaps decades. Sportswriting, however, is a life. This workshop is meant to open students' eyes to the world of professional opportunities surrounding the games they watch.

Access to ballplayers is the hook. For our workshop the students are granted media credentials and conduct interviews in a major league clubhouse, just like the pros. But the workshop is not all fun and games. In Session 1, we sort through possible angles and prepare for our interviews. Session 2 takes place at the ballpark, and consists of collecting interviews and organizing notebooks. In Session 3, we read and react, as a group, to feature articles generated by the students in the interim. Professionalism is paramount, and deadlines are enforced. Just like in real life.

We've the class on access to the San Francisco Giants, but theoretically any sport franchise will do the trick. It doesn't have to be a professional team; even Little League or the school badminton team can offer great stories. The key is a working relationship with the media relations manager, whose job boils down

to protecting his or her athletes from distractions. You will need to earn the manager's trust to have any chance of prying a credential or three from his or her grasp.

You may also need to recruit some extra chaperones for Session 2. It minimizes strays at the ballpark, and keeps the students in line. The potential for disaster in a major league clubhouse is not to be minimized. And the entire point is for the students to have a good first impression of the profession. They can learn the sparky parts later.

## Session 1

In our first session we describe our jobs and tell the students what a sportswriter's life is really like. Yes, there's a lot of sports—but there's also a lot of writing. We discuss the sports beat versus features and columns, big markets versus small, high school sports versus the major leagues, and how to break into the business. It might be worth making a call to your local newspaper to see if a sportswriter can come tell the class a bit about the job.

Next we talk "chops." We discuss what makes a good piece. How do you know a good story when you see one? How do you find an angle? How do you balance entertainment value versus substance? We look through the sports section for good examples. We ask what grabs their interest and why. Then we touch on the basics of solid sportswriting, for example, how to structure a story and write a good lead. For more tips, www.highschooljournalism.org is a great resource.

Then we get the students ready to start writing themselves. We give them an assignment: prepare to interview a sports figure. If you have access to a local team, the students can pick a local player. If not, they'll have the fun of conducting an imaginary interview, so the sky's the limit—they can interview Ted Williams or Babe Ruth or anyone they like.

Before we turn them loose we go over interview basics. We tell them how to land an interview and how to act once you do. The first step is research. You need to find out as much as you can about your subject. Good places to start looking are on the Internet and in newspaper archives. Then we talk about writing good questions. Questions with yes or no answers are out, as are really obvious ones. You want to ask the relevant questions that no one else has thought of. You also want to ask questions that lead to other questions. It's important to keep the conversation going. Maintain good eye contact. Really *listen* for the story. Maybe you go in thinking you're interviewing a player about his batting average and the discussion veers off toward injuries. Maybe he has a past you didn't know about. Maybe *that's* your story instead. We also discuss taking notes versus taping (both have their conveniences and hassles). Finally, we spend a little time on etiquette and dress. We know Oscar Madison was a sportswriter, but you probably don't want to show up to your interview dressed like him.

Their homework for tonight: do research on their interview subject and write up interview questions.

## Session 2

For our second class we bring the students into the press box at the Giants game. Yep, this is pretty much the best class ever. But even if you don't have an in with a major league team, you can still have a sportswriting experience. Have the class convene at a school game or local sports event. Remind them that they're sportswriters for the night, so they need to dress and act the part.

They're there to get a story. They can either report on the game or interview a local player (and use the questions they prepared in the previous assignment). They should be taking notes and thinking of good angles.

Their homework: write the story. It should be 800–1,200 words (just like a newspaper feature). They submit via e-mail against a real deadline.

## Session 3

In the last session, they get to experience the editing process just like a real sportswriter. This is definitely not as much fun as hanging out with ballplayers and eating nachos, but it's good for students to know that even the pros go through this process. Editors are like coaches for your writing, and they want you to win.

In our class we use peer feedback. Each student reads another student's work out loud, then we discuss it as a group. Was the angle successful? Were there good quotes and supporting details? Was the story well constructed, and did it hold the reader's attention? Then the teacher weighs in. If peer feedback sounds like a recipe for disaster with your students, you can just meet with them one-on-one.

Then they revise just like real writers. Once they've got a polished piece, it's time to think about publication. We discuss outlets for their work: the school paper, the local paper, other publications. We show them an example of a pitch letter, and then we turn them loose, on their way to sportswriting stardom—or, at the very least, their first byline.

# HOW TO WRITE A FAN LETTER WITHOUT GETTING A RESTRAINING ORDER

*by* LISA LUTZ

1 SESSION, 90 MINUTES

MANY WRITERS—EVEN SOME EXPERIENCED ONES—THINK OF WRITING mostly as a way of expressing themselves, as opposed to communicating with other human beings. Having your students write a fan letter is a great way to encourage them to express their feelings while also considering those of the reader. This lesson is intended to explain both what a fan letter is and what it isn't. The exercises are meant to be both sincere and tongue-in-cheek, giving the students a creative and fun outlet to figure out the right balance of enthusiasm and the appropriate manner in which to share their feelings with a complete stranger. The handout provides a quick course on the nature of fan letters, three class exercises, and an extra-credit assignment.

# WHAT IS A FAN LETTER?

Sometimes we like a person so much that we simply must put our feelings into words and send those words off to the object of our affection. If this person we admire is not a close acquaintance, this type of epistle is called a fan letter. While it may seem simple enough, a fan letter is a delicate art that requires an understanding of human nature, etiquette, spell check, and basic Internet research.

The most salient ingredient in a fan letter is the understanding that there's nothing in it for you. A true fan letter is intended to compliment the recipient and leave it at that. If your expectations are to develop a lifelong friendship with the musician, author, actor, politician, or other celebrity, then you have already failed this assignment. The intention of the letter should be to make its recipient feel valued, to express the pleasure he or she has brought to your life.

Sometimes we find fault even with people we greatly admire. How many times have you listened to the third album of your favorite band and wished they'd stop branching out? It is absolutely your right to write a letter expressing your disappointment, but that, my friend, is not a fan letter. That is a *you've-disappointed-me letter*. Please make sure you understand the distinction.

Another pitfall in fan letters is not finding the right balance between fan and superfan (a.k.a. stalker). You want to make the recipient of the letter feel good, not afraid. But sometimes, if you like someone so much you need to write it down and send off a missive, you lose perspective and go too far. That is perhaps the biggest mistake that most authors of fan letters make.

Here are a few exercises that might help you exercise some restraint.

**CLASS EXERCISE**

**1. Write a letter to a celebrity in whom you have a decided lack of interest. For my example I will use Justin Bieber (you are free to write to someone else):**

Dear Justin Bieber (Mr. Bieber would also be fine):

Hello. We have never met. I doubt we ever will. Honestly, I'm cool with that. I only recently learned of your existence, but your existence is fairly recent compared to mine, so I think that's understandable. You have certainly done quite well for yourself and have made many powerful friends. Congratulations. I am happy for you. I must admit that I am unfamiliar with your music, but many people are quite fond of it, I hear. Especially young girls. Your parents must be so proud.

I saw on my Internet homepage that you got a haircut recently. I think I like it, but I was impressed by how long you managed to rock the bowl cut.

I wish you the best in all your future endeavors.

Sincerely,

Lisa Lutz

Please note that I began the letter formally to show respect. I offered encouragement and complimented his hair. Since I do not like his music, I stayed off that subject. When writing a sincere fan letter, there still may be things you don't like about your idol. Keep them to yourself. I assure you, if your admired has a mother, a father, an ornery attorney, or other fans, they've heard it all.

*[On a personal note, if you are writing to an author, and the book has been out for more than six months, please, please, please do not mention that you've spotted a typo. She's heard about it already. Probably at least a dozen times.]*

Now that you've learned restraint, it's time to move on to the next exercise.

**CLASS EXERCISE**

**2. Practice writing a fan letter to someone you may like quite a bit, but who is not a celebrity. For instance, one of the following individuals:**

- Librarian
- Postal worker
- Bus driver
- Instructor of this class
- A fellow classmate

For my example, I will use a bus driver.

> Dear Female Bus Driver on the 49 Muni Line:
>
> I was riding your bus just last Thursday and I have to tell you, I think you are awesome. When the fare-ditcher got on the bus, you made a valiant effort to make her pay up because we all have to pay. But once you realized it was a lost cause, you patiently let it go. Her excuse was that the government had invaded her body. While I think that was unlikely, and you seemed to agree, there was no way to prove otherwise in the middle of rush-hour traffic. You then were kind enough to apologize to the other passengers for the delay, which I thought gracious, but unnecessary, and then we were on our way.
>
> Best wishes from a devoted passenger,
> Lisa Lutz

Now you're ready for the real deal. I don't want to influence your own fan letter experience, so I will not provide an example. However, I will give you a list of dos and don'ts to review before you embark on your assignment.

## Don't

- Mention that you live near the recipient of the letter.
- Use words like "die," "kill," "death," and the like.
- Ask for money.
- Suggest you go for coffee.
- Mistake your fan letter recipient for someone else. When in doubt, Google.
- Mention your criminal past.
- Mention your idol's criminal past.
- Send edible items.

## Do

- Use spell check. You don't want the recipient to feel diminished by the low quality of fans.
- Be specific. Mention a book, song, film, whatever, and why you were fond of it.
- If you live far away, totally let him or her know. If you live in Canada, by all means mention that. For reasons I can't explain Canadians generally come off as unthreatening.
- If it's an e-mail fan letter and you get a response, it's fine to respond again if the e-mail includes a question or an invitation to respond. If it is merely a thank-you for a fan letter, responding to that would be like writing a thank-you letter to a thank-you letter. Please do not set this never-ending cycle in motion.

Congratulations! You now have all the tools you need to write a simple, nonthreatening, noninsulting fan letter. Remember, if you work hard, stay in school (or drop out at just the right moment), and find infamy yourself, one day you too might be the recipient of one.

### CLASS EXERCISE

**3. Write fan letter.**

### EXTRA CREDIT:

- Write a fan letter to yourself that you would like to receive.
- Write a fan letter to yourself that you would NOT like to receive.

# (45)

# EXQUISITE STORY LINES

*by* JEREMY WILSON AND KAIT STEELE

**1 SESSION, 2 HOURS**

SOMETIMES THE BEST STORIES ARE spontaneous, and there's nothing like a little collaboration to get those creative juices flowing. In this workshop, students work in teams to create offbeat, original stories. Using the technique of the Exquisite Corpse, this class emphasizes the importance of character traits and the parts of a story, as well.

We start the class with a brief discussion of the Exquisite Corpse, a popular parlor game that the Surrealists used to create art at the beginning of the twentieth century. Players begin with part of a drawing or poem, then pass their creation to their neighbor, who adds the next part of the image or composition—generally without seeing much or any of what has already been done. This repeats until everyone has had a turn. The result is a hodgepodge of spontaneous art, which is often entertaining, and sometimes filled with surprising connections. André Breton, the principal founder of the Surrealists, called these games "the most fabulous source of unfindable images." We couldn't agree more.

After a bit of discussion on the idea of spontaneous art, students get in teams of three to create their own Exquisite Corpse drawing. (If the class does not divide easily into groups of three, two students may work together. This workshop is all about the serendipity of collaboration!)

In their teams, students count off as "1," "2," and "3," and each is given a piece of drawing paper. Without looking at what their teammates are doing, students will each be responsible for creating a part of their character. **Student 1** will draw the head of a person or animal. **Student 2** will draw the arms and torso. **Student 3** will draw the legs and feet (or fins or claws or roller skates). Students then tape their drawings together to see what they have created, with incredibly original and often hilarious results.

In their teams, students come up with a list of specific character traits and descriptions about their character to share with the class. Since they've already done a bang-up job of creating a visual representation of their character, we often emphasize that the character traits they compile should really be about what makes these characters tick. What are their characters' desires or fears? What are their secrets? What do they do for fun? What song do they hum while they're making their favorite sandwich? The more specific, the better! These details will ultimately be the connecting factors in the stories the students create. Once students have given their characters some winning traits, each team takes a turn introducing their character to the rest of the class.

As a group, we then go over what makes a solid story line, emphasizing which parts of a basic story typically fall in the beginning (introduction of character and setting), the middle (rising action, conflict, and climax), and the end (resolution, falling action, and conclusion). This is also a great time to ask students what makes a story interesting to *them*. Is it figurative language and sensory details? Action and suspense? More humor than you can shake a stick at? See what advice students have for each other on how to create a truly epic tale.

Once we have our story arc solidly in mind, students return to their teams and simultaneously create a story about their character using the following prompts:

Student 1 writes THE BEGINNING: This was going to be a big day for (Character).

Student 2 writes THE MIDDLE: But as (Character) discovered, there was a major problem.

Student 3 writes THE END: (Character) knew what he or she had to do.

Parts of the story are loosely connected by the common character, with students using their character traits to help with description and motivation. Because students don't see what their teammates are writing, these tales are often bizarre and always amusing.

Once students have completed their first story, we repeat the activity with a twist. In this version, all three students sit in a circle and simultaneously write THE BEGINNING to their story, starting with the same line: *This was going to be a big day for (Character).* Once everyone has written a beginning, students pass their beginnings to the teammate on their left. After they have taken a moment to read what their neighbor has written, students continue with THE MIDDLE: *But as (Character) discovered, there was a major problem.* Students pass the stories to their left once more, and each teammate reads only the middle written by his or her neighbor. Once everyone has done this, it's time to write THE END: *(Character) knew what he or she had to do.*

At the end of both activities, each team will have four stories written about their unique character: one created through simultaneous writing and three created by passing stories around the group. Have students share these with the class and discuss how writing worked differently in each method. Which did they prefer? What was cool or challenging about either activity? How was it different working on a collaborative story instead of writing independently? The first method might not make sense, but it often opens students up to the fun and the uncanny connections of spontaneous writing. The second method especially emphasizes the importance of a solid story arc and how it works. Both activities highlight the power of compelling character traits and encourage students to let their ideas come from unlikely places. With this in mind, students should leave the workshop filled with a great mix of knowledge and exquisite inspiration.

# SOUL PROWLERS

## THE ART OF WRITING NEWSPAPER PROFILES

*by* RONA MARECH

3 SESSIONS, 90 MINUTES EACH
MATERIALS: *A visitor to interview*

WHAT COULD BE MORE INTERESTING for a reporter than writing about people—about their quirks and longings, contradictions and flaws, dreams and disappointments? Celebrities can be fascinating (though beware, they may not be). And ordinary-seeming people often have extraordinary, heroic stories—it just takes curiosity and will to excavate them. In this class, students learn about how to identify good subjects, find inspiration in the details of a life, and write compelling stories about both regular and famous people.

## Session 1: How to Interview

What is a profile? Students usually know a profile involves using words to paint a portrait of someone. I like to throw out a range of examples—stories I've written or read—to show the wide world of possibility. I've written profiles about such people as a former football star who ended up at a local shelter, a blues harmonica player, a mother of sixteen children, a renowned coffee roaster, a successful sculptor with Down syndrome, and a fish salesman.

What are some profiles that students have read recently? What drew them in? What details were conspicuously missing? What famous person would they love to interview?

With the ice broken, you can get down to the first order of business: conducting interviews. How do they do it?

For the rest of the session, they are going to imagine they are newspaper reporters. An editor has just handed them a profile assignment—what's the very first thing they should do? This is not an open-ended question! They should always, always, check the clips and find out everything they can about their subject. Then they must prepare a list of interview questions.

SOME DISCUSSION TOPICS TO COVER

- How do they listen and write at the same time?

- Should they write down everything a speaker is saying or should they be selective in their note taking?

- What kind of questions best draw out a subject?

☞ What are the advantages and disadvantages of using a tape recorder?

☞ What's the difference between interviewing a celebrity or a public official and interviewing a private individual?

### SOME INTERVIEWING TIPS TO COVER

Students should:

☞ Focus on what the source is saying, not on formulating the next question.

☞ Be responsive: ask questions based on what the subject just said.

☞ Feel free to refer to their list of questions (I like to pull it out at the end to make sure I have hit the important items) but avoid being overly rigid about it.

☞ Avoid asking the hardest questions first. It is better to wait until the right moment—likely late in the interview.

☞ Ask a source to repeat a good quote or an important fact if necessary. That's acceptable!

☞ Go over their notes as soon as possible after the interview.

Once students know a few things about interviewing techniques, you can introduce the first activity—an interview with a special guest visitor with whom you've made arrangements in advance. It's fun to snag a journalist—especially a highfalutin' journalist such as someone who, say, covers the White House—but anyone interesting will do. You could invite a local politician, a religious leader, a filmmaker, or an author. Maybe an amazing character who sells doughnuts on the corner has a fascinating life story he is willing to share. Hand out biographical information about the visitor. This could be published stories (if you've got a known or known-ish person) or a LinkedIn profile or a short biography the visitor sent you. Give students time to read the material and prepare questions and then quickly go over them.

OK! They're ready to roll. Make sure they have pens and plenty of paper. Introduce the guest and then hand the floor over to the students. Step in, if necessary, to offer some direction or to make sure everyone is getting a chance to ask at least one question, but they should be able to pull this off on their own. If there is time, use the last minutes of class to debrief. How did it go?

Their homework assignment is to interview someone. It could be a family member or someone from school. It could be a 10-year-old phenom or a 90-year-old with a century's worth of stories. Students should prepare questions in advance and take careful notes they will bring to the next session.

**Additional materials:** Carole Rich's *Writing and Reporting News: A Coaching Method* is an excellent resource. The book has a useful section about interviewing techniques with tips about listening and note taking.

## Session 2: The Elements of a Profile

So how do students turn some scribbled questions and answers into a profile? What does a great profile look like? We start this session by reading a couple samples. One story I have used because it has a very clear structure and tends to intrigue students is a 1992 *Philadelphia Inquirer* piece by Donna St. George about a woman who survived a difficult childhood and went on to become one of the most successful homicide detectives in New Orleans. I also like to use a profile that was published very recently—that day or week.

First: Discuss! Why is the person they just read about a good subject for a profile? What details in the piece are effective? Do the quotes advance the story and add texture to it? What is the function of quotations from sources other than the subject?

Next up: A quickie training in how to write a newspaper story. What is a lead—or "lede," as old-timey newspaper reporters usually put it? (It's the initial hook that entices the reader to continue reading.) What are different kinds of leads writers can use in a feature story? (For example: in a descriptive lead, the writer homes in on a person, place, or event; or in an anecdotal lead, the writer begins with a story.) What is a nut graph—"nut graf" in newspaper parlance? (It's a paragraph explaining the focus or main point of a story. In a profile, the nut graph usually clarifies why readers should care about the subject.) Talk about physical descriptions of subjects— what sort of details are helpful and what is inappropriate? If words are inside quotation marks does that mean the speaker said it *exactly* that way? When should students paraphrase? What makes a strong story ending?

Using the two sample profiles as tools, have students examine the leads, nut graphs, quotes, organization, physical descriptions, and endings. (You can also pass out copies of that day's newspaper and ask them to identify leads and nut graphs for extra practice.)

Finally, go over the interviews they conducted for homework. What did they find out that they didn't know before? Were some questions difficult to ask? Have them share good quotes or anecdotes from their interviews.

At the end of the class, students can begin turning their notes into profiles, starting with a lead and nut graph and picking a quote they want to use high in the story. Slacker alternative: students who didn't do the homework can write about the special guest from the first session.

Homework: Students follow up on the previous assignment by interviewing one or two people who know their profile subject—they could choose a friend (or enemy), a family member, a neighbor, or a colleague. They must take notes, of course, and bring them to the final session.

## Session 3: Putting It All Together

So you've got two options here:

Scenario one: students conducted terrific interviews, took thorough notes, and are gung-ho about writing up profiles, which they can submit to a school newspaper or another publication. Start the session by reviewing their work from the previous week. Ask students to swap papers or read their initial efforts aloud so their peers can offer feedback. Are their leads effectively drawing in readers? Is it clear why readers should give a hoot about the profile subject? Inspired and swimming in fresh ideas, students return to their pieces to write and revise, write and revise. Students should leave with an impressive chunk of a story and enough information to finish their pieces outside of class.

Scenario two: students flaked out, forgot notes, are uninspired by their own interviews, or don't seem to have enough material to write a profile (or part of one) during the session. No worries—skip to plan B. The following activity will give students a chance to practice the whole process of profile writing at high speed.

You will need to come to class with a fairly in-depth question-and-answer style interview you've found in a magazine or another publication. Or, better yet, if you're a journalist, bring in the transcript of an interview you've conducted. Pass out background material on the Q&A subject (you could even include photos if possible) and give students a chance to prepare questions. You know what's coming: the students are the interviewers and you play the role of the interviewee, reading your answers from the article (and fudging or improvising where necessary). They should be scribbling in their notebooks like mad when you're talking, but cut them a break at the end and pass out copies of your script so they can get quotes or other details exactly right. Encourage students to make an outline and then have them dig in and start writing a profile. They should write, write, write as if they're on a deadline. Stop, share leads, give feedback.

It's nice to send students home with copies of one of your favorite profiles—a long and juicy story that says something meaningful about human nature and the world. Hand out a piece you love but don't have time to read in class as an inspiring parting gift!

# HOMESTYLE

## WRITING ABOUT THE PLACE WHERE YOU LIVE

*by* TOM MOLANPHY

1 SESSION, 2 HOURS

IT'S BEEN OUR EXPERIENCE THAT ALL STUDENTS THINK HOME IS HOPELESSLY dull. They could live in a Yemenite ziggurat, an Alaskan igloo, or Versailles, and still report that there was nothing special about it. Although routine can be comforting, it can also pound the imagination like a rubber mallet. This lesson teaches students to see home in a fresh way, to walk through doors and open windows they never noticed, and to find the stories that home holds.

We begin by brainstorming on the board. The abstract notion of home can easily be taken for granted, so the first task is to rediscover why a home became home in the first place. The following questions can help unlock this answer:

☞ Why is home a special place?

☞ What makes a home memorable?

☞ What makes home different from everywhere else?

☞ What's weird about it? Exciting?

☞ What are its secrets?

If discussion lags, I ask what makes our school a "special" place. They usually have something to say about that.

Next, we read page one of Sandra Cisneros's *The House on Mango Street* and ask how home defines us. Would you be different if, say, you'd grown up on a dude ranch? In a New York high-rise? In Buckingham Palace?

Then I distribute the handout and give them their assignment: to write about home. Home can be anywhere: the house they live in, or their block, their city, or a vacation spot they especially love. Encourage small, specific locales, though; the constraints of a place force the students to consider the smallest aspects and avoid sweeping generalizations.

If there's time, I have them break into pairs to discuss the place they call home. A one-on-one discussion with a peer can jiggle the imagination to allow a new perspective on an old place to emerge. After the discussion, the students complete the handout and share their work in class.

Encourage specific detail throughout the process, but remind students that they're not writing an apartment listing for a newspaper. Hinting at the magic of home is the best any of us can do, and students shouldn't shy away from allowing residual mystery to linger in their descriptions. The role of the creative writer is to spark the reader's imagination, not replace it.

# WRITE ABOUT THE PLACE WHERE YOU LIVE

Life's a voyage that's homeward bound.

—Herman Melville

Write about the place you consider home. Here are some things to think about:

- Do the people in your house make that place a home?
- What's the first thing you imagine when you hear the word "home"? Think small and specific.
- What's the most surprising thing about this home?
- How does this home make you feel?
- Pretend you're a visitor and you're seeing this home for the first time. How would you describe it to someone else?

Discuss these questions with a partner, and then write about your home below (or on a separate piece of paper). Remember that everyone has a different concept of home, and that it's up to you to deliver your unique and important concept of home.

_____

_____

_____

_____

_____

_____

_____

_____

_____

_____

_____

# AGITATE! PROPAGANDIZE!

*by* JULIUS DIAZ PANORIŃGAN

1 SESSION, 2 HOURS

MOST OF US THINK OF PROPAGANDA IN a political or nationalistic context; this lesson does not. Although there's much to be gained from understanding political propaganda, widening the scope here, I think, is better for students' overall media literacy and critical media consumption. By the end of this lesson, students will have explored a lot of the things that make propaganda tick, via the production of some of their own.

## Part I: A Brief Introduction (15 minutes)

Here, we're just getting our feet wet. I like to start by asking a class what they think propaganda is. I've been surprised by the responses from even younger students to whom I've taught versions of this lesson. Usually, someone will answer with at the very least a near miss: "It's like in politics when someone tries to make you think a certain way" (OK, that's not a miss at all) or "It's sort of like advertising." Take this opportunity to have a little discussion, making sure to hit the following three points:

☞ Propaganda is about ideas, unlike advertising, which is about products.

☞ It's usually political in nature.

☞ It's neither always political nor always misleading. In theory, it's not always necessarily a bad thing. I provide the Merriam-Webster definition: "The spreading of ideas, information, or rumor for the purpose of helping or injuring an institution, a cause, or a person." (If someone wants to spread get-out-the-vote propaganda, it's not necessarily bad/unfair/partial/partisan. Of course, it is if it's tied to a particular cause.)

Knowing what propaganda is offers a bridge into demonstrating how it works. I like to have a bunch of examples on hand. It's pretty easy to find wartime propaganda or anti-communist propaganda, which you should definitely get, but I like to include these flu materials from the CDC: www.cdc.gov/flu/freeresources/additional_print.htm.

Use the examples to illustrate the following important point:

☞ In practice, propaganda's usually a bad thing. Information is often nonexistent, incomplete, or, worst of all, intentionally misleading.

For a good chunk of the flu propaganda, for instance, the information is usually very much oversimplified.

## Part II: Warming Up (45 minutes)

Before starting, I find it very important to set boundaries for the remainder of the lesson. For students who are still in middle school, I have everyone recite the following Propagandist's Pledge:

> I do so solemnly swear,
>
> knowing that the power of propaganda may be used for deception and evil,
>
> that I will use what I learn in this class only for good,
>
> or, at worst, for mild-to-moderate mischief.

Your mileage may vary. Do what's appropriate for your students, whether it be this playful pledge or some snappy direct guideline setting.

Next, take about 5 minutes to let your students think of causes to propagandize for or against, and then another 5 to let them share with the larger group. This part of the lesson runs smoothly enough.

And now, we start to reveal some of propaganda's secrets.

I put the following three Greek words on the board, in very large letters: ἦθος (ethos), λόγος (logos), and πάθος (pathos), and a give a brief explanation of each.

- Ethos is an appeal that relies on using the speaker's authority or character.

- Logos is an appeal using reasoning and logic.

- Pathos is an appeal to the audience's emotion.

Then I ask which the class thinks propaganda relies on, and they correctly answer pathos every time.

At this point, for fun, I like to show one or two video clips. One has to do with advertising, not propaganda, but it gets the point across. It's *Sesame Street*'s send-up of *Mad Men*: www.youtube.com/watch?v=YgvKCfZqxrQ. The other is most definitely propaganda related; it's Dwight's speech at the paper convention, from "Dwight's Speech," a second-season episode of the U.S. version of *The Office*. Both are a little silly, but neither is far from the truth.

Now, take 10–12 minutes and have your class come up with a list of emotions. Things will start out pretty simple—happiness, anger—and usually they'll move on to things more complicated and nuanced—regret, nostalgia, patriotism. Ask your students which are the strongest emotions, and point out how great they would be in propaganda. Happy families with puppies sway minds very well, as do regular joes who are angry about the way things are. Even regret's useful; if a large section of the population regrets voting for someone or something in the last election, you can definitely tap into that. This exercise may take a little thinking on your feet, but it's worth it.

Next, give the students about 15 minutes to make a rough sketch of a propaganda poster, one that uses emotional imagery and goes light on the actual information. Bonus points for catchy slogans. Also give them a few minutes to share with their classmates.

## Part III: Oh, Boy (What Have We Done?) (60 minutes)

Once the poster fun is over, we've got even more work to do. I hope you have more propaganda examples, 'cause you'll need 'em. (I've got some for you too.)

Spend another 15–20 minutes going over more propaganda examples. You'll want to hit the following points:

☞ *Propaganda* uses meaningless, empty, overly general language. For this one, I like to pull out the Obama and McCain campaign posters from the 2008 election: www.photoshophow.com/photoshop-john-mccains-campaign-poster. I make a huge show, generally, and flail my arms about, asking, "What does 'Change we can believe in' mean?! What does 'Peace is born of wisdom' mean?!" The answer: they don't really mean anything, and neither candidate makes a case for why he's an advocate for change, or a wise mediator, or whatever either claims to be.

☞ *Symbolism.* This point was already touched on in the poster section, but here, it has to do more with speeches. Look up some grade-level-appropriate propaganda speeches (or queue up Dwight's speech again) and point out the symbolism, often of patriotism, war, and/or victory. This is the usual symbolic route, and though there are others, isn't it great to feel like a winner?

☞ *Here's the big one: **fear.*** All you need to do here, probably, is revisit examples from earlier in the lesson. So much of the best propaganda (in the sense of being effective) preys on people's fears. My favorite example to bring up here is the "Are you at risk?" flu poster. Even though it's for a good cause, it uses some shady propaganda techniques.

At this point in the class, you're free to set your students loose. Once again, they'll be propagandizing for some cause, but the medium will be different. There are two options that work here; you can give one or both. You can have your students work on a propaganda pamphlet, which builds on the poster idea but requires some additional planning of pacing and narrative. (Classic example: the cover and first inside flap paint a dystopian future; the inside presents a vision of utopia led by me.) Alternately, have your students write a speech, where their goal is to say as little of substance as possible while taking the audience on an emotional rollercoaster of their design.

# TASTY MEDICINE FOR WRITER'S BLOCK

## MINDFUL WRITING EXERCISES

BRAD WOLFE AND REBECCA STERN

**4 SESSIONS, 10 MINUTES EACH**
**MATERIALS:** *See each activity's instructions*

HOW OFTEN DO YOU GET TO TRULY TASTE your food, savoring and experiencing each morsel as it turns in your mouth? How often do you really listen to the multitude of sounds that constantly surround you? If your life is busy and fast-paced, like ours, you probably don't get to slow down and take in all that's around you very frequently. And chances are, your students have never consciously done these things before.

Being hyper-aware of your senses allows you to notice minute details that normally whiz right by. Your students' writing will become stronger if they learn to first recognize, and then capture on paper, these microscopic feelings, smells, sights, and sounds.

The following activities combine creative writing with mindfulness practice, thus helping your students to become more aware, both in their everyday lives and in their writing. They are designed to take about 10 minutes each, and can be done back-to-back, or on separate days.

We found Jon Kabat-Zinn's definition of mindfulness to be the most succinct and clear. He says, "Mindfulness means paying attention in a particular way: on purpose, in the present moment, and nonjudgmentally." Before you begin the activities, share this quote with your students and ask them what they think Kabat-Zinn means.

These activities also work well when they are framed as an antidote to writer's block. The writer's block rut often occurs because we get stuck in patterns that make life seem dull and uninteresting. However, if we slow down and pay more attention, even to the "normal" elements of our lives, we begin to see them in an entirely new, interesting, and writing-worthy way. Poof! Writer's block averted.

## Activities

### 1. Mindful Eating

The goal of this activity is to show your students that they have the power to control their attention and their focus and that, in doing so, they can taste their food in a new way. In addition, they will write a poem, using descriptive language that will articulate what they tasted, felt, and experienced while they were eating.

**MATERIALS:** *Pick one of the following (or have several available and allow each student to pick one): orange slices, M&Ms, apple slices, chocolate squares, or some other food that can be eaten slowly*
*Timer*
*Paper and pencils or pens*

## PROCEDURE

Tell your students that they are going to receive one small piece of food and that their challenge is not only to eat as slowly as possible, but also to try to focus on the flavors, textures, and feelings in their mouths.

Ask the students how long they think they can keep an M&M (or whatever food you're using) in their mouths. Set the timer for a minute and tell them that during this minute they should put all of their focus and awareness on the food in their mouths.

Next, pass out the food, but tell them not to start because they will all begin at the same time. Once everyone has a morsel, turn the lights down low and tell the students to begin tasting their food.

Once the minute is up, turn the lights on. Tell the students to write down as many words as possible to describe the food they've just eaten—flavors, textures, and so forth. They can also jot down how they were feeling or what they noticed during that minute. Then, ask them what it was like to eat as slowly as possible. Was it a challenge? Easy? Next, ask them to share some of the things that they wrote down. Record their answers on the board.

Finally, have students write a poem or paragraph about what they tasted, felt, experienced. They can use the words that they recorded earlier, or choose new words.

## 2. Hello Left Hand, Meet Right Hand . . . A Conversation Between Dominant and Nondominant

This activity will challenge the students to write with both their dominant and nondominant hands. Studies have shown that writing (or engaging in other fine-motor activities) with the nondominant hand can strengthen and create new neural connections. This activity will also help your students to notice how, by freeing ourselves from the writing routines we take for granted and reverting back to a more "childlike" writing state, we might find ourselves actually thinking differently.

**MATERIALS:** *Pencils and paper*

## PROCEDURE

Explain to the students that they are about to have a conversation with themselves in writing, switching back and forth between hands. A self-interview tends to work best when the dominant hand asks the questions and the nondominant hand responds in detail. Right-handed students, for example, ask questions with their right hand and then move the pen to their left for a response, switching back and forth for each new question and answer. The key is to relax and let the conversation between hands flow as freely as possible. The dominant hand can follow up on the prior question and start a dialogue or ask totally new questions.

At first, the students should not be surprised if the answers are one word or are scribbled. It may take a minute to warm up. It also helps if the students ask themselves open-ended questions. What do you want to do when you grow up and why? What do you really wish you could do that you can't? Suggest asking about a problem they are facing. Keep asking questions! After 10 minutes or so of letting the students write, have a conversation with the class. How did their body and mind feel—did they notice a difference in mind or body when they were writing with the nondominant hand? Were they surprised by any of their answers? What were they surprised by, or what did they discover?

### 3. That Made You Think of WHAT?

This is a fun word-association game that gets students thinking in new ways and shows them how just one word can spark so many different thoughts and ideas.

This activity is meant for classes of about eighteen students. If your class has more than that, you might want to break them into two equal groups.

> **MATERIALS:** *1 four-by-six-inch slip of paper per student (size of paper doesn't really matter; it should just be large enough to write one word on)*
> *Pens or pencils*

#### PROCEDURE

If it's not too disruptive, have your students sit in a circle on the floor—they should bring a pen or pencil with them. Give each student a slip of paper. Pick one student to start. She should write one word down on her paper. It can be any word. Then she passes it to the person next to her. That person reads the word to himself, and is given 10 seconds to write the first word that pops into his head on his slip of paper. He then passes that slip to the next person, and holds on to the slip that was initially passed to him. This continues around the circle until everyone has written a word.

After the last person finishes, ask the student who started to say her word aloud. Then, go around the circle and have each student say the word that he or she wrote, and why he or she wrote that word. For example, if the starting word is "blue," and Charlie went next, writing "Mohawk" on his slip, he should say why blue made him think of a Mohawk (Charlie might say this his brother has a blue Mohawk, so blue made him think of his brother's hair). At the very end, point out the obvious: how completely different the first word or idea was from the last.

### 4. I Can Hear You but I Can't See You! Hearing What We Normally Block Out . . .

This is a simple listening exercise to heighten students' ability to notice what often goes unheard.

> **MATERIALS:** *Blindfolds for each student if possible (closing eyes works too, but is a bit less fun)*
> *Pencils and paper*

Turn the lights down low and have students put on their blindfolds or close their eyes for 3–5 minutes. Instruct them to stay silent while paying attention to and remembering EVERY sound they hear. The students should be able not only to identify the sounds using nouns but also to think about the sounds descriptively in their minds, with adjectives or metaphors. After a few minutes of silence, feel free to make some normal "teacherly" movements to add some new sounds to the mix. Turn on the overhead projector, use the blackboard, walk to your desk, and so on.

When time is up, have the students remove their blindfolds, open their eyes, and pull out their pencils and paper. Then have them jot down every sound they can remember, along with descriptions of each.

# HIGH SCHOOL INK

## GETTING PUBLISHED

*by* LARA ZIELIN

1 SESSION, 2 HOURS

THINK YOU HAVE TO WAIT UNTIL YOU'RE 30 YEARS OLD AND HAVE A SIX-FIGURE book contract to get your writing published? Hardly. There are lots of ways kids can see their work in print—starting now. The trick to publishing is twofold: (1) make the work awesome; and (2) know good places within the publishing market to submit. This workshop is geared toward publishing works of fiction (short stories or novels), though there are resources at the very end for kids who want to publish poetry and nonfiction.

## Make It Awesome

What is it about *Harry Potter* or *The Hunger Games* or *The Lightning Thief* that keeps us turning pages, staying up until the wee morning hours so we can find out what happens? I start by asking kids what they love about their favorite stories, and we spend some time talking about *characters*. Creating memorable people that hook readers and draw them into the story is an important step toward creating publishable works.

## Character Work

The best way to write compelling characters is to know them, inside and out. If students are working on a story—or thinking about one—I ask them to flesh out their characters using the "Character Work" worksheet. Not everything about the characters they come up with has to go into the story, but the more they know them, the more their characters will come alive on the pages.

Once they've completed it, I ask for kids who are willing to share their favorite parts about their characters.

## Plotting Along

Now, we have to find out what happens to these amazing characters! I start by asking the students what they love about the plots in their favorite books. Is it that they don't know what will happen? Or that the character they're rooting for makes good decisions (and sometimes bad)? What they come up with organically can be folded into the overarching plot principal, outlined in the "Plotting Along" handout.

When students are ready to start imagining their own plots, ask them to think about what their following, using italics where indicated: characters *want,* and how it's different from what they *have currently.* For example, Katniss (*The Hunger Games*) wants to be able to provide for her family and keep them safe. The Hunger Games threaten her ability to protect her sister. She not only must take her sister's place in the games, but also must survive to ensure that her sister (and family and community) are safe in the long term. What Katniss wants: safety. What Katniss actually has: lots of danger. The plot follows her struggle to transition from what she *has* to what she *wants.*

You can use any examples you wish, but the point is to get students thinking about not just what *happens* to their characters, but how their characters actively change their circumstances to achieve their goals. Using the worksheet, have them think about what it is their characters will experience and accomplish in the story.

## Editing

No matter what they're writing, encourage all students to find a trusted friend or teacher or parent who can help them edit their work. Ask them to think about what kinds of comments will be constructive for them to both get—and give—on writing projects.

Here, I like to quote from author Christopher Paolini in an interview he did on www .teenreads.com. He talked about the process of writing *Eragon,* which he started when he was a teen. Telling Paolini's story (or one like it) helps show that teens can write and get published—though it does require a good amount of work and determination. As Paolini says: "Editing and revision are two of the most important tools for forging a great book. With my parents' advice, I was able to clarify my descriptions, streamline my logic, and quicken the pace of the story so that *Eragon* read the way that I had intended it to."

## Encouragement

"EVEN AT A YOUNG AGE I ENJOYED WRITING SHORT STORIES AND POEMS, . . . THOUGH MOST OF THEM WERE QUITE AWFUL."

—C. PAOLINI

I love using additional quotations from Paolini throughout the workshop because it shows (a) that he wasn't totally a rock star writer at first and (b) that he had to practice at writing a lot. More good quotations and early interviews with Paolini can be found here: www.teen-reads.com/authors/au-paolini-christopher.asp.

## Market Info

Now that students have worked to make their story the best it can be, what do they do with it? The "Get Your Work Out There!" handout lists some online sites and print publications that primarily accept work by teens and that also offer resources to teen writers. I usually share the list, then ask kids to talk about which venues look good to them and why. If they have fear or trepidation about submitting their work, more encouragement can go a long way. I personally share rejection letters I've received from publishers and magazines to let them know that rejection is part of the process, but it doesn't mean that their work isn't any good, or that publishing is impossible.

# CHARACTER WORK

Character's name:

_____

Date of birth:

_____

Favorite food:

_____

Favorite song:

_____

Worst thing that ever happened to this character:

_____

_____

Best thing that ever happened to him or her:

_____

_____

Most dominant character trait (examples: angry, bubbly, excitable, nervous, timid, courageous)—what happened to make him or her like that?

_____

_____

What the character wants to be when he or she grows up:

_____

Favorite clothing item:

_____

Hobbies:

_____

# PLOTTING ALONG

What is the character's situation when the story starts?

_____

_____

_____

What does he or she want that is different from the current situation?

_____

_____

_____

How will the character achieve his or her goals?

_____

_____

_____

How will he or she change in the process?

_____

_____

_____

# GET YOUR WORK OUT THERE!

Here are some places to submit your work

**ONLINE**

## www.teenink.com

*Teen Ink Magazine* is for teens, written by teens, about teens. You can submit your work electronically for their site, and they also occasionally publish books. You can friend them on Facebook, follow them on Twitter, and subscribe to their newsletter to get information, participate in contests, and more.

## www.kidsonthenet.org.uk/

**Kids on the Net** has a creative writing site where you can share your work with others, and get tips on how to write. Your writing is available for others to read and comment on.

## www.write4fun.net/

**Write for Fun** has great contests you can enter for free to win cash and prizes.

## www.tinyurl.com/krpmad

**Poets.org** has launched an online site for teens. You can get help writing poems, and you can create and submit "poetry notebooks" that others can read and share.

## www.weeklyreader.com/spc

For kids who like to write nonfiction, *Weekly Reader* magazine has a nonfiction student publishing contest, and other ways to share work on the site.

## www.teenlit.com/teens.php

**Teen Lit** is a place to read and write book reviews, not to mention read and share work. They also have writing tips and contests.

**PRINT**

Teen Voices
(for girls between the ages of 13 and 19)
P.O. Box 120027
Boston, MA 02112–0027
www.teenvoices.com

Merlyn's Pen
The publication is still largely print, though you can submit your work online here: www .merlynspen.org/write/submit.php

Stone Soup
Submissions Dept.
P.O. Box 83
Santa Cruz, CA 95063
www.stonesoup.com

**LEARN MORE**

*Teen's Guide to Getting Published for Profit, Recognition, and Academic Success by Jessica Dunn*
Austin, Texas: Prufrock Press, 2006.

## BEWARE THE SCAMS!

If anyone wants money from you in the publishing process, it's probably a scam. No one should ever have to pay to see his or her work published. Some contests do require an entry fee, but most contests for teens do not. If anyone ever asks you for money to publish your work, show the request to an adult or teacher to find out if it's legit.

# APPENDIX

# Middle School Evaluation Rubric

| | Structure | | Style | Grammar & Usage |
|---|---|---|---|---|
| | **Nonfiction** | **Fiction** | | |
| **Great** | • Sticks closely to topic<br>• Topic is inventive and original<br>• Organization is strong and apparent<br>• Ideas are well supported<br>• Ideas flow logically from paragraph to paragraph<br>• Has a strong conclusion | • Setting, characters and plot are fully fleshed out, vibrant, and connected<br>• Action flows logically or naturally<br>• Dialogue is effective and believable<br>• Ending is effective and fitting | • Includes lots of descriptive detail<br>• Writing reflects a unique, consistent personal voice<br>• Word choice is inventive and appropriate | • Uses advanced punctuation, like semicolons and dashes<br>• Advanced words are spelled correctly<br>• Sentence structure is varied |
| **Good** | • Has a fairly strong thesis and sticks to it somewhat<br>• Organization is apparent and generally strong, with some weaker points<br>• Uses paragraphs, though transitions may be rough<br>• Has a definite conclusion, but may end on a weak note | • Setting, characters, and plot are fairly well rounded but underdeveloped or disconnected at points<br>• Dialogue is generally strong with some weak spots<br>• Ending is fairly strong but may feel somewhat sudden or disjointed | • Includes some descriptive detail<br>• Writing may reflect a personal voice but it may not be consistent<br>• Word choice is occasionally inventive | • Uses correct punctuation<br>• Most words are spelled correctly<br>• Sentences are complete |
| **Basic** | • Lacks a strong thesis<br>• Organization is weak<br>• Expresses feelings and ideas, but may not have development or support<br>• Little or no use of paragraphs<br>• Conclusion is weak or missing | • Story features characters, setting, and a plot, but they may not be developed or connected<br>• Dialogue is lacking or unrealistic<br>• Ending is missing or very abrupt | • Includes little descriptive detail<br>• Personal voice is weak or inconsistent<br>• Word choice is flat or stale | • Many words are used or spelled incorrectly<br>• Lacks punctuation in places<br>Sentences may be fragmented |

# High School Evaluation Rubric

| | Structure | | Style | Grammar & Usage |
|---|---|---|---|---|
| | **Nonfiction** | **Fiction** | | |
| **Great** | • Has a strong thesis and sticks closely to it<br>• Topic is inventive and original<br>• Organization is strong and apparent<br>• Ideas are well supported and researched<br>• Ideas flow logically from paragraph to paragraph<br>• Has a strong conclusion | • Setting, characters, and plot are fully fleshed out, vibrant, and connected<br>• Action flows logically or naturally<br>• May have multiple subplots<br>• May use symbolism or subtext<br>• Dialogue is effective and believable<br>• Ending is effective and fitting | • Includes lots of descriptive detail<br>• Writing reflects a unique, consistent personal voice<br>• May experiment successfully with different styles, like stream-of-consciousness or magic realism<br>• Word choice is inventive and appropriate | • Uses advanced punctuation, like semicolons and dashes<br>• Advanced words are spelled correctly<br>• Sentence structure is varied and complex |
| **Good** | • Has a thesis and sticks to it most of the time<br>• Organization is apparent and generally strong<br>• Ideas are sometimes supported and researched<br>• Uses paragraphs, though transitions may be rough<br>• Has a definite conclusion, but may end on a weak note | • Setting, characters, and plot are fairly well rounded but underdeveloped or disconnected at points<br>• May have a subplot<br>• Dialogue is generally strong with some weak spots<br>• Ending may feel sudden or disjointed | • Includes some descriptive detail<br>• Writing may reflect a personal voice that in strong at times<br>• Word choice is occasionally inventive | • Uses correct punctuation<br>• Most words are spelled correctly<br>• Sentences are complete |
| **Basic** | • Has a topic, though may wander off<br>• Organization is weak<br>• Expresses feelings and ideas, but may not have development or support<br>• Little or no use of paragraphs<br>• Conclusion is weak or missing | • Story features characters, setting, and a plot, but they may not be developed or connected<br>• Dialogue may sound unnatural<br>• Ending is missing or very abrupt | • Includes little descriptive detail<br>• Personal voice is weak or inconsistent<br>• Word choice is flat or stale | • Words are frequently misspelled<br>• Punctuation is occasionally misused<br>• Sentences may be fragmented |

# Middle School Self-Assessment Checklist—Nonfiction

- ☐ My paper has an inventive, original topic.

- ☐ My paper sticks closely to the topic idea.

- ☐ My introduction draws the reader in.

- ☐ My paper is well organized.

- ☐ My ideas are well supported.

- ☐ I show the reader that I know a lot about my topic.

- ☐ My ideas flow logically from paragraph to paragraph.

- ☐ I included a lot of descriptive detail.

- ☐ I used colorful, energetic words, instead of bland words like "nice."

- ☐ I edited out hesitant words like "sort of" and "seems to."

- ☐ I wrote in a unique personal voice.

- ☐ I used correct punctuation.

- ☐ I used some advanced punctuation, like semi-colons and dashes.

- ☐ I spelled all the words correctly. When I didn't know how to spell something, I looked it up.

- ☐ There are no run-on sentences.

- ☐ My sentence structure is sometimes complex and varied.

- ☐ My paper has a strong conclusion.

- ☐ I proofread my paper.

# Middle School Self-Assessment Checklist—Fiction

☐ My introduction draws the reader in.

☐ The plot is well thought out and includes an introduction, climax, and conclusion.

☐ The characters are well rounded, believable, and interesting.

☐ The setting, characters, and plot are well integrated.

☐ The action flows logically or naturally.

☐ The dialogue is effective and believable.

☐ I included a lot of descriptive detail.

☐ I used colorful, energetic words, instead of bland words like "nice."

☐ I used strong, active language instead of hesitant words like "sort of" and "seems to."

☐ I wrote in a unique personal voice.

☐ I used correct punctuation.

☐ I used some advanced punctuation, like semi-colons and dashes.

☐ I spelled all the words correctly. When I didn't know how to spell something, I looked it up.

☐ There are no run-on sentences.

☐ My sentence structure is sometimes complex and varied.

☐ My ending is strong and fitting.

☐ I proofread my story.

# High School Self-Assessment Checklist—Nonfiction

☐ My paper has a strong, original thesis.

☐ My paper sticks closely to my thesis.

☐ My introduction draws the reader in.

☐ My paper is well organized.

☐ My ideas are well supported.

☐ I show the reader that I researched my topic well.

☐ My ideas flow logically from paragraph to paragraph.

☐ I included a lot of descriptive detail.

☐ My word choice is inventive and appropriate.

☐ I used strong, active language instead of hesitant phrases like "sort of" and "seems to."

☐ I wrote in a unique personal voice.

☐ I used correct punctuation.

☐ I used some advanced punctuation, like semi-colons and dashes.

☐ I checked my spelling.

☐ There are no run-on sentences.

☐ My sentence structure is complex and varied.

☐ My paper has a strong conclusion that gives the reader something to think about.

☐ I proofread my paper.

# High School Self-Assessment Checklist—Fiction

- ☐ My introduction draws the reader in.
- ☐ The plot is well thought out and includes an introduction, climax, and conclusion.
- ☐ The characters are well rounded, believable, and interesting.
- ☐ The setting, characters, and plot are well integrated.
- ☐ The action flows logically or naturally.
- ☐ My story may have multiple subplots.
- ☐ My story may use symbolism or subtext.
- ☐ The dialogue is effective and believable.
- ☐ My story might experiment with different techniques, like magic realism or stream-of-consciousness.
- ☐ I included a lot of descriptive detail.
- ☐ My word choice is inventive and appropriate. I avoided bland words like "nice."
- ☐ I used strong, active language instead of hesitant phrases like "sort of" and "seems to."
- ☐ I wrote in a unique personal voice.
- ☐ I used correct punctuation.
- ☐ I used some advanced punctuation, like semi-colons and dashes.
- ☐ I checked my spelling.
- ☐ There are no run-on sentences.
- ☐ My sentence structure is complex and varied.
- ☐ The ending is effective and fitting.
- ☐ I proofread my story.

# Common Core Curriculum Standards

To help ensure you're satisfying necessary standards, we've prepared charts to show you which of the Common Core Curriculum Standards each lesson plan meets. The standards were created as part of the Common Core State Standards Initiative, which aims to align diverse state standards and curricula. Forty-eight states are members of the initiative, and most states have adopted the standards.

Some grades have been combined here for convenience, occasionally with slight modifications. You can read the full text of the standards and learn more about them at www .corestandards.org.

| | Write arguments to support claims with clear reasons and relevant evidence. • Introduce claim(s) and organize the reasons and evidence clearly. • Support claim(s) with clear reasons and relevant evidence, using credible sources and demonstrating an understanding of the topic or text. • Use words, phrases, and clauses to clarify the relationships among claim(s) and reasons. • Establish and maintain a formal style. • Provide a concluding statement or section that follows from the argument presented. | Write informative/explanatory texts to examine a topic and convey ideas, concepts, and information through the selection, organization, and analysis of relevant content. • Introduce a topic; organize ideas, concepts, and information, using strategies such as definition, classification, comparison/contrast, and cause/effect; include formatting (e.g., headings), graphics (e.g., charts, tables), and multimedia when useful to aiding comprehension. • Develop the topic with relevant facts, definitions, concrete details, quotations, or other information and examples. • Use appropriate transitions to clarify the relationships among ideas and concepts. • Use precise language and domain-specific vocabulary to inform about or explain the topic. • Establish and maintain a formal style. Provide a concluding statement or section that follows from the information or explanation presented. | Write narratives to develop real or imagined experiences or events using effective technique, relevant descriptive details, and well-structured event sequences. • Engage and orient the reader by establishing a context and introducing a narrator and/or characters; organize an event sequence that unfolds naturally and logically. • Use narrative techniques, such as dialogue, pacing, and description, to develop experiences, events, and/or characters. • Use a variety of transition words, phrases, and clauses to convey sequence and signal shifts from one time frame or setting to another. • Use precise words and phrases, relevant descriptive details, and sensory language to convey experiences and events. Provide a conclusion that follows from the narrated experiences or events. |
|---|---|---|---|
| DETAILS (GOLDEN), CHARACTER (IMMORTAL), AND SETTING (RURAL INDIA) | | ❖ | ❖ |
| LITERARY FACEBOOKS | | | ❖ |
| SUBURBAN EPICS | | | ❖ |
| BUSTED | | ❖ | ❖ |
| HOW TO WRITE SCIENCE FICTION | | ❖ | ❖ |
| WRITING FROM EXPERIENCE | | ❖ | ❖ |
| TOO MUCH MONEY! AN ETHICAL WRITING EXERCISE IN 10 EASY STEPS | ❖ | ❖ | ❖ |
| THE TALK SHOW CIRCUIT | | ❖ | ❖ |
| THE FIRST DRAFT IS MY ENEMY: REVISIONS | ❖ | ❖ | ❖ |
| SEE YOU AGAIN YESTERDAY: PLAYING WITH TIME | | | ❖ |
| LOOK SMART FAST: COLLEGE APPLICATION ESSAY BOOT CAMP | ❖ | ❖ | ❖ |
| WRITING ABOUT PAINFUL THINGS | | ❖ | ❖ |
| MUTANT SHAKESPEARE | | | ❖ |

| | Produce clear and coherent writing in which the development, organization, and style are appropriate to task, purpose, and audience. (Grade-specific expectations for writing types are defined in standards 1–3 above.) | With some guidance and support from peers and adults, develop and strengthen writing as needed by planning, revising, editing, rewriting, or trying a new approach. | Use technology, including the Internet, to produce and publish writing as well as to interact and collaborate with others; demonstrate sufficient command of keyboarding skills to type a minimum of three pages in a single sitting. |
|---|---|---|---|
| DETAILS (GOLDEN), CHARACTER (IMMORTAL), AND SETTING (RURAL INDIA) | ❖ | ❖ | |
| LITERARY FACEBOOKS | ❖ | ❖ | ❖ |
| SUBURBAN EPICS | ❖ | ❖ | |
| BUSTED | ❖ | ❖ | |
| HOW TO WRITE SCIENCE FICTION | ❖ | ❖ | ❖ |
| WRITING FROM EXPERIENCE | ❖ | ❖ | |
| TOO MUCH MONEY! AN ETHICAL WRITING EXERCISE IN 10 EASY STEPS | ❖ | ❖ | |
| THE TALK SHOW CIRCUIT | ❖ | ❖ | |
| THE FIRST DRAFT IS MY ENEMY: REVISIONS | ❖ | ❖ | |
| SEE YOU AGAIN YESTERDAY: PLAYING WITH TIME | ❖ | ❖ | |
| LOOK SMART FAST: COLLEGE APPLICATION ESSAY BOOT CAMP | ❖ | ❖ | |
| WRITING ABOUT PAINFUL THINGS | ❖ | ❖ | |
| MUTANT SHAKESPEARE | ❖ | ❖ | |

| SIXTH GRADE | RESEARCH TO BUILD AND PRESENT KNOWLEDGE | | | RANGE OF WRITING |
|---|---|---|---|---|
| | Conduct short research projects to answer a question, drawing on several sources and refocusing the inquiry when appropriate. | Gather relevant information from multiple print and digital sources; assess the credibility of each source; and quote or paraphrase the data and conclusions of others while avoiding plagiarism and providing basic bibliographic information for sources. | Draw evidence from literary or informational texts to support analysis, reflection, and research.<br>• Apply grade 6 reading standards to literature (e.g., "Compare and contrast texts in different forms or genres [e.g., stories and poems; historical novels and fantasy stories] in terms of their approaches to similar themes and topics").<br>• Apply grade 6 reading standards to literary nonfiction (e.g., "Trace and evaluate the argument and specific claims in a text, distinguishing claims that are supported by reasons and evidence from claims that are not"). | Write routinely over extended time frames (time for research, reflection, and revision) and shorter time frames (a single sitting or a day or two) for a range of discipline-specific tasks, purposes, and audiences. |
| DETAILS (GOLDEN), CHARACTER (IMMORTAL), AND SETTING (RURAL INDIA) | ◆ | ◆ | ◆ | ◆ |
| LITERARY FACEBOOKS | ◆ | ◆ | ◆ | ◆ |
| SUBURBAN EPICS | ◆ | | | ◆ |
| BUSTED | | | | ◆ |
| HOW TO WRITE SCIENCE FICTION | | | | ◆ |
| WRITING FROM EXPERIENCE | ◆ | ◆ | | ◆ |
| TOO MUCH MONEY! AN ETHICAL WRITING EXERCISE IN 10 EASY STEPS | | | ◆ | ◆ |
| THE TALK SHOW CIRCUIT | | | | ◆ |
| THE FIRST DRAFT IS MY ENEMY: REVISIONS | ◆ | ◆ | ◆ | ◆ |
| SEE YOU AGAIN YESTERDAY: PLAYING WITH TIME | | | | ◆ |
| LOOK SMART FAST: COLLEGE APPLICATION ESSAY BOOT CAMP | | | | ◆ |
| WRITING ABOUT PAINFUL THINGS | ◆ | ◆ | | ◆ |
| MUTANT SHAKESPEARE | ◆ | | ◆ | ◆ |

| | Write arguments to support claims with clear reasons and relevant evidence. <br>• Introduce claim(s) and organize the reasons and evidence clearly. <br>• Support claim(s) with clear reasons and relevant evidence, using credible sources and demonstrating an understanding of the topic or text. <br>• Use words, phrases, and clauses to clarify the relationships among claim(s) and reasons. <br>• Establish and maintain a formal style. <br>• Provide a concluding statement or section that follows from the argument presented. | Write informative/explanatory texts to examine a topic and convey ideas, concepts, and information through the selection, organization, and analysis of relevant content. <br>• Introduce a topic; organize ideas, concepts, and information, using strategies such as definition, classification, comparison/contrast, and cause/effect; include formatting (e.g., headings), graphics (e.g., charts, tables), and multimedia when useful to aiding comprehension. <br>• Develop the topic with relevant facts, definitions, concrete details, quotations, or other information and examples. <br>• Use appropriate transitions to clarify the relationships among ideas and concepts. <br>• Use precise language and domain-specific vocabulary to inform about or explain the topic. <br>• Establish and maintain a formal style. <br>Provide a concluding statement or section that follows from the information or explanation presented. | Write narratives to develop real or imagined experiences or events using effective technique, relevant descriptive details, and well-structured event sequences. <br>• Engage and orient the reader by establishing a context and introducing a narrator and/or characters; organize an event sequence that unfolds naturally and logically. <br>• Use narrative techniques, such as dialogue, pacing, and description, to develop experiences, events, and/or characters. <br>• Use a variety of transition words, phrases, and clauses to convey sequence and signal shifts from one time frame or setting to another. <br>• Use precise words and phrases, relevant descriptive details, and sensory language to convey experiences and events. <br>Provide a conclusion that follows from the narrated experiences or events. |
|---|---|---|---|
| HOW TO WRITE A ONE-PERSON SHOW ABOUT A HISTORICAL FIGURE | | ❖ | ❖ |
| WRITING FOR GAMERS | | | ❖ |
| HUMOR WRITING: AN EXERCISE IN ALCHEMY | | ❖ | ❖ |
| ON PINING: WRITE A VERSE TO MAKE THEM STAY | ❖ | | ❖ |
| ADDING INSULT TO POETRY | ❖ | | ❖ |
| BAD WRITING | | | ❖ |
| WHERE STORIES COME FROM | | | |
| WORD KARAOKE | | | ❖ |
| TALL TALES AND SHORT STORIES | | | |
| WELCOME TO THE FUNHOUSE: WRITING FUNNY SCENES | | ❖ | ❖ |
| VOICEMAILS FROM MY FUTURE SELF | | ❖ | ❖ |
| HOW SHORT IS SHORT? | | | |
| COMIC COMPOSITION CHALLENGE! | | | ❖ |
| MY BORING LIFE | | ❖ | ❖ |

| SIXTH GRADE | PRODUCTION AND DISTRIBUTION OF WRITING | | |
|---|---|---|---|
| | Produce clear and coherent writing in which the development, organization, and style are appropriate to task, purpose, and audience. (Grade-specific expectations for writing types are defined in standards 1–3 above.) | With some guidance and support from peers and adults, develop and strengthen writing as needed by planning, revising, editing, rewriting, or trying a new approach. | Use technology, including the Internet, to produce and publish writing and present the relationships between information and ideas efficiently as well as to interact and collaborate with others, including linking to and citing sources. |
| HOW TO WRITE A ONE-PERSON SHOW ABOUT A HISTORICAL FIGURE | ❖ | ❖ | |
| WRITING FOR GAMERS | ❖ | ❖ | ❖ |
| HUMOR WRITING: AN EXERCISE IN ALCHEMY | ❖ | ❖ | |
| ON PINING: WRITE A VERSE TO MAKE THEM STAY | ❖ | ❖ | |
| ADDING INSULT TO POETRY | ❖ | ❖ | |
| BAD WRITING | ❖ | ❖ | |
| WHERE STORIES COME FROM | ❖ | ❖ | |
| WORD KARAOKE | ❖ | ❖ | |
| TALL TALES AND SHORT STORIES | ❖ | ❖ | |
| WELCOME TO THE FUNHOUSE: WRITING FUNNY SCENES | ❖ | ❖ | |
| VOICEMAILS FROM MY FUTURE SELF | ❖ | ❖ | |
| HOW SHORT IS SHORT? | ❖ | ❖ | |
| COMIC COMPOSITION CHALLENGE! | ❖ | ❖ | |
| MY BORING LIFE | ❖ | ❖ | |

| SIXTH GRADE | RESEARCH TO BUILD AND PRESENT KNOWLEDGE | | | RANGE OF WRITING |
|---|---|---|---|---|
| | Conduct short research projects to answer a question, drawing on several sources and refocusing the inquiry when appropriate. | Gather relevant information from multiple print and digital sources; assess the credibility of each source; and quote or paraphrase the data and conclusions of others while avoiding plagiarism and providing basic bibliographic information for sources. | Draw evidence from literary or informational texts to support analysis, reflection, and research.<br>• Apply grade 6 reading standards to literature (e.g., "Compare and contrast texts in different forms or genres [e.g., stories and poems; historical novels and fantasy stories] in terms of their approaches to similar themes and topics").<br>• Apply grade 6 reading standards to literary nonfiction (e.g., "Trace and evaluate the argument and specific claims in a text, distinguishing claims that are supported by reasons and evidence from claims that are not"). | Write routinely over extended time frames (time for research, reflection, and revision) and shorter time frames (a single sitting or a day or two) for a range of discipline-specific tasks, purposes, and audiences. |
| HOW TO WRITE A ONE-PERSON SHOW ABOUT A HISTORICAL FIGURE | ❖ | ❖ | ❖ | ❖ |
| WRITING FOR GAMERS | | | ❖ | ❖ |
| HUMOR WRITING: AN EXERCISE IN ALCHEMY | | | ❖ | ❖ |
| ON PINING: WRITE A VERSE TO MAKE THEM STAY | | | | ❖ |
| ADDING INSULT TO POETRY | | | | ❖ |
| BAD WRITING | ❖ | ❖ | ❖ | ❖ |
| WHERE STORIES COME FROM | ❖ | ❖ | ❖ | ❖ |
| WORD KARAOKE | | | | ❖ |
| TALL TALES AND SHORT STORIES | ❖ | ❖ | ❖ | ❖ |
| WELCOME TO THE FUNHOUSE: WRITING FUNNY SCENES | | | ❖ | ❖ |
| VOICEMAILS FROM MY FUTURE SELF | ❖ | ❖ | | ❖ |
| HOW SHORT IS SHORT? | ❖ | ❖ | ❖ | ❖ |
| COMIC COMPOSITION CHALLENGE! | ❖ | ❖ | ❖ | ❖ |
| MY BORING LIFE | ❖ | ❖ | | ❖ |

| | Write arguments to support claims with clear reasons and relevant evidence. | Write informative/explanatory texts to examine a topic and convey ideas, concepts, and information through the selection, organization, and analysis of relevant content. | Write narratives to develop real or imagined experiences or events using effective technique, relevant descriptive details, and well-structured event sequences. |
|---|---|---|---|
| | • Introduce claim(s) and organize the reasons and evidence clearly.<br>• Support claim(s) with clear reasons and relevant evidence, using credible sources and demonstrating an understanding of the topic or text.<br>• Use words, phrases, and clauses to clarify the relationships among claim(s) and reasons.<br>• Establish and maintain a formal style.<br>• Provide a concluding statement or section that follows from the argument presented. | • Introduce a topic; organize ideas, concepts, and information, using strategies such as definition, classification, comparison/contrast, and cause/effect; include formatting (e.g., headings), graphics (e.g., charts, tables), and multimedia when useful to aiding comprehension.<br>• Develop the topic with relevant facts, definitions, concrete details, quotations, or other information and examples.<br>• Use appropriate transitions to clarify the relationships among ideas and concepts.<br>• Use precise language and domain-specific vocabulary to inform about or explain the topic.<br>• Establish and maintain a formal style.<br>Provide a concluding statement or section that follows from the information or explanation presented. | • Engage and orient the reader by establishing a context and introducing a narrator and/or characters; organize an event sequence that unfolds naturally and logically.<br>• Use narrative techniques, such as dialogue, pacing, and description, to develop experiences, events, and/or characters.<br>• Use a variety of transition words, phrases, and clauses to convey sequence and signal shifts from one time frame or setting to another.<br>• Use precise words and phrases, relevant descriptive details, and sensory language to convey experiences and events.<br>Provide a conclusion that follows from the narrated experiences or events. |
| COLONEL MUSTARD IN THE LIBRARY WITH A CANDLESTICK | | | ❖ |
| CREATING CHARACTERS | | | ❖ |
| HIGH SCHOOL CONFIDENTIAL | | | ❖ |
| GET YOUR HAIKU ON | | | ❖ |
| THE ESSAY | ❖ | ❖ | ❖ |
| THE STORY OF ME | | ❖ | ❖ |
| MEET YOUR PROTAGONIST! | | | ❖ |
| ALL WITNESSES EVENTUALLY DIE | | ❖ | ❖ |
| WICKED STYLE AND HOW TO GET IT | | | ❖ |
| PRESIDENT TAKES MARTIAN BRIDE | | ❖ | ❖ |
| LYING FOR FUN AND PROFIT | | | |
| THIS CLASS SUCKS | ❖ | ❖ | ❖ |

| | Produce clear and coherent writing in which the development, organization, and style are appropriate to task, purpose, and audience. (Grade-specific expectations for writing types are defined in standards 1–3 above.) | With some guidance and support from peers and adults, develop and strengthen writing as needed by planning, revising, editing, rewriting, or trying a new approach. | Use technology, including the Internet, to produce and publish writing and present the relationships between information and ideas efficiently as well as to interact and collaborate with others, including linking to and citing sources. |
|---|---|---|---|
| COLONEL MUSTARD IN THE LIBRARY WITH A CANDLESTICK | ❖ | ❖ | |
| CREATING CHARACTERS | ❖ | ❖ | |
| HIGH SCHOOL CONFIDENTIAL | ❖ | ❖ | |
| GET YOUR HAIKU ON | ❖ | ❖ | |
| THE ESSAY | ❖ | ❖ | |
| THE STORY OF ME | ❖ | ❖ | |
| MEET YOUR PROTAGONIST! | ❖ | ❖ | |
| ALL WITNESSES EVENTUALLY DIE | ❖ | ❖ | |
| WICKED STYLE AND HOW TO GET IT | ❖ | ❖ | |
| PRESIDENT TAKES MARTIAN BRIDE | ❖ | ❖ | |
| LYING FOR FUN AND PROFIT | ❖ | ❖ | |
| THIS CLASS SUCKS | ❖ | ❖ | ❖ |

| Sixth Grade | Research to Build and Present Knowledge | | | Range of Writing |
|---|---|---|---|---|
| | Conduct short research projects to answer a question, drawing on several sources and refocusing the inquiry when appropriate. | Gather relevant information from multiple print and digital sources; assess the credibility of each source; and quote or paraphrase the data and conclusions of others while avoiding plagiarism and providing basic bibliographic information for sources. | Draw evidence from literary or informational texts to support analysis, reflection, and research.<br>• Apply grade 6 reading standards to literature (e.g., "Compare and contrast texts in different forms or genres [e.g., stories and poems; historical novels and fantasy stories] in terms of their approaches to similar themes and topics").<br>• Apply grade 6 reading standards to literary nonfiction (e.g., "Trace and evaluate the argument and specific claims in a text, distinguishing claims that are supported by reasons and evidence from claims that are not"). | Write routinely over extended time frames (time for research, reflection, and revision) and shorter time frames (a single sitting or a day or two) for a range of discipline-specific tasks, purposes, and audiences. |
| Colonel Mustard in the Library with a Candlestick | | | | ◆ |
| Creating Characters | | | | ◆ |
| High School Confidential | | | | ◆ |
| Get Your Haiku On | | | | ◆ |
| The Essay | ◆ | ◆ | ◆ | ◆ |
| The Story of Me | ◆ | ◆ | | ◆ |
| Meet Your Protagonist! | | | | ◆ |
| All Witnesses Eventually Die | ◆ | ◆ | | ◆ |
| Wicked Style and How to Get It | ◆ | ◆ | ◆ | ◆ |
| President Takes Martian Bride | | | ◆ | ◆ |
| Lying for Fun and Profit | ◆ | ◆ | ◆ | ◆ |
| This Class Sucks | ◆ | ◆ | ◆ | ◆ |

| | Write arguments to support claims with clear reasons and relevant evidence. | Write informative/explanatory texts to examine a topic and convey ideas, concepts, and information through the selection, organization, and analysis of relevant content. | Write narratives to develop real or imagined experiences or events using effective technique, relevant descriptive details, and well-structured event sequences. |
|---|---|---|---|
| | • Introduce claim(s) and organize the reasons and evidence clearly.<br>• Support claim(s) with clear reasons and relevant evidence, using credible sources and demonstrating an understanding of the topic or text.<br>• Use words, phrases, and clauses to clarify the relationships among claim(s) and reasons.<br>• Establish and maintain a formal style.<br>• Provide a concluding statement or section that follows from the argument presented. | • Introduce a topic; organize ideas, concepts, and information, using strategies such as definition, classification, comparison/ contrast, and cause/effect; include formatting (e.g., headings), graphics (e.g., charts, tables), and multimedia when useful to aiding comprehension.<br>• Develop the topic with relevant facts, definitions, concrete details, quotations, or other information and examples.<br>• Use appropriate transitions to clarify the relationships among ideas and concepts.<br>• Use precise language and domain-specific vocabulary to inform about or explain the topic.<br>• Establish and maintain a formal style.<br>Provide a concluding statement or section that follows from the information or explanation presented. | • Engage and orient the reader by establishing a context and introducing a narrator and/ or characters; organize an event sequence that unfolds naturally and logically.<br>• Use narrative techniques, such as dialogue, pacing, and description, to develop experiences, events, and/or characters.<br>• Use a variety of transition words, phrases, and clauses to convey sequence and signal shifts from one time frame or setting to another.<br>• Use precise words and phrases, relevant descriptive details, and sensory language to convey experiences and events.<br>Provide a conclusion that follows from the narrated experiences or events. |
| SCREENWRITING | | ◆ | ◆ |
| HOW TO WRITE A GHOST STORY | | | ◆ |
| 826 UNPLUGGED | | | ◆ |
| SPORTSWRITING | | ◆ | ◆ |
| HOW TO WRITE A FAN LETTER | ◆ | ◆ | ◆ |
| EXQUISITE STORY LINES | | | |
| SOUL PROWLERS | | ◆ | ◆ |
| HOMESTYLE | | ◆ | ◆ |
| AGITATE! PROPAGANDIZE! | ◆ | ◆ | ◆ |
| TASTY MEDICINE FOR WRITER'S BLOCK | | ◆ | ◆ |
| HIGH SCHOOL INK | | ◆ | ◆ |

| | Produce clear and coherent writing in which the development, organization, and style are appropriate to task, purpose, and audience. (Grade-specific expectations for writing types are defined in standards 1–3 above.) | With some guidance and support from peers and adults, develop and strengthen writing as needed by planning, revising, editing, rewriting, or trying a new approach. | Use technology, including the Internet, to produce and publish writing and present the relationships between information and ideas efficiently as well as to interact and collaborate with others, including linking to and citing sources. |
|---|---|---|---|
| SCREENWRITING | ❖ | ❖ | ❖ |
| HOW TO WRITE A GHOST STORY | ❖ | ❖ | |
| 826 UNPLUGGED | ❖ | ❖ | |
| SPORTSWRITING | ❖ | ❖ | ❖ |
| HOW TO WRITE A FAN LETTER | ❖ | ❖ | ❖ |
| EXQUISITE STORY LINES | ❖ | ❖ | |
| SOUL PROWLERS | ❖ | ❖ | |
| HOMESTYLE | ❖ | ❖ | |
| AGITATE! PROPAGANDIZE! | ❖ | ❖ | |
| TASTY MEDICINE FOR WRITER'S BLOCK | ❖ | ❖ | |
| HIGH SCHOOL INK | ❖ | ❖ | ❖ |

| Sixth Grade | Research to Build and Present Knowledge | | | Range of Writing |
|---|---|---|---|---|
| | Conduct short research projects to answer a question, drawing on several sources and refocusing the inquiry when appropriate. | Gather relevant information from multiple print and digital sources; assess the credibility of each source; and quote or paraphrase the data and conclusions of others while avoiding plagiarism and providing basic bibliographic information for sources. | Draw evidence from literary or informational texts to support analysis, reflection, and research.<br>• Apply grade 6 reading standards to literature (e.g., "Compare and contrast texts in different forms or genres [e.g., stories and poems; historical novels and fantasy stories] in terms of their approaches to similar themes and topics").<br>• Apply grade 6 reading standards to literary nonfiction (e.g., "Trace and evaluate the argument and specific claims in a text, distinguishing claims that are supported by reasons and evidence from claims that are not"). | Write routinely over extended time frames (time for research, reflection, and revision) and shorter time frames (a single sitting or a day or two) for a range of discipline-specific tasks, purposes, and audiences. |
| Screenwriting | | | | ❖ |
| How to Write a Ghost Story | | | | ❖ |
| 826 Unplugged | | | | ❖ |
| Sportswriting | ❖ | ❖ | | ❖ |
| How to Write a Fan Letter | | | | ❖ |
| Exquisite Story Lines | ❖ | ❖ | ❖ | ❖ |
| Soul Prowlers | ❖ | ❖ | | ❖ |
| Homestyle | ❖ | ❖ | ❖ | ❖ |
| Agitate! Propagandize! | ❖ | ❖ | ❖ | ❖ |
| Tasty Medicine for Writer's Block | ❖ | ❖ | | ❖ |
| High School Ink | | | | ❖ |

| | Write arguments to support claims with clear reasons and relevant evidence. <br>• Introduce claim(s) and organize the reasons and evidence clearly. <br>• Support claim(s) with clear reasons and relevant evidence, using credible sources and demonstrating an understanding of the topic or text. <br>• Use words, phrases, and clauses to clarify the relationships among claim(s) and reasons. <br>• Establish and maintain a formal style. <br>• Provide a concluding statement or section that follows from the argument presented. | Write informative/explanatory texts to examine a topic and convey ideas, concepts, and information through the selection, organization, and analysis of relevant content. <br>• Introduce a topic; organize ideas, concepts, and information, using strategies such as definition, classification, comparison/contrast, and cause/effect; include formatting (e.g., headings), graphics (e.g., charts, tables), and multimedia when useful to aiding comprehension. <br>• Develop the topic with relevant facts, definitions, concrete details, quotations, or other information and examples. <br>• Use appropriate transitions to clarify the relationships among ideas and concepts. <br>• Use precise language and domain-specific vocabulary to inform about or explain the topic. <br>• Establish and maintain a formal style. <br>• Provide a concluding statement or section that follows from the information or explanation presented. | Write narratives to develop real or imagined experiences or events using effective technique, relevant descriptive details, and well-structured event sequences. <br>• Engage and orient the reader by establishing a context and introducing a narrator and/or characters; organize an event sequence that unfolds naturally and logically. <br>• Use narrative techniques, such as dialogue, pacing, and description, to develop experiences, events, and/or characters. <br>• Use a variety of transition words, phrases, and clauses to convey sequence and signal shifts from one time frame or setting to another. <br>• Use precise words and phrases, relevant descriptive details, and sensory language to convey experiences and events. <br>• Provide a conclusion that follows from the narrated experiences or events. |
|---|---|---|---|
| DETAILS (GOLDEN), CHARACTER (IMMORTAL), AND SETTING (RURAL INDIA) | | ❖ | ❖ |
| LITERARY FACEBOOKS | | | ❖ |
| SUBURBAN EPICS | | | ❖ |
| BUSTED | | ❖ | ❖ |
| HOW TO WRITE SCIENCE FICTION | | ❖ | ❖ |
| WRITING FROM EXPERIENCE | | ❖ | ❖ |
| TOO MUCH MONEY! AN ETHICAL WRITING EXERCISE IN 10 EASY STEPS | ❖ | ❖ | ❖ |
| THE TALK SHOW CIRCUIT | | ❖ | ❖ |
| THE FIRST DRAFT IS MY ENEMY: REVISIONS | ❖ | ❖ | ❖ |
| SEE YOU AGAIN YESTERDAY: PLAYING WITH TIME | | | ❖ |
| LOOK SMART FAST: COLLEGE APPLICATION ESSAY BOOT CAMP | ❖ | ❖ | ❖ |

| | Produce clear and coherent writing in which the development, organization, and style are appropriate to task, purpose, and audience. (Grade-specific expectations for writing types are defined in standards 1–3 above.) | With some guidance and support from peers and adults, develop and strengthen writing as needed by planning, revising, editing, rewriting, or trying a new approach. | Use technology, including the Internet, to produce and publish writing and present the relationships between information and ideas efficiently as well as to interact and collaborate with others, including linking to and citing sources. |
|---|---|---|---|
| Details (Golden), Character (Immortal), and Setting (Rural India) | ❖ | ❖ | |
| Literary Facebooks | ❖ | ❖ | ❖ |
| Suburban Epics | ❖ | ❖ | |
| Busted | ❖ | ❖ | |
| How to Write Science Fiction | ❖ | ❖ | ❖ |
| Writing from Experience | ❖ | ❖ | |
| Too Much Money! An Ethical Writing Exercise in 10 Easy Steps | ❖ | ❖ | |
| The Talk Show Circuit | ❖ | ❖ | |
| The First Draft Is My Enemy: Revisions | ❖ | ❖ | |
| See You Again Yesterday: Playing with Time | ❖ | ❖ | |
| Look Smart Fast: College Application Essay Boot Camp | ❖ | ❖ | |

| Seventh–Eighth Grade | Research to Build and Present Knowledge | | | Range of Writing |
|---|---|---|---|---|
| | Conduct short research projects to answer a question, drawing on several sources and refocusing the inquiry when appropriate. | Gather relevant information from multiple print and digital sources; assess the credibility of each source; and quote or paraphrase the data and conclusions of others while avoiding plagiarism and providing basic bibliographic information for sources. | Draw evidence from literary or informational texts to support analysis, reflection, and research. • Apply grade 6 reading standards to literature (e.g., "Compare and contrast texts in different forms or genres [e.g., stories and poems; historical novels and fantasy stories] in terms of their approaches to similar themes and topics"). • Apply grade 6 reading standards to literary nonfiction (e.g., "Trace and evaluate the argument and specific claims in a text, distinguishing claims that are supported by reasons and evidence from claims that are not"). | Write routinely over extended time frames (time for research, reflection, and revision) and shorter time frames (a single sitting or a day or two) for a range of discipline-specific tasks, purposes, and audiences. |
| Details (Golden), Character (Immortal), and Setting (Rural India) | ◈ | ◈ | ◈ | ◈ |
| Literary Facebooks | ◈ | ◈ | ◈ | ◈ |
| Suburban Epics | ◈ | | | ◈ |
| Busted | | | | ◈ |
| How to Write Science Fiction | | | | ◈ |
| Writing from Experience | ◈ | ◈ | | ◈ |
| Too Much Money! An Ethical Writing Exercise in 10 Easy Steps | | | ◈ | ◈ |
| The Talk Show Circuit | | | | ◈ |
| The First Draft Is My Enemy: Revisions | ◈ | ◈ | ◈ | ◈ |
| See You Again Yesterday: Playing with Time | | | | ◈ |
| Look Smart Fast: College Application Essay Boot Camp | | | | ◈ |

| | Write arguments to support claims with clear reasons and relevant evidence. <br>• Introduce claim(s) and organize the reasons and evidence clearly. <br>• Support claim(s) with clear reasons and relevant evidence, using credible sources and demonstrating an understanding of the topic or text. <br>• Use words, phrases, and clauses to clarify the relationships among claim(s) and reasons. <br>• Establish and maintain a formal style. <br>• Provide a concluding statement or section that follows from the argument presented. | Write informative/explanatory texts to examine a topic and convey ideas, concepts, and information through the selection, organization, and analysis of relevant content. <br>• Introduce a topic; organize ideas, concepts, and information, using strategies such as definition, classification, comparison/contrast, and cause/effect; include formatting (e.g., headings), graphics (e.g., charts, tables), and multimedia when useful to aiding comprehension. <br>• Develop the topic with relevant facts, definitions, concrete details, quotations, or other information and examples. <br>• Use appropriate transitions to clarify the relationships among ideas and concepts. <br>• Use precise language and domain-specific vocabulary to inform about or explain the topic. <br>• Establish and maintain a formal style. <br>• Provide a concluding statement or section that follows from the information or explanation presented. | Write narratives to develop real or imagined experiences or events using effective technique, relevant descriptive details, and well-structured event sequences. <br>• Engage and orient the reader by establishing a context and introducing a narrator and/or characters; organize an event sequence that unfolds naturally and logically. <br>• Use narrative techniques, such as dialogue, pacing, and description, to develop experiences, events, and/or characters. <br>• Use a variety of transition words, phrases, and clauses to convey sequence and signal shifts from one time frame or setting to another. <br>• Use precise words and phrases, relevant descriptive details, and sensory language to convey experiences and events. <br>• Provide a conclusion that follows from the narrated experiences or events. |
|---|---|---|---|
| WRITING ABOUT PAINFUL THINGS | | ❖ | ❖ |
| MUTANT SHAKESPEARE | | | ❖ |
| HOW TO WRITE A ONE-PERSON SHOW ABOUT A HISTORICAL FIGURE | | ❖ | ❖ |
| WRITING FOR GAMERS | | | ❖ |
| HUMOR WRITING: AN EXERCISE IN ALCHEMY | | ❖ | ❖ |
| ON PINING: WRITE A VERSE TO MAKE THEM STAY | ❖ | | ❖ |
| ADDING INSULT TO POETRY | ❖ | | ❖ |
| BAD WRITING | | | ❖ |
| WHERE STORIES COME FROM | | | |
| WORD KARAOKE | | | ❖ |
| TALL TALES AND SHORT STORIES | | | |
| WELCOME TO THE FUNHOUSE: WRITING FUNNY SCENES | | ❖ | ❖ |

PRODUCTION AND DISTRIBUTION OF WRITING

| | Produce clear and coherent writing in which the development, organization, and style are appropriate to task, purpose, and audience. (Grade-specific expectations for writing types are defined in standards 1–3 above.) | With some guidance and support from peers and adults, develop and strengthen writing as needed by planning, revising, editing, rewriting, or trying a new approach. | Use technology, including the Internet, to produce and publish writing and present the relationships between information and ideas efficiently as well as to interact and collaborate with others, including linking to and citing sources. |
|---|---|---|---|
| WRITING ABOUT PAINFUL THINGS | ❖ | ❖ | |
| MUTANT SHAKESPEARE | ❖ | ❖ | |
| HOW TO WRITE A ONE-PERSON SHOW ABOUT A HISTORICAL FIGURE | ❖ | ❖ | |
| WRITING FOR GAMERS | ❖ | ❖ | ❖ |
| HUMOR WRITING: AN EXERCISE IN ALCHEMY | ❖ | ❖ | |
| ON PINING: WRITE A VERSE TO MAKE THEM STAY | ❖ | ❖ | |
| ADDING INSULT TO POETRY | ❖ | ❖ | |
| BAD WRITING | ❖ | ❖ | |
| WHERE STORIES COME FROM | ❖ | ❖ | |
| WORD KARAOKE | ❖ | ❖ | |
| TALL TALES AND SHORT STORIES | ❖ | ❖ | |
| WELCOME TO THE FUNHOUSE: WRITING FUNNY SCENES | ❖ | ❖ | |

| SEVENTH–EIGHTH GRADE | RESEARCH TO BUILD AND PRESENT KNOWLEDGE | | | RANGE OF WRITING |
| --- | --- | --- | --- | --- |
| | Conduct short research projects to answer a question, drawing on several sources and refocusing the inquiry when appropriate. | Gather relevant information from multiple print and digital sources; assess the credibility of each source; and quote or paraphrase the data and conclusions of others while avoiding plagiarism and providing basic bibliographic information for sources. | Draw evidence from literary or informational texts to support analysis, reflection, and research.<br>• Apply grade 6 reading standards to literature (e.g., "Compare and contrast texts in different forms or genres [e.g., stories and poems; historical novels and fantasy stories] in terms of their approaches to similar themes and topics").<br>• Apply grade 6 reading standards to literary nonfiction (e.g., "Trace and evaluate the argument and specific claims in a text, distinguishing claims that are supported by reasons and evidence from claims that are not"). | Write routinely over extended time frames (time for research, reflection, and revision) and shorter time frames (a single sitting or a day or two) for a range of discipline-specific tasks, purposes, and audiences. |
| WRITING ABOUT PAINFUL THINGS | ✦ | ✦ | | ✦ |
| MUTANT SHAKESPEARE | ✦ | | ✦ | ✦ |
| HOW TO WRITE A ONE-PERSON SHOW ABOUT A HISTORICAL FIGURE | ✦ | ✦ | ✦ | ✦ |
| WRITING FOR GAMERS | | | ✦ | ✦ |
| HUMOR WRITING: AN EXERCISE IN ALCHEMY | | | ✦ | ✦ |
| ON PINING: WRITE A VERSE TO MAKE THEM STAY | | | | ✦ |
| ADDING INSULT TO POETRY | | | | ✦ |
| BAD WRITING | ✦ | ✦ | ✦ | ✦ |
| WHERE STORIES COME FROM | ✦ | ✦ | ✦ | ✦ |
| WORD KARAOKE | | | | ✦ |
| TALL TALES AND SHORT STORIES | ✦ | ✦ | ✦ | ✦ |
| WELCOME TO THE FUNHOUSE: WRITING FUNNY SCENES | | | ✦ | ✦ |

TEXT TYPES AND PURPOSES

| | Write arguments to support claims with clear reasons and relevant evidence. • Introduce claim(s) and organize the reasons and evidence clearly. • Support claim(s) with clear reasons and relevant evidence, using credible sources and demonstrating an understanding of the topic or text. • Use words, phrases, and clauses to clarify the relationships among claim(s) and reasons. • Establish and maintain a formal style. • Provide a concluding statement or section that follows from the argument presented. | Write informative/explanatory texts to examine a topic and convey ideas, concepts, and information through the selection, organization, and analysis of relevant content. • Introduce a topic; organize ideas, concepts, and information, using strategies such as definition, classification, comparison/contrast, and cause/effect; include formatting (e.g., headings), graphics (e.g., charts, tables), and multimedia when useful to aiding comprehension. • Develop the topic with relevant facts, definitions, concrete details, quotations, or other information and examples. • Use appropriate transitions to clarify the relationships among ideas and concepts. • Use precise language and domain-specific vocabulary to inform about or explain the topic. • Establish and maintain a formal style. • Provide a concluding statement or section that follows from the information or explanation presented. | Write narratives to develop real or imagined experiences or events using effective technique, relevant descriptive details, and well-structured event sequences. • Engage and orient the reader by establishing a context and introducing a narrator and/or characters; organize an event sequence that unfolds naturally and logically. • Use narrative techniques, such as dialogue, pacing, and description, to develop experiences, events, and/or characters. • Use a variety of transition words, phrases, and clauses to convey sequence and signal shifts from one time frame or setting to another. • Use precise words and phrases, relevant descriptive details, and sensory language to convey experiences and events. • Provide a conclusion that follows from the narrated experiences or events. |
|---|---|---|---|
| VOICEMAILS FROM MY FUTURE SELF | | ❖ | ❖ |
| HOW SHORT IS SHORT? | | | |
| COMIC COMPOSITION CHALLENGE! | | | ❖ |
| MY BORING LIFE | | ❖ | ❖ |
| COLONEL MUSTARD IN THE LIBRARY WITH A CANDLESTICK | | | ❖ |
| CREATING CHARACTERS | | | ❖ |
| HIGH SCHOOL CONFIDENTIAL | | | ❖ |
| GET YOUR HAIKU ON | | | ❖ |
| THE ESSAY | ❖ | ❖ | ❖ |
| THE STORY OF ME | | ❖ | ❖ |
| MEET YOUR PROTAGONIST! | | | ❖ |
| ALL WITNESSES EVENTUALLY DIE | | ❖ | ❖ |
| WICKED STYLE AND HOW TO GET IT | | | ❖ |

| SEVENTH–EIGHTH GRADE | Produce clear and coherent writing in which the development, organization, and style are appropriate to task, purpose, and audience. (Grade-specific expectations for writing types are defined in standards 1–3 above.) | With some guidance and support from peers and adults, develop and strengthen writing as needed by planning, revising, editing, rewriting, or trying a new approach. | Use technology, including the Internet, to produce and publish writing and present the relationships between information and ideas efficiently as well as to interact and collaborate with others, including linking to and citing sources. |
|---|---|---|---|
| VOICEMAILS FROM MY FUTURE SELF | ❖ | ❖ | |
| HOW SHORT IS SHORT? | ❖ | ❖ | |
| COMIC COMPOSITION CHALLENGE! | ❖ | ❖ | |
| MY BORING LIFE | ❖ | ❖ | |
| COLONEL MUSTARD IN THE LIBRARY WITH A CANDLESTICK | ❖ | ❖ | |
| CREATING CHARACTERS | ❖ | ❖ | |
| HIGH SCHOOL CONFIDENTIAL | ❖ | ❖ | |
| GET YOUR HAIKU ON | ❖ | ❖ | |
| THE ESSAY | ❖ | ❖ | |
| THE STORY OF ME | ❖ | ❖ | |
| MEET YOUR PROTAGONIST! | ❖ | ❖ | |
| ALL WITNESSES EVENTUALLY DIE | ❖ | ❖ | |
| WICKED STYLE AND HOW TO GET IT | ❖ | ❖ | |

| SEVENTH–EIGHTH GRADE | Conduct short research projects to answer a question, drawing on several sources and refocusing the inquiry when appropriate. | Gather relevant information from multiple print and digital sources; assess the credibility of each source; and quote or paraphrase the data and conclusions of others while avoiding plagiarism and providing basic bibliographic information for sources. | Draw evidence from literary or informational texts to support analysis, reflection, and research. • Apply grade 6 reading standards to literature (e.g., "Compare and contrast texts in different forms or genres [e.g., stories and poems; historical novels and fantasy stories] in terms of their approaches to similar themes and topics"). • Apply grade 6 reading standards to literary nonfiction (e.g., "Trace and evaluate the argument and specific claims in a text, distinguishing claims that are supported by reasons and evidence from claims that are not"). | Write routinely over extended time frames (time for research, reflection, and revision) and shorter time frames (a single sitting or a day or two) for a range of discipline-specific tasks, purposes, and audiences. |
|---|---|---|---|---|
| VOICEMAILS FROM MY FUTURE SELF | ❖ | ❖ | | ❖ |
| HOW SHORT IS SHORT? | ❖ | ❖ | ❖ | ❖ |
| COMIC COMPOSITION CHALLENGE! | ❖ | ❖ | ❖ | ❖ |
| MY BORING LIFE | ❖ | ❖ | | ❖ |
| COLONEL MUSTARD IN THE LIBRARY WITH A CANDLESTICK | | | | ❖ |
| CREATING CHARACTERS | | | | ❖ |
| HIGH SCHOOL CONFIDENTIAL | | | | ❖ |
| GET YOUR HAIKU ON | | | | ❖ |
| THE ESSAY | ❖ | ❖ | ❖ | ❖ |
| THE STORY OF ME | ❖ | ❖ | | ❖ |
| MEET YOUR PROTAGONIST! | | | | ❖ |
| ALL WITNESSES EVENTUALLY DIE | ❖ | ❖ | | ❖ |
| WICKED STYLE AND HOW TO GET IT | ❖ | ❖ | ❖ | ❖ |

**TEXT TYPES AND PURPOSES**

| | Write arguments to support claims with clear reasons and relevant evidence. | Write informative/explanatory texts to examine a topic and convey ideas, concepts, and information through the selection, organization, and analysis of relevant content. | Write narratives to develop real or imagined experiences or events using effective technique, relevant descriptive details, and well-structured event sequences. |
|---|---|---|---|
| | • Introduce claim(s) and organize the reasons and evidence clearly.<br>• Support claim(s) with clear reasons and relevant evidence, using credible sources and demonstrating an understanding of the topic or text.<br>• Use words, phrases, and clauses to clarify the relationships among claim(s) and reasons.<br>• Establish and maintain a formal style.<br>• Provide a concluding statement or section that follows from the argument presented. | • Introduce a topic; organize ideas, concepts, and information, using strategies such as definition, classification, comparison/contrast, and cause/effect; include formatting (e.g., headings), graphics (e.g., charts, tables), and multimedia when useful to aiding comprehension.<br>• Develop the topic with relevant facts, definitions, concrete details, quotations, or other information and examples.<br>• Use appropriate transitions to clarify the relationships among ideas and concepts.<br>• Use precise language and domain-specific vocabulary to inform about or explain the topic.<br>• Establish and maintain a formal style.<br>• Provide a concluding statement or section that follows from the information or explanation presented. | • Engage and orient the reader by establishing a context and introducing a narrator and/or characters; organize an event sequence that unfolds naturally and logically.<br>• Use narrative techniques, such as dialogue, pacing, and description, to develop experiences, events, and/or characters.<br>• Use a variety of transition words, phrases, and clauses to convey sequence and signal shifts from one time frame or setting to another.<br>• Use precise words and phrases, relevant descriptive details, and sensory language to convey experiences and events.<br>• Provide a conclusion that follows from the narrated experiences or events. |
| **PRESIDENT TAKES MARTIAN BRIDE** | | ◆ | ◆ |
| **LYING FOR FUN AND PROFIT** | | | |
| **THIS CLASS SUCKS** | ◆ | ◆ | ◆ |
| **SCREENWRITING** | | ◆ | ◆ |
| **HOW TO WRITE A GHOST STORY** | | | ◆ |
| **826 UNPLUGGED** | | | ◆ |
| **SPORTSWRITING** | | ◆ | ◆ |
| **HOW TO WRITE A FAN LETTER** | ◆ | ◆ | ◆ |
| **EXQUISITE STORY LINES** | | | |
| **SOUL PROWLERS** | | ◆ | ◆ |
| **HOMESTYLE** | | ◆ | ◆ |
| **AGITATE! PROPAGANDIZE!** | ◆ | ◆ | ◆ |
| **TASTY MEDICINE FOR WRITER'S BLOCK** | | ◆ | ◆ |
| **HIGH SCHOOL INK** | | ◆ | ◆ |

PRODUCTION AND DISTRIBUTION OF WRITING

| | Produce clear and coherent writing in which the development, organization, and style are appropriate to task, purpose, and audience. (Grade-specific expectations for writing types are defined in standards 1–3 above.) | With some guidance and support from peers and adults, develop and strengthen writing as needed by planning, revising, editing, rewriting, or trying a new approach. | Use technology, including the Internet, to produce and publish writing and present the relationships between information and ideas efficiently as well as to interact and collaborate with others, including linking to and citing sources. |
|---|---|---|---|
| PRESIDENT TAKES MARTIAN BRIDE | ❖ | ❖ | |
| LYING FOR FUN AND PROFIT | ❖ | ❖ | |
| THIS CLASS SUCKS | ❖ | ❖ | ❖ |
| SCREENWRITING | ❖ | ❖ | ❖ |
| HOW TO WRITE A GHOST STORY | ❖ | ❖ | |
| 826 UNPLUGGED | ❖ | ❖ | |
| SPORTSWRITING | ❖ | ❖ | ❖ |
| HOW TO WRITE A FAN LETTER | ❖ | ❖ | ❖ |
| EXQUISITE STORY LINES | ❖ | ❖ | |
| SOUL PROWLERS | ❖ | ❖ | |
| HOMESTYLE | ❖ | ❖ | |
| AGITATE! PROPAGAN-DIZE! | ❖ | ❖ | |
| TASTY MEDICINE FOR WRITER'S BLOCK | ❖ | ❖ | |
| HIGH SCHOOL INK | ❖ | ❖ | ❖ |

| | Conduct short research projects to answer a question, drawing on several sources and refocusing the inquiry when appropriate. | Gather relevant information from multiple print and digital sources; assess the credibility of each source; and quote or paraphrase the data and conclusions of others while avoiding plagiarism and providing basic bibliographic information for sources. | Draw evidence from literary or informational texts to support analysis, reflection, and research. • Apply grade 6 reading standards to literature (e.g., "Compare and contrast texts in different forms or genres [e.g., stories and poems; historical novels and fantasy stories] in terms of their approaches to similar themes and topics"). • Apply grade 6 reading standards to literary nonfiction (e.g., "Trace and evaluate the argument and specific claims in a text, distinguishing claims that are supported by reasons and evidence from claims that are not"). | Write routinely over extended time frames (time for research, reflection, and revision) and shorter time frames (a single sitting or a day or two) for a range of discipline-specific tasks, purposes, and audiences. |
|---|---|---|---|---|
| PRESIDENT TAKES MARTIAN BRIDE | | | ❖ | ❖ |
| LYING FOR FUN AND PROFIT | ❖ | ❖ | ❖ | ❖ |
| THIS CLASS SUCKS | ❖ | ❖ | ❖ | ❖ |
| SCREENWRITING | | | | ❖ |
| HOW TO WRITE A GHOST STORY | | | | ❖ |
| 826 UNPLUGGED | | | | ❖ |
| SPORTSWRITING | ❖ | ❖ | | ❖ |
| HOW TO WRITE A FAN LETTER | | | | ❖ |
| EXQUISITE STORY LINES | ❖ | ❖ | ❖ | ❖ |
| SOUL PROWLERS | ❖ | ❖ | | ❖ |
| HOMESTYLE | ❖ | ❖ | ❖ | ❖ |
| AGITATE! PROPAGANDIZE! | ❖ | ❖ | ❖ | ❖ |
| TASTY MEDICINE FOR WRITER'S BLOCK | ❖ | ❖ | | ❖ |
| HIGH SCHOOL INK | | | | ❖ |

| | Write arguments to support claims with clear reasons and relevant evidence. <br>• Introduce claim(s) and organize the reasons and evidence clearly. <br>• Support claim(s) with clear reasons and relevant evidence, using credible sources and demonstrating an understanding of the topic or text. <br>• Use words, phrases, and clauses to clarify the relationships among claim(s) and reasons. <br>• Establish and maintain a formal style. <br>• Provide a concluding statement or section that follows from the argument presented. | Write informative/explanatory texts to examine a topic and convey ideas, concepts, and information through the selection, organization, and analysis of relevant content. <br>• Introduce a topic; organize ideas, concepts, and information, using strategies such as definition, classification, comparison/contrast, and cause/effect; include formatting (e.g., headings), graphics (e.g., charts, tables), and multimedia when useful to aiding comprehension. <br>• Develop the topic with relevant facts, definitions, concrete details, quotations, or other information and examples. <br>• Use appropriate transitions to clarify the relationships among ideas and concepts. <br>• Use precise language and domain-specific vocabulary to inform about or explain the topic. <br>• Establish and maintain a formal style. <br>Provide a concluding statement or section that follows from the information or explanation presented. | Write narratives to develop real or imagined experiences or events using effective technique, relevant descriptive details, and well-structured event sequences. <br>• Engage and orient the reader by establishing a context and introducing a narrator and/or characters; organize an event sequence that unfolds naturally and logically. <br>• Use narrative techniques, such as dialogue, pacing, and description, to develop experiences, events, and/or characters. <br>• Use a variety of transition words, phrases, and clauses to convey sequence and signal shifts from one time frame or setting to another. <br>• Use precise words and phrases, relevant descriptive details, and sensory language to convey experiences and events. <br>Provide a conclusion that follows from the narrated experiences or events. |
|---|---|---|---|
| DETAILS (GOLDEN), CHARACTER (IMMORTAL), AND SETTING (RURAL INDIA) | | ❖ | ❖ |
| LITERARY FACEBOOKS | | | ❖ |
| SUBURBAN EPICS | | | ❖ |
| BUSTED | | ❖ | ❖ |
| HOW TO WRITE SCIENCE FICTION | | ❖ | ❖ |
| WRITING FROM EXPERIENCE | | ❖ | ❖ |
| TOO MUCH MONEY! AN ETHICAL WRITING EXERCISE IN 10 EASY STEPS | ❖ | ❖ | ❖ |
| THE TALK SHOW CIRCUIT | | ❖ | ❖ |
| THE FIRST DRAFT IS MY ENEMY: REVISIONS | ❖ | ❖ | ❖ |
| SEE YOU AGAIN YESTERDAY: PLAYING WITH TIME | | | ❖ |
| LOOK SMART FAST: COLLEGE APPLICATION ESSAY BOOT CAMP | ❖ | ❖ | ❖ |
| WRITING ABOUT PAINFUL THINGS | | ❖ | ❖ |

| | Produce clear and coherent writing in which the development, organization, and style are appropriate to task, purpose, and audience. (Grade-specific expectations for writing types are defined in standards 1–3 above.) | With some guidance and support from peers and adults, develop and strengthen writing as needed by planning, revising, editing, rewriting, or trying a new approach. | Use technology, including the Internet, to produce and publish writing and present the relationships between information and ideas efficiently as well as to interact and collaborate with others, including linking to and citing sources. |
| --- | --- | --- | --- |
| DETAILS (GOLDEN), CHARACTER (IMMORTAL), AND SETTING (RURAL INDIA) | ❖ | ❖ | |
| LITERARY FACEBOOKS | ❖ | ❖ | ❖ |
| SUBURBAN EPICS | ❖ | ❖ | |
| BUSTED | ❖ | ❖ | |
| HOW TO WRITE SCIENCE FICTION | ❖ | ❖ | ❖ |
| WRITING FROM EXPERIENCE | ❖ | ❖ | |
| TOO MUCH MONEY! AN ETHICAL WRITING EXERCISE IN 10 EASY STEPS | ❖ | ❖ | |
| THE TALK SHOW CIRCUIT | ❖ | ❖ | |
| THE FIRST DRAFT IS MY ENEMY: REVISIONS | ❖ | ❖ | |
| SEE YOU AGAIN YESTERDAY: PLAYING WITH TIME | ❖ | ❖ | |
| LOOK SMART FAST: COLLEGE APPLICATION ESSAY BOOT CAMP | ❖ | ❖ | |
| WRITING ABOUT PAINFUL THINGS | ❖ | ❖ | |

| | Conduct short research projects to answer a question, drawing on several sources and refocusing the inquiry when appropriate. | Gather relevant information from multiple print and digital sources; assess the credibility of each source; and quote or paraphrase the data and conclusions of others while avoiding plagiarism and providing basic bibliographic information for sources. | Draw evidence from literary or informational texts to support analysis, reflection, and research.<br>• Apply grade 6 reading standards to literature (e.g., "Compare and contrast texts in different forms or genres [e.g., stories and poems; historical novels and fantasy stories] in terms of their approaches to similar themes and topics").<br>• Apply grade 6 reading standards to literary nonfiction (e.g., "Trace and evaluate the argument and specific claims in a text, distinguishing claims that are supported by reasons and evidence from claims that are not"). | Write routinely over extended time frames (time for research, reflection, and revision) and shorter time frames (a single sitting or a day or two) for a range of discipline-specific tasks, purposes, and audiences. |
|---|---|---|---|---|
| **DETAILS (GOLDEN), CHARACTER (IMMORTAL), AND SETTING (RURAL INDIA)** | ◈ | ◈ | ◈ | ◈ |
| **LITERARY FACEBOOKS** | ◈ | ◈ | ◈ | ◈ |
| **SUBURBAN EPICS** | ◈ | | | ◈ |
| **BUSTED** | | | | ◈ |
| **HOW TO WRITE SCIENCE FICTION** | | | | ◈ |
| **WRITING FROM EXPERIENCE** | ◈ | ◈ | | ◈ |
| **TOO MUCH MONEY! AN ETHICAL WRITING EXERCISE IN 10 EASY STEPS** | | | ◈ | ◈ |
| **THE TALK SHOW CIRCUIT** | | | | ◈ |
| **THE FIRST DRAFT IS MY ENEMY: REVISIONS** | ◈ | ◈ | ◈ | ◈ |
| **SEE YOU AGAIN YESTERDAY: PLAYING WITH TIME** | | | | ◈ |
| **LOOK SMART FAST: COLLEGE APPLICATION ESSAY BOOT CAMP** | | | | ◈ |
| **WRITING ABOUT PAINFUL THINGS** | ◈ | ◈ | | ◈ |

| | Write arguments to support claims with clear reasons and relevant evidence. <br>• Introduce claim(s) and organize the reasons and evidence clearly. <br>• Support claim(s) with clear reasons and relevant evidence, using credible sources and demonstrating an understanding of the topic or text. <br>• Use words, phrases, and clauses to clarify the relationships among claim(s) and reasons. <br>• Establish and maintain a formal style. <br>• Provide a concluding statement or section that follows from the argument presented. | Write informative/explanatory texts to examine a topic and convey ideas, concepts, and information through the selection, organization, and analysis of relevant content. <br>• Introduce a topic; organize ideas, concepts, and information, using strategies such as definition, classification, comparison/contrast, and cause/effect; include formatting (e.g., headings), graphics (e.g., charts, tables), and multimedia when useful to aiding comprehension. <br>• Develop the topic with relevant facts, definitions, concrete details, quotations, or other information and examples. <br>• Use appropriate transitions to clarify the relationships among ideas and concepts. <br>• Use precise language and domain-specific vocabulary to inform about or explain the topic. <br>• Establish and maintain a formal style. <br>Provide a concluding statement or section that follows from the information or explanation presented. | Write narratives to develop real or imagined experiences or events using effective technique, relevant descriptive details, and well-structured event sequences. <br>• Engage and orient the reader by establishing a context and introducing a narrator and/or characters; organize an event sequence that unfolds naturally and logically. <br>• Use narrative techniques, such as dialogue, pacing, and description, to develop experiences, events, and/or characters. <br>• Use a variety of transition words, phrases, and clauses to convey sequence and signal shifts from one time frame or setting to another. <br>• Use precise words and phrases, relevant descriptive details, and sensory language to convey experiences and events. <br>Provide a conclusion that follows from the narrated experiences or events. |
|---|---|---|---|
| MUTANT SHAKESPEARE | | | ◆ |
| HOW TO WRITE A ONE-PERSON SHOW ABOUT A HISTORICAL FIGURE | | ◆ | ◆ |
| WRITING FOR GAMERS | | | ◆ |
| HUMOR WRITING: AN EXERCISE IN ALCHEMY | | ◆ | ◆ |
| ON PINING: WRITE A VERSE TO MAKE THEM STAY | ◆ | | ◆ |
| ADDING INSULT TO POETRY | ◆ | | ◆ |
| BAD WRITING | | | ◆ |
| WHERE STORIES COME FROM | | | |
| WORD KARAOKE | | | ◆ |
| TALL TALES AND SHORT STORIES | | | |
| WELCOME TO THE FUNHOUSE: WRITING FUNNY SCENES | | ◆ | ◆ |
| VOICEMAILS FROM MY FUTURE SELF | | ◆ | ◆ |
| HOW SHORT IS SHORT? | | | |

| | Produce clear and coherent writing in which the development, organization, and style are appropriate to task, purpose, and audience. (Grade-specific expectations for writing types are defined in standards 1–3 above.) | With some guidance and support from peers and adults, develop and strengthen writing as needed by planning, revising, editing, rewriting, or trying a new approach. | Use technology, including the Internet, to produce and publish writing and present the relationships between information and ideas efficiently as well as to interact and collaborate with others, including linking to and citing sources. |
|---|---|---|---|
| MUTANT SHAKESPEARE | ❖ | ❖ | |
| HOW TO WRITE A ONE-PERSON SHOW ABOUT A HISTORICAL FIGURE | ❖ | ❖ | |
| WRITING FOR GAMERS | ❖ | ❖ | ❖ |
| HUMOR WRITING: AN EXERCISE IN ALCHEMY | ❖ | ❖ | |
| ON PINING: WRITE A VERSE TO MAKE THEM STAY | ❖ | ❖ | |
| ADDING INSULT TO POETRY | ❖ | ❖ | |
| BAD WRITING | ❖ | ❖ | |
| WHERE STORIES COME FROM | ❖ | ❖ | |
| WORD KARAOKE | ❖ | ❖ | |
| TALL TALES AND SHORT STORIES | ❖ | ❖ | |
| WELCOME TO THE FUNHOUSE: WRITING FUNNY SCENES | ❖ | ❖ | |
| VOICEMAILS FROM MY FUTURE SELF | ❖ | ❖ | |
| HOW SHORT IS SHORT? | ❖ | ❖ | |

| | Conduct short research projects to answer a question, drawing on several sources and refocusing the inquiry when appropriate. | Gather relevant information from multiple print and digital sources; assess the credibility of each source; and quote or paraphrase the data and conclusions of others while avoiding plagiarism and providing basic bibliographic information for sources. | Draw evidence from literary or informational texts to support analysis, reflection, and research.<br>• Apply grade 6 reading standards to literature (e.g., "Compare and contrast texts in different forms or genres [e.g., stories and poems; historical novels and fantasy stories] in terms of their approaches to similar themes and topics").<br>• Apply grade 6 reading standards to literary nonfiction (e.g., "Trace and evaluate the argument and specific claims in a text, distinguishing claims that are supported by reasons and evidence from claims that are not"). | Write routinely over extended time frames (time for research, reflection, and revision) and shorter time frames (a single sitting or a day or two) for a range of discipline-specific tasks, purposes, and audiences. |
|---|---|---|---|---|
| MUTANT SHAKESPEARE | ✦ | | ✦ | ✦ |
| HOW TO WRITE A ONE-PERSON SHOW ABOUT A HISTORICAL FIGURE | ✦ | ✦ | ✦ | ✦ |
| WRITING FOR GAMERS | | | ✦ | ✦ |
| HUMOR WRITING: AN EXERCISE IN ALCHEMY | | | ✦ | ✦ |
| ON PINING: WRITE A VERSE TO MAKE THEM STAY | | | | ✦ |
| ADDING INSULT TO POETRY | | | | ✦ |
| BAD WRITING | ✦ | ✦ | ✦ | ✦ |
| WHERE STORIES COME FROM | ✦ | ✦ | ✦ | ✦ |
| WORD KARAOKE | | | | ✦ |
| TALL TALES AND SHORT STORIES | ✦ | ✦ | ✦ | ✦ |
| WELCOME TO THE FUNHOUSE: WRITING FUNNY SCENES | | | ✦ | ✦ |
| VOICEMAILS FROM MY FUTURE SELF | ✦ | ✦ | | ✦ |
| HOW SHORT IS SHORT? | ✦ | ✦ | ✦ | ✦ |

| | Write arguments to support claims with clear reasons and relevant evidence. | Write informative/explanatory texts to examine a topic and convey ideas, concepts, and information through the selection, organization, and analysis of relevant content. | Write narratives to develop real or imagined experiences or events using effective technique, relevant descriptive details, and well-structured event sequences. |
|---|---|---|---|
| | • Introduce claim(s) and organize the reasons and evidence clearly.<br>• Support claim(s) with clear reasons and relevant evidence, using credible sources and demonstrating an understanding of the topic or text.<br>• Use words, phrases, and clauses to clarify the relationships among claim(s) and reasons.<br>• Establish and maintain a formal style.<br>• Provide a concluding statement or section that follows from the argument presented. | • Introduce a topic; organize ideas, concepts, and information, using strategies such as definition, classification, comparison/contrast, and cause/effect; include formatting (e.g., headings), graphics (e.g., charts, tables), and multimedia when useful to aiding comprehension.<br>• Develop the topic with relevant facts, definitions, concrete details, quotations, or other information and examples.<br>• Use appropriate transitions to clarify the relationships among ideas and concepts.<br>• Use precise language and domain-specific vocabulary to inform about or explain the topic.<br>• Establish and maintain a formal style.<br>Provide a concluding statement or section that follows from the information or explanation presented. | • Engage and orient the reader by establishing a context and introducing a narrator and/or characters; organize an event sequence that unfolds naturally and logically.<br>• Use narrative techniques, such as dialogue, pacing, and description, to develop experiences, events, and/or characters.<br>• Use a variety of transition words, phrases, and clauses to convey sequence and signal shifts from one time frame or setting to another.<br>• Use precise words and phrases, relevant descriptive details, and sensory language to convey experiences and events.<br>Provide a conclusion that follows from the narrated experiences or events. |
| COMIC COMPOSITION CHALLENGE! | | | ❖ |
| MY BORING LIFE | | ❖ | ❖ |
| COLONEL MUSTARD IN THE LIBRARY WITH A CANDLESTICK | | | ❖ |
| CREATING CHARACTERS | | | ❖ |
| HIGH SCHOOL CONFIDENTIAL | | | ❖ |
| GET YOUR HAIKU ON | | | ❖ |
| THE ESSAY | ❖ | ❖ | ❖ |
| THE STORY OF ME | | ❖ | ❖ |
| MEET YOUR PROTAGONIST! | | | ❖ |
| ALL WITNESSES EVENTUALLY DIE | | ❖ | ❖ |
| WICKED STYLE AND HOW TO GET IT | | | ❖ |
| PRESIDENT TAKES MARTIAN BRIDE | | ❖ | ❖ |
| LYING FOR FUN AND PROFIT | | | |

| | Produce clear and coherent writing in which the development, organization, and style are appropriate to task, purpose, and audience. (Grade-specific expectations for writing types are defined in standards 1–3 above.) | With some guidance and support from peers and adults, develop and strengthen writing as needed by planning, revising, editing, rewriting, or trying a new approach. | Use technology, including the Internet, to produce and publish writing and present the relationships between information and ideas efficiently as well as to interact and collaborate with others, including linking to and citing sources. |
|---|---|---|---|
| COMIC COMPOSITION CHALLENGE! | ❖ | ❖ | |
| MY BORING LIFE | ❖ | ❖ | |
| COLONEL MUSTARD IN THE LIBRARY WITH A CANDLESTICK | ❖ | ❖ | |
| CREATING CHARACTERS | ❖ | ❖ | |
| HIGH SCHOOL CONFIDENTIAL | ❖ | ❖ | |
| GET YOUR HAIKU ON | ❖ | ❖ | |
| THE ESSAY | ❖ | ❖ | |
| THE STORY OF ME | ❖ | ❖ | |
| MEET YOUR PROTAGONIST! | ❖ | ❖ | |
| ALL WITNESSES EVENTUALLY DIE | ❖ | ❖ | |
| WICKED STYLE AND HOW TO GET IT | ❖ | ❖ | |
| PRESIDENT TAKES MARTIAN BRIDE | ❖ | ❖ | |
| LYING FOR FUN AND PROFIT | ❖ | ❖ | |

| | Conduct short research projects to answer a question, drawing on several sources and refocusing the inquiry when appropriate. | Gather relevant information from multiple print and digital sources; assess the credibility of each source; and quote or paraphrase the data and conclusions of others while avoiding plagiarism and providing basic bibliographic information for sources. | Draw evidence from literary or informational texts to support analysis, reflection, and research.<br>• Apply grade 6 reading standards to literature (e.g., "Compare and contrast texts in different forms or genres [e.g., stories and poems; historical novels and fantasy stories] in terms of their approaches to similar themes and topics").<br>• Apply grade 6 reading standards to literary nonfiction (e.g., "Trace and evaluate the argument and specific claims in a text, distinguishing claims that are supported by reasons and evidence from claims that are not"). | Write routinely over extended time frames (time for research, reflection, and revision) and shorter time frames (a single sitting or a day or two) for a range of discipline-specific tasks, purposes, and audiences. |
|---|---|---|---|---|
| COMIC COMPOSITION CHALLENGE! | ✦ | ✦ | ✦ | ✦ |
| MY BORING LIFE | ✦ | ✦ | | ✦ |
| COLONEL MUSTARD IN THE LIBRARY WITH A CANDLESTICK | | | | ✦ |
| CREATING CHARACTERS | | | | ✦ |
| HIGH SCHOOL CONFIDENTIAL | | | | ✦ |
| GET YOUR HAIKU ON | | | | ✦ |
| THE ESSAY | ✦ | ✦ | ✦ | ✦ |
| THE STORY OF ME | ✦ | ✦ | | ✦ |
| MEET YOUR PROTAGONIST! | | | | ✦ |
| ALL WITNESSES EVENTUALLY DIE | ✦ | ✦ | | ✦ |
| WICKED STYLE AND HOW TO GET IT | ✦ | ✦ | ✦ | ✦ |
| PRESIDENT TAKES MARTIAN BRIDE | | | ✦ | ✦ |
| LYING FOR FUN AND PROFIT | ✦ | ✦ | ✦ | ✦ |

| | Write arguments to support claims with clear reasons and relevant evidence. | Write informative/explanatory texts to examine a topic and convey ideas, concepts, and information through the selection, organization, and analysis of relevant content. | Write narratives to develop real or imagined experiences or events using effective technique, relevant descriptive details, and well-structured event sequences. |
|---|---|---|---|
| | • Introduce claim(s) and organize the reasons and evidence clearly.<br>• Support claim(s) with clear reasons and relevant evidence, using credible sources and demonstrating an understanding of the topic or text.<br>• Use words, phrases, and clauses to clarify the relationships among claim(s) and reasons.<br>• Establish and maintain a formal style.<br>• Provide a concluding statement or section that follows from the argument presented. | • Introduce a topic; organize ideas, concepts, and information, using strategies such as definition, classification, comparison/contrast, and cause/effect; include formatting (e.g., headings), graphics (e.g., charts, tables), and multimedia when useful to aiding comprehension.<br>• Develop the topic with relevant facts, definitions, concrete details, quotations, or other information and examples.<br>• Use appropriate transitions to clarify the relationships among ideas and concepts.<br>• Use precise language and domain-specific vocabulary to inform about or explain the topic.<br>• Establish and maintain a formal style.<br>Provide a concluding statement or section that follows from the information or explanation presented. | • Engage and orient the reader by establishing a context and introducing a narrator and/or characters; organize an event sequence that unfolds naturally and logically.<br>• Use narrative techniques, such as dialogue, pacing, and description, to develop experiences, events, and/or characters.<br>• Use a variety of transition words, phrases, and clauses to convey sequence and signal shifts from one time frame or setting to another.<br>• Use precise words and phrases, relevant descriptive details, and sensory language to convey experiences and events.<br>Provide a conclusion that follows from the narrated experiences or events. |
| THIS CLASS SUCKS | ◈ | ◈ | ◈ |
| SCREENWRITING | | ◈ | ◈ |
| HOW TO WRITE A GHOST STORY | | | ◈ |
| 826 UNPLUGGED | | | ◈ |
| SPORTSWRITING | | ◈ | ◈ |
| HOW TO WRITE A FAN LETTER | ◈ | ◈ | ◈ |
| EXQUISITE STORY LINES | | | |
| SOUL PROWLERS | | ◈ | ◈ |
| HOMESTYLE | | ◈ | ◈ |
| AGITATE! PROPAGANDIZE! | ◈ | ◈ | ◈ |
| TASTY MEDICINE FOR WRITER'S BLOCK | | ◈ | ◈ |
| HIGH SCHOOL INK | | ◈ | ◈ |

| | Produce clear and coherent writing in which the development, organization, and style are appropriate to task, purpose, and audience. (Grade-specific expectations for writing types are defined in standards 1–3 above.) | With some guidance and support from peers and adults, develop and strengthen writing as needed by planning, revising, editing, rewriting, or trying a new approach. | Use technology, including the Internet, to produce and publish writing and present the relationships between information and ideas efficiently as well as to interact and collaborate with others, including linking to and citing sources. |
|---|:---:|:---:|:---:|
| THIS CLASS SUCKS | ❖ | ❖ | ❖ |
| SCREENWRITING | ❖ | ❖ | ❖ |
| HOW TO WRITE A GHOST STORY | ❖ | ❖ | |
| 826 UNPLUGGED | ❖ | ❖ | |
| SPORTSWRITING | ❖ | ❖ | ❖ |
| HOW TO WRITE A FAN LETTER | ❖ | ❖ | ❖ |
| EXQUISITE STORY LINES | ❖ | ❖ | |
| SOUL PROWLERS | ❖ | ❖ | |
| HOMESTYLE | ❖ | ❖ | |
| AGITATE! PROPAGANDIZE! | ❖ | ❖ | |
| TASTY MEDICINE FOR WRITER'S BLOCK | ❖ | ❖ | |
| HIGH SCHOOL INK | ❖ | ❖ | ❖ |

| | Conduct short research projects to answer a question, drawing on several sources and refocusing the inquiry when appropriate. | Gather relevant information from multiple print and digital sources; assess the credibility of each source; and quote or paraphrase the data and conclusions of others while avoiding plagiarism and providing basic bibliographic information for sources. | Draw evidence from literary or informational texts to support analysis, reflection, and research. • Apply grade 6 reading standards to literature (e.g., "Compare and contrast texts in different forms or genres [e.g., stories and poems; historical novels and fantasy stories] in terms of their approaches to similar themes and topics"). • Apply grade 6 reading standards to literary nonfiction (e.g., "Trace and evaluate the argument and specific claims in a text, distinguishing claims that are supported by reasons and evidence from claims that are not"). | Write routinely over extended time frames (time for research, reflection, and revision) and shorter time frames (a single sitting or a day or two) for a range of discipline-specific tasks, purposes, and audiences. |
|---|---|---|---|---|
| THIS CLASS SUCKS | ◆ | ◆ | ◆ | ◆ |
| SCREENWRITING | | | | ◆ |
| HOW TO WRITE A GHOST STORY | | | | ◆ |
| 826 UNPLUGGED | | | | ◆ |
| SPORTSWRITING | ◆ | ◆ | | ◆ |
| HOW TO WRITE A FAN LETTER | | | | ◆ |
| EXQUISITE STORY LINES | ◆ | ◆ | ◆ | ◆ |
| SOUL PROWLERS | ◆ | ◆ | | ◆ |
| HOMESTYLE | ◆ | ◆ | ◆ | ◆ |
| AGITATE! PROPAGANDIZE! | ◆ | ◆ | ◆ | ◆ |
| TASTY MEDICINE FOR WRITER'S BLOCK | ◆ | ◆ | | ◆ |
| HIGH SCHOOL INK | | | | ◆ |

| | Write arguments to support claims with clear reasons and relevant evidence.<br>• Introduce claim(s) and organize the reasons and evidence clearly.<br>• Support claim(s) with clear reasons and relevant evidence, using credible sources and demonstrating an understanding of the topic or text.<br>• Use words, phrases, and clauses to clarify the relationships among claim(s) and reasons.<br>• Establish and maintain a formal style.<br>• Provide a concluding statement or section that follows from the argument presented. | Write informative/explanatory texts to examine a topic and convey ideas, concepts, and information through the selection, organization, and analysis of relevant content.<br>• Introduce a topic; organize ideas, concepts, and information, using strategies such as definition, classification, comparison/contrast, and cause/effect; include formatting (e.g., headings), graphics (e.g., charts, tables), and multimedia when useful to aiding comprehension.<br>• Develop the topic with relevant facts, definitions, concrete details, quotations, or other information and examples.<br>• Use appropriate transitions to clarify the relationships among ideas and concepts.<br>• Use precise language and domain-specific vocabulary to inform about or explain the topic.<br>• Establish and maintain a formal style.<br>Provide a concluding statement or section that follows from the information or explanation presented. | Write narratives to develop real or imagined experiences or events using effective technique, relevant descriptive details, and well-structured event sequences.<br>• Engage and orient the reader by establishing a context and introducing a narrator and/or characters; organize an event sequence that unfolds naturally and logically.<br>• Use narrative techniques, such as dialogue, pacing, and description, to develop experiences, events, and/or characters.<br>• Use a variety of transition words, phrases, and clauses to convey sequence and signal shifts from one time frame or setting to another.<br>• Use precise words and phrases, relevant descriptive details, and sensory language to convey experiences and events.<br>Provide a conclusion that follows from the narrated experiences or events. |
|---|---|---|---|
| DETAILS (GOLDEN), CHARACTER (IMMORTAL), AND SETTING (RURAL INDIA) | | ♦ | ♦ |
| LITERARY FACEBOOKS | | | ♦ |
| SUBURBAN EPICS | | | ♦ |
| BUSTED | | ♦ | ♦ |
| HOW TO WRITE SCIENCE FICTION | | ♦ | ♦ |
| WRITING FROM EXPERIENCE | | ♦ | ♦ |
| TOO MUCH MONEY! AN ETHICAL WRITING EXERCISE IN 10 EASY STEPS | ♦ | ♦ | ♦ |
| THE TALK SHOW CIRCUIT | | ♦ | ♦ |
| THE FIRST DRAFT IS MY ENEMY: REVISIONS | ♦ | ♦ | ♦ |
| SEE YOU AGAIN YESTERDAY: PLAYING WITH TIME | | | ♦ |
| LOOK SMART FAST: COLLEGE APPLICATION ESSAY BOOT CAMP | ♦ | ♦ | ♦ |
| WRITING ABOUT PAINFUL THINGS | | ♦ | ♦ |

PRODUCTION AND DISTRIBUTION OF WRITING

| | Produce clear and coherent writing in which the development, organization, and style are appropriate to task, purpose, and audience. (Grade-specific expectations for writing types are defined in standards 1–3 above.) | With some guidance and support from peers and adults, develop and strengthen writing as needed by planning, revising, editing, rewriting, or trying a new approach. | Use technology, including the Internet, to produce and publish writing and present the relationships between information and ideas efficiently as well as to interact and collaborate with others, including linking to and citing sources. |
|---|---|---|---|
| DETAILS (GOLDEN), CHARACTER (IMMORTAL), AND SETTING (RURAL INDIA) | ❖ | ❖ | |
| LITERARY FACEBOOKS | ❖ | ❖ | ❖ |
| SUBURBAN EPICS | ❖ | ❖ | |
| BUSTED | ❖ | ❖ | |
| HOW TO WRITE SCIENCE FICTION | ❖ | ❖ | ❖ |
| WRITING FROM EXPERIENCE | ❖ | ❖ | |
| TOO MUCH MONEY! AN ETHICAL WRITING EXERCISE IN 10 EASY STEPS | ❖ | ❖ | |
| THE TALK SHOW CIRCUIT | ❖ | ❖ | |
| THE FIRST DRAFT IS MY ENEMY: REVISIONS | ❖ | ❖ | |
| SEE YOU AGAIN YESTERDAY: PLAYING WITH TIME | ❖ | ❖ | |
| LOOK SMART FAST: COLLEGE APPLICATION ESSAY BOOT CAMP | ❖ | ❖ | |
| WRITING ABOUT PAINFUL THINGS | ❖ | ❖ | |

| ELEVENTH–TWELFTH GRADE | Conduct short research projects to answer a question, drawing on several sources and refocusing the inquiry when appropriate. | Gather relevant information from multiple print and digital sources; assess the credibility of each source; and quote or paraphrase the data and conclusions of others while avoiding plagiarism and providing basic bibliographic information for sources. | Draw evidence from literary or informational texts to support analysis, reflection, and research.<br>• Apply grade 6 reading standards to literature (e.g., "Compare and contrast texts in different forms or genres [e.g., stories and poems; historical novels and fantasy stories] in terms of their approaches to similar themes and topics").<br>• Apply grade 6 reading standards to literary nonfiction (e.g., "Trace and evaluate the argument and specific claims in a text, distinguishing claims that are supported by reasons and evidence from claims that are not"). | Write routinely over extended time frames (time for research, reflection, and revision) and shorter time frames (a single sitting or a day or two) for a range of discipline-specific tasks, purposes, and audiences. |
|---|---|---|---|---|
| DETAILS (GOLDEN), CHARACTER (IMMORTAL), AND SETTING (RURAL INDIA) | ❖ | ❖ | ❖ | ❖ |
| LITERARY FACEBOOKS | ❖ | ❖ | ❖ | ❖ |
| SUBURBAN EPICS | ❖ | | | ❖ |
| BUSTED | | | | ❖ |
| HOW TO WRITE SCIENCE FICTION | | | | ❖ |
| WRITING FROM EXPERIENCE | ❖ | ❖ | | ❖ |
| TOO MUCH MONEY! AN ETHICAL WRITING EXERCISE IN 10 EASY STEPS | | | ❖ | ❖ |
| THE TALK SHOW CIRCUIT | | | | ❖ |
| THE FIRST DRAFT IS MY ENEMY: REVISIONS | ❖ | ❖ | ❖ | ❖ |
| SEE YOU AGAIN YESTERDAY: PLAYING WITH TIME | | | | ❖ |
| LOOK SMART FAST: COLLEGE APPLICATION ESSAY BOOT CAMP | | | | ❖ |
| WRITING ABOUT PAINFUL THINGS | ❖ | ❖ | | ❖ |

| | Write arguments to support claims with clear reasons and relevant evidence. <br>• Introduce claim(s) and organize the reasons and evidence clearly. <br>• Support claim(s) with clear reasons and relevant evidence, using credible sources and demonstrating an understanding of the topic or text. <br>• Use words, phrases, and clauses to clarify the relationships among claim(s) and reasons. <br>• Establish and maintain a formal style. <br>• Provide a concluding statement or section that follows from the argument presented. | Write informative/explanatory texts to examine a topic and convey ideas, concepts, and information through the selection, organization, and analysis of relevant content. <br>• Introduce a topic; organize ideas, concepts, and information, using strategies such as definition, classification, comparison/contrast, and cause/effect; include formatting (e.g., headings), graphics (e.g., charts, tables), and multimedia when useful to aiding comprehension. <br>• Develop the topic with relevant facts, definitions, concrete details, quotations, or other information and examples. <br>• Use appropriate transitions to clarify the relationships among ideas and concepts. <br>• Use precise language and domain-specific vocabulary to inform about or explain the topic. <br>• Establish and maintain a formal style. <br>Provide a concluding statement or section that follows from the information or explanation presented. | Write narratives to develop real or imagined experiences or events using effective technique, relevant descriptive details, and well-structured event sequences. <br>• Engage and orient the reader by establishing a context and introducing a narrator and/or characters; organize an event sequence that unfolds naturally and logically. <br>• Use narrative techniques, such as dialogue, pacing, and description, to develop experiences, events, and/or characters. <br>• Use a variety of transition words, phrases, and clauses to convey sequence and signal shifts from one time frame or setting to another. <br>• Use precise words and phrases, relevant descriptive details, and sensory language to convey experiences and events. <br>Provide a conclusion that follows from the narrated experiences or events. |
|---|---|---|---|
| MUTANT SHAKESPEARE | | | ❖ |
| HOW TO WRITE A ONE-PERSON SHOW ABOUT A HISTORICAL FIGURE | | ❖ | ❖ |
| WRITING FOR GAMERS | | | ❖ |
| HUMOR WRITING: AN EXERCISE IN ALCHEMY | | ❖ | ❖ |
| ON PINING: WRITE A VERSE TO MAKE THEM STAY | ❖ | | ❖ |
| ADDING INSULT TO POETRY | ❖ | | ❖ |
| BAD WRITING | | | ❖ |
| WHERE STORIES COME FROM | | | |
| WORD KARAOKE | | | ❖ |
| TALL TALES AND SHORT STORIES | | | |
| WELCOME TO THE FUNHOUSE: WRITING FUNNY SCENES | | ❖ | ❖ |
| VOICEMAILS FROM MY FUTURE SELF | | ❖ | ❖ |

PRODUCTION AND DISTRIBUTION OF WRITING

|  | Produce clear and coherent writing in which the development, organization, and style are appropriate to task, purpose, and audience. (Grade-specific expectations for writing types are defined in standards 1–3 above.) | With some guidance and support from peers and adults, develop and strengthen writing as needed by planning, revising, editing, rewriting, or trying a new approach. | Use technology, including the Internet, to produce and publish writing and present the relationships between information and ideas efficiently as well as to interact and collaborate with others, including linking to and citing sources. |
|---|---|---|---|
| MUTANT SHAKESPEARE | ❖ | ❖ | |
| HOW TO WRITE A ONE-PERSON SHOW ABOUT A HISTORICAL FIGURE | ❖ | ❖ | |
| WRITING FOR GAMERS | ❖ | ❖ | ❖ |
| HUMOR WRITING: AN EXERCISE IN ALCHEMY | ❖ | ❖ | |
| ON PINING: WRITE A VERSE TO MAKE THEM STAY | ❖ | ❖ | |
| ADDING INSULT TO POETRY | ❖ | ❖ | |
| BAD WRITING | ❖ | ❖ | |
| WHERE STORIES COME FROM | ❖ | ❖ | |
| WORD KARAOKE | ❖ | ❖ | |
| TALL TALES AND SHORT STORIES | ❖ | ❖ | |
| WELCOME TO THE FUNHOUSE: WRITING FUNNY SCENES | ❖ | ❖ | |
| VOICEMAILS FROM MY FUTURE SELF | ❖ | ❖ | |

| ELEVENTH–TWELFTH GRADE | RESEARCH TO BUILD AND PRESENT KNOWLEDGE | | | RANGE OF WRITING |
|---|---|---|---|---|
| | Conduct short research projects to answer a question, drawing on several sources and refocusing the inquiry when appropriate. | Gather relevant information from multiple print and digital sources; assess the credibility of each source; and quote or paraphrase the data and conclusions of others while avoiding plagiarism and providing basic bibliographic information for sources. | Draw evidence from literary or informational texts to support analysis, reflection, and research. • Apply grade 6 reading standards to literature (e.g., "Compare and contrast texts in different forms or genres [e.g., stories and poems; historical novels and fantasy stories] in terms of their approaches to similar themes and topics"). • Apply grade 6 reading standards to literary nonfiction (e.g., "Trace and evaluate the argument and specific claims in a text, distinguishing claims that are supported by reasons and evidence from claims that are not"). | Write routinely over extended time frames (time for research, reflection, and revision) and shorter time frames (a single sitting or a day or two) for a range of discipline-specific tasks, purposes, and audiences. |
| MUTANT SHAKESPEARE | ◆ | | ◆ | ◆ |
| HOW TO WRITE A ONE-PERSON SHOW ABOUT A HISTORICAL FIGURE | ◆ | ◆ | ◆ | ◆ |
| WRITING FOR GAMERS | | | ◆ | ◆ |
| HUMOR WRITING: AN EXERCISE IN ALCHEMY | | | ◆ | ◆ |
| ON PINING: WRITE A VERSE TO MAKE THEM STAY | | | | ◆ |
| ADDING INSULT TO POETRY | | | | ◆ |
| BAD WRITING | ◆ | ◆ | ◆ | ◆ |
| WHERE STORIES COME FROM | ◆ | ◆ | ◆ | ◆ |
| WORD KARAOKE | | | | ◆ |
| TALL TALES AND SHORT STORIES | ◆ | ◆ | ◆ | ◆ |
| WELCOME TO THE FUNHOUSE: WRITING FUNNY SCENES | | | ◆ | ◆ |
| VOICEMAILS FROM MY FUTURE SELF | ◆ | ◆ | | ◆ |

| | Write arguments to support claims with clear reasons and relevant evidence.<br>• Introduce claim(s) and organize the reasons and evidence clearly.<br>• Support claim(s) with clear reasons and relevant evidence, using credible sources and demonstrating an understanding of the topic or text.<br>• Use words, phrases, and clauses to clarify the relationships among claim(s) and reasons.<br>• Establish and maintain a formal style.<br>• Provide a concluding statement or section that follows from the argument presented. | Write informative/explanatory texts to examine a topic and convey ideas, concepts, and information through the selection, organization, and analysis of relevant content.<br>• Introduce a topic; organize ideas, concepts, and information, using strategies such as definition, classification, comparison/contrast, and cause/effect; include formatting (e.g., headings), graphics (e.g., charts, tables), and multimedia when useful to aiding comprehension.<br>• Develop the topic with relevant facts, definitions, concrete details, quotations, or other information and examples.<br>• Use appropriate transitions to clarify the relationships among ideas and concepts.<br>• Use precise language and domain-specific vocabulary to inform about or explain the topic.<br>• Establish and maintain a formal style.<br>Provide a concluding statement or section that follows from the information or explanation presented. | Write narratives to develop real or imagined experiences or events using effective technique, relevant descriptive details, and well-structured event sequences.<br>• Engage and orient the reader by establishing a context and introducing a narrator and/or characters; organize an event sequence that unfolds naturally and logically.<br>• Use narrative techniques, such as dialogue, pacing, and description, to develop experiences, events, and/or characters.<br>• Use a variety of transition words, phrases, and clauses to convey sequence and signal shifts from one time frame or setting to another.<br>• Use precise words and phrases, relevant descriptive details, and sensory language to convey experiences and events.<br>Provide a conclusion that follows from the narrated experiences or events. |
|---|---|---|---|
| HOW SHORT IS SHORT? | | | |
| COMIC COMPOSITION CHALLENGE! | | | ◆ |
| MY BORING LIFE | | ◆ | ◆ |
| COLONEL MUSTARD IN THE LIBRARY WITH A CANDLESTICK | | | ◆ |
| CREATING CHARACTERS | | | ◆ |
| HIGH SCHOOL CONFIDENTIAL | | | ◆ |
| GET YOUR HAIKU ON | | | ◆ |
| THE ESSAY | ◆ | ◆ | ◆ |
| THE STORY OF ME | | ◆ | ◆ |
| MEET YOUR PROTAGONIST! | | | ◆ |
| ALL WITNESSES EVENTUALLY DIE | | ◆ | ◆ |
| WICKED STYLE AND HOW TO GET IT | | | ◆ |
| PRESIDENT TAKES MARTIAN BRIDE | | ◆ | ◆ |

| ELEVENTH–TWELFTH GRADE | PRODUCTION AND DISTRIBUTION OF WRITING | | |
|---|---|---|---|
| | Produce clear and coherent writing in which the development, organization, and style are appropriate to task, purpose, and audience. (Grade-specific expectations for writing types are defined in standards 1–3 above.) | With some guidance and support from peers and adults, develop and strengthen writing as needed by planning, revising, editing, rewriting, or trying a new approach. | Use technology, including the Internet, to produce and publish writing and present the relationships between information and ideas efficiently as well as to interact and collaborate with others, including linking to and citing sources. |
| HOW SHORT IS SHORT? | ❖ | ❖ | |
| COMIC COMPOSITION CHALLENGE! | ❖ | ❖ | |
| MY BORING LIFE | ❖ | ❖ | |
| COLONEL MUSTARD IN THE LIBRARY WITH A CANDLESTICK | ❖ | ❖ | |
| CREATING CHARACTERS | ❖ | ❖ | |
| HIGH SCHOOL CONFIDENTIAL | ❖ | ❖ | |
| GET YOUR HAIKU ON | ❖ | ❖ | |
| THE ESSAY | ❖ | ❖ | |
| THE STORY OF ME | ❖ | ❖ | |
| MEET YOUR PROTAGONIST! | ❖ | ❖ | |
| ALL WITNESSES EVENTUALLY DIE | ❖ | ❖ | |
| WICKED STYLE AND HOW TO GET IT | ❖ | ❖ | |
| PRESIDENT TAKES MARTIAN BRIDE | ❖ | ❖ | |

| ELEVENTH–TWELFTH GRADE | RESEARCH TO BUILD AND PRESENT KNOWLEDGE | | | RANGE OF WRITING |
|---|---|---|---|---|
| | Conduct short research projects to answer a question, drawing on several sources and refocusing the inquiry when appropriate. | Gather relevant information from multiple print and digital sources; assess the credibility of each source; and quote or paraphrase the data and conclusions of others while avoiding plagiarism and providing basic bibliographic information for sources. | Draw evidence from literary or informational texts to support analysis, reflection, and research. • Apply grade 6 reading standards to literature (e.g., "Compare and contrast texts in different forms or genres [e.g., stories and poems; historical novels and fantasy stories] in terms of their approaches to similar themes and topics"). • Apply grade 6 reading standards to literary nonfiction (e.g., "Trace and evaluate the argument and specific claims in a text, distinguishing claims that are supported by reasons and evidence from claims that are not"). | Write routinely over extended time frames (time for research, reflection, and revision) and shorter time frames (a single sitting or a day or two) for a range of discipline-specific tasks, purposes, and audiences. |
| HOW SHORT IS SHORT? | ◈ | ◈ | ◈ | ◈ |
| COMIC COMPOSITION CHALLENGE! | ◈ | ◈ | ◈ | ◈ |
| MY BORING LIFE | ◈ | ◈ | | ◈ |
| COLONEL MUSTARD IN THE LIBRARY WITH A CANDLESTICK | | | | ◈ |
| CREATING CHARACTERS | | | | ◈ |
| HIGH SCHOOL CONFIDENTIAL | | | | ◈ |
| GET YOUR HAIKU ON | | | | ◈ |
| THE ESSAY | ◈ | ◈ | ◈ | ◈ |
| THE STORY OF ME | ◈ | ◈ | | ◈ |
| MEET YOUR PROTAGONIST! | | | | ◈ |
| ALL WITNESSES EVENTUALLY DIE | ◈ | ◈ | | ◈ |
| WICKED STYLE AND HOW TO GET IT | ◈ | ◈ | ◈ | ◈ |
| PRESIDENT TAKES MARTIAN BRIDE | | | ◈ | ◈ |

| | Write arguments to support claims with clear reasons and relevant evidence. | Write informative/explanatory texts to examine a topic and convey ideas, concepts, and information through the selection, organization, and analysis of relevant content. | Write narratives to develop real or imagined experiences or events using effective technique, relevant descriptive details, and well-structured event sequences. |
|---|---|---|---|
| | • Introduce claim(s) and organize the reasons and evidence clearly.<br>• Support claim(s) with clear reasons and relevant evidence, using credible sources and demonstrating an understanding of the topic or text.<br>• Use words, phrases, and clauses to clarify the relationships among claim(s) and reasons.<br>• Establish and maintain a formal style.<br>• Provide a concluding statement or section that follows from the argument presented. | • Introduce a topic; organize ideas, concepts, and information, using strategies such as definition, classification, comparison/contrast, and cause/effect; include formatting (e.g., headings), graphics (e.g., charts, tables), and multimedia when useful to aiding comprehension.<br>• Develop the topic with relevant facts, definitions, concrete details, quotations, or other information and examples.<br>• Use appropriate transitions to clarify the relationships among ideas and concepts.<br>• Use precise language and domain-specific vocabulary to inform about or explain the topic.<br>• Establish and maintain a formal style.<br>Provide a concluding statement or section that follows from the information or explanation presented. | • Engage and orient the reader by establishing a context and introducing a narrator and/or characters; organize an event sequence that unfolds naturally and logically.<br>• Use narrative techniques, such as dialogue, pacing, and description, to develop experiences, events, and/or characters.<br>• Use a variety of transition words, phrases, and clauses to convey sequence and signal shifts from one time frame or setting to another.<br>• Use precise words and phrases, relevant descriptive details, and sensory language to convey experiences and events.<br>Provide a conclusion that follows from the narrated experiences or events. |
| LYING FOR FUN AND PROFIT | | | |
| THIS CLASS SUCKS | ◆ | ◆ | ◆ |
| SCREENWRITING | | ◆ | ◆ |
| HOW TO WRITE A GHOST STORY | | | ◆ |
| 826 UNPLUGGED | | | ◆ |
| SPORTSWRITING | | ◆ | ◆ |
| HOW TO WRITE A FAN LETTER | ◆ | ◆ | ◆ |
| EXQUISITE STORY LINES | | | |
| SOUL PROWLERS | | ◆ | ◆ |
| HOMESTYLE | | ◆ | ◆ |
| AGITATE! PROPAGANDIZE! | ◆ | ◆ | ◆ |
| TASTY MEDICINE FOR WRITER'S BLOCK | | ◆ | ◆ |
| HIGH SCHOOL INK | | ◆ | ◆ |

PRODUCTION AND DISTRIBUTION OF WRITING

| | Produce clear and coherent writing in which the development, organization, and style are appropriate to task, purpose, and audience. (Grade-specific expectations for writing types are defined in standards 1–3 above.) | With some guidance and support from peers and adults, develop and strengthen writing as needed by planning, revising, editing, rewriting, or trying a new approach. | Use technology, including the Internet, to produce and publish writing and present the relationships between information and ideas efficiently as well as to interact and collaborate with others, including linking to and citing sources. |
|---|---|---|---|
| LYING FOR FUN AND PROFIT | ❖ | ❖ | |
| THIS CLASS SUCKS | ❖ | ❖ | ❖ |
| SCREENWRITING | ❖ | ❖ | ❖ |
| HOW TO WRITE A GHOST STORY | ❖ | ❖ | |
| 826 UNPLUGGED | ❖ | ❖ | |
| SPORTSWRITING | ❖ | ❖ | ❖ |
| HOW TO WRITE A FAN LETTER | ❖ | ❖ | ❖ |
| EXQUISITE STORY LINES | ❖ | ❖ | |
| SOUL PROWLERS | ❖ | ❖ | |
| HOMESTYLE | ❖ | ❖ | |
| AGITATE! PROPAGANDIZE! | ❖ | ❖ | |
| TASTY MEDICINE FOR WRITER'S BLOCK | ❖ | ❖ | |
| HIGH SCHOOL INK | ❖ | ❖ | ❖ |

## RESEARCH TO BUILD AND PRESENT KNOWLEDGE

## RANGE OF WRITING

| ELEVENTH–TWELFTH GRADE | Conduct short research projects to answer a question, drawing on several sources and refocusing the inquiry when appropriate. | Gather relevant information from multiple print and digital sources; assess the credibility of each source; and quote or paraphrase the data and conclusions of others while avoiding plagiarism and providing basic bibliographic information for sources. | Draw evidence from literary or informational texts to support analysis, reflection, and research.<br>• Apply grade 6 reading standards to literature (e.g., "Compare and contrast texts in different forms or genres [e.g., stories and poems; historical novels and fantasy stories] in terms of their approaches to similar themes and topics").<br>• Apply grade 6 reading standards to literary nonfiction (e.g., "Trace and evaluate the argument and specific claims in a text, distinguishing claims that are supported by reasons and evidence from claims that are not"). | Write routinely over extended time frames (time for research, reflection, and revision) and shorter time frames (a single sitting or a day or two) for a range of discipline-specific tasks, purposes, and audiences. |
|---|---|---|---|---|
| LYING FOR FUN AND PROFIT | ◆ | ◆ | ◆ | ◆ |
| THIS CLASS SUCKS | ◆ | ◆ | ◆ | ◆ |
| SCREENWRITING | | | | ◆ |
| HOW TO WRITE A GHOST STORY | | | | ◆ |
| 826 UNPLUGGED | | | | ◆ |
| SPORTSWRITING | ◆ | ◆ | | ◆ |
| HOW TO WRITE A FAN LETTER | | | | ◆ |
| EXQUISITE STORY LINES | ◆ | ◆ | ◆ | ◆ |
| SOUL PROWLERS | ◆ | ◆ | | ◆ |
| HOMESTYLE | ◆ | ◆ | ◆ | ◆ |
| AGITATE! PROPAGANDIZE! | ◆ | ◆ | ◆ | ◆ |
| TASTY MEDICINE FOR WRITER'S BLOCK | ◆ | ◆ | | ◆ |
| HIGH SCHOOL INK | | | | ◆ |

# 826 Centers and Staff

## 826 National

826 Valencia Street
San Francisco, CA 94110
(415) 730–7526

*Staff:* Gerald Richards, Erin Archuleta, Jen Benka, Ryan Lewis, Mariama Lockington

*Board of Directors:* Joel Arquillos, Jennifer Bunshoft, Howard Cutler, Jonathan Dearman, Dave Eggers, Brian Gray, Reece Hirsch, Daniel Kuruna, Pam McEwan, Tynnetta McIntosh, Amir Mokari, Scott Seeley, Amanda Uhle, Kevin Whalen

———◆———

## 826 Valencia

826 Valencia Street
San Francisco, CA 94110
(415) 642–5905
www.826valencia.org

*Staff:* Leigh Lehman, Raúl Alcantar, Justin Carder, Emilie Coulson, Anne Farrah, Margaret McCarthy, María Inés Montes, Cherylle Taylor, Miranda Tsang, Vickie Vertiz

*Board of Directors:* Barb Bersche, Nínive Calegari, Dave Eggers, Brian Gray, Thomas Mike, Abner Morales, Bita Nazarian, Alexandra Quinn, Mary Schaefer, Vendela Vida, Richard Wolfgram

———◆———

## 826NYC

372 Fifth Avenue
Brooklyn, NY 11215
(718) 499–9884
www.826nyc.org

*Staff:* Scott Seeley, Kate Ackerman, Joan Kim, Joshua Martin, Anthony Mascorro, Sarah Pollock, Chris Roberti

*Board of Directors:* Nínive Calegari, Brenda Chan Casimir, Dave Eggers, Bill Heinzen, Jeanette Lee, Tynnetta McIntosh, Jon Scieszka, Sarah Vowell, Sean Wilsey

———◆———

## 826LA

**826LA East**
1714 W. Sunset Blvd.
Echo Park, CA 90026
(213) 413–3388

**826LA West**
SPARC Building
685 Venice Blvd.
Venice, CA 90291
(310) 305–8418

*Staff:* Joel Arquillos, Bonnie Chau, Christina Galante, Marisa Gedney, Danny Hom, Julius Diaz Panoriñgan

*Board of Directors:* Miguel Arteta, Mac Barnett, Joshuah Bearman, Nínive Calegari, Dave Eggers, Jodie Evans, John T. Gilbertson, Naomi Foner Gyllenhaal, Keith Knight, Melissa Mathison, Salvador Plascencia, Sally Willcox

———◆———

## 826CHI
1331 N. Milwaukee Avenue
Chicago, IL 60622
(773) 772–8108
www.826chi.org

*Staff:* Mara Fuller O'Brien, Zach Duffy, Patrick Shaffner, Kait Steele

*Board of Directors:* Stephanie D'Alessandro, Staci Davidson, Monica Eng, Larry Feinberg, Ira Glass, Justine Jentes, Trista Hertz, Dan Kuruna, Kyra Kyles, Mara O'Brien, Matt Schrecengost, Jan Zasowski

———◆———

## 826 Seattle
8414 Greenwood Avenue North
Seattle, Washington 98103
(206) 725–2625
www.826seattle.org

*Staff:* Teri Hein, Samar Abulhassan, Justin Allan, Alex Allred, Toffer Lehnherr, Sarah Beecroft

*Board of Directors:* Sherman Alexie, David Brotherton, Elizabeth Duffell, Teri Hein, Pam MacEwan, Shawn Rediger, Ann Senechal, Joan Hiller, Matthew Leavenworth

———◆———

**826michigan**
115 East Liberty Street
Ann Arbor, MI 48104
(734) 761–3463
www.826michigan.org

*Staff:* Amanda Uhle, Amy Sumerto, Catherine Calabro

*Board of Directors:* Vicky Henry, Keith Hood, Angela Kujava, Laura London, Jeff Meyers, Jeremy Peters, Jacqui Robbins, Julia Sheill, Christopher Taylor, Jennifer Traig, Laura Wagner, Richard Weise

---

**826 Boston**
3035 Washington St.
Roxbury, MA 02119
(617) 442–5400
www.826boston.org

*Staff:* Daniel Johnson, Lindsey Plait Jones, Karen Sama, Ryan Smith

*Board of Directors:* Kevin Feeney, Jon Fullerton, John Giordano, Helen Jacobson, Paul Oh, Junia Yearwood

---

**826DC**
3233 14th St., NW
Washington, D.C. 20010
(202) 525–1074
www.826dc.org

*Staff:* Joe Callahan, Mariam Al-Shawaf, Kira Wisniewski

*Board of Directors:* Holly Jones, Matthew Klam, Steven Oxman, Marcela Sanchez, David Wakelyn